ANAPHORA AND SEMANTIC INTERPRETATION

CROOM HELM LINGUISTICS SERIES
Edited by James R. Hurford and John A. Hawkins

Anaphora
and Semantic Interpretation

TANYA REINHART

CROOM HELM
London & Canberra

© 1983 Tanya Reinhart
Croom Helm Ltd, Provident House, Burrell Row,
Beckenham, Kent BR3 1AT

British Library Cataloguing in Publication Data

Reinhart, Tanya
    Anaphora and semantic interpretation. –
    (Croom Helm linguistics series)
    1. Anaphora (Linguistics)
    I. Title
    410   PA295.A5

    ISBN 0-7099-2237-X

Printed and bound in Great Britain
by Billing & Sons Limited, Worcester.

CONTENTS

To Albert, Chalil, Rita and Salim
of the Palestinian Beer Zeit University

EDITORIAL STATEMENT

CROOM HELM LTD are publishing a Linguistics Series under the joint editorship of James Hurford (University of Edinburgh) and John Hawkins (Max-Planck-Institut für Psycholinguistik). These editors wish to draw this series to the attention of scholars, who are invited to submit manuscripts to Jim Hurford or to John Hawkins. Following is a statement of editorial intent:

The series will not specialise in any one area of language study, nor will it limit itself to any one theoretical approach. Synchronic and diachronic descriptive studies, either syntactic, semantic, phonological or morphological, will be welcomed, as will more theoretical 'model-building' studies, and studies in sociolinguistics or psycholinguistics. The criterion for acceptance will be quality and potential contribution to the relevant field. All monographs published must advance our understanding of the nature of language in areas of substantial interest to major sectors of the linguistic research community. Traditional scholarly standards, such as clarity of presentation, factual and logical soundness of argumentation, and a thorough and reasoned orientation to other relevant work, must also be adhered to. Within these indispensible limitations we welcome the submission of creative and original contributions to the study of language.

James R. Hurford, Department of Linguistics, University of Edinburgh, Adam Ferguson Building, George Square, Edinburgh EH8 9LL. John A. Hawkins, Max-Planck-Institut für Psycholinguistik, Berg en Dalseweg 79, NL-6522 BC, Nijmegen, The Netherlands.

PREFACE

In recent years, anaphora has become a central issue in linguistic theory, since it lies at a crossroad between several major problems. It is believed, on the one hand (see, e.g. Chomsky, 1980, 1981), that the same conditions that govern the interpretation of anaphora (or coindexing) also govern syntactic movement rules, i.e. they filter out inappropriate derivations as uninterpretable. The precise formulation of these conditions is therefore of much broader linguistic relevance. On the other hand, while anaphora is known to interact with various discourse and semantic considerations, it also provides a clear instance of the dependency of the semantic interpretation of sentences upon syntactic properties of natural language. So it is a test case for competing hypotheses concerning the relations between syntax, semantics and pragmatics in linguistic theory.

This book has two major goals: the first is a comprehensive analysis of sentence-level anaphora that addresses the questions posed above, and the second is an examination of the broader issue of the relations between the structural properties of sentences and their semantic interpretation within the hypotheses of the autonomy of syntax and of interpretative semantics developed by Chomsky. I argue that the anaphora restrictions themselves obey more general syntactic conditions on all interpretative rules, and, in fact, on all sentence-level linguistic rules. If this is so, these conditions may reflect properties of the processing ability of the mind, and I conclude, in Chapter 10, with the question to what extent we may find correlations between these conditions and the actual processing of sentences.

The structural conditions I propose here, and the definitions of 'syntactic domains' and 'c-command' are a development of the analysis in my dissertation (Reinhart, 1976) and a few subsequent articles (references are given in the relevant sections). These notions have since been largely assumed in the Extended Standard Theory, and I therefore include a survey of the way they are incorporated into the indexing system of this framework (in Chapters 6 and 7), as well as an evaluation of the difference in some details of the definitions.

Regarding the overall organisation of the anaphora picture, however, this book departs radically from my dissertation. I assumed there, following Chomsky (1973) and Lasnik (1976), that anaphora is governed by non-coreference or disjoint-reference rules. I believe now that such rules should be abandoned, and I argue further that the many problems of current anaphora analyses result from neglecting the semantics of anaphora. A distinction is needed between pragmatic coreference and bound anaphora, i.e. the interpretation of pronouns as bound variables, with only the latter directly restricted by sentence-level rules. Consequently, the problem of definite NP coreference which was the major issue in my dissertation (and was summarised in Reinhart, 1981a), was incorrectly stated to begin with, and many of the facts in this area actually fall outside of the grammar. However, in its empirical results, the analysis I propose now is largely equivalent to my previous analysis of definite-NP coreference. (The way this works is explained in Chapter 7.) Furthermore, I believe it is still important to have an overview of the coreference options of definite NPs, first since it was this problem that traditionally motivated the anaphora studies, and secondly, because it still supports (although indirectly) the syntactic approach to anaphora over functionally-oriented approaches, as we see in Chapter 4. I therefore devote Chapters 2–4 to definite-NP coreference, along the lines of my previous analysis; the problems are then restated in Chapter 7.

It would hardly be possible to acknowledge all those who helped me form the ideas in this book. The list would probably overlap to a large extent with the list of authors of the references. However, I would like to thank again the many people acknowledged in my dissertation, particularly Morris Halle, Paul Kiparsky, Susumu Kuno, Dick Oehrle and Haj Ross. Many of my later ideas were inspired by extensive discussions with Ed Keenan. My debt to Noam Chomsky goes far beyond his supervision of my dissertation. His linguistic work as well as his personal inspiration provided me with the framework for my research.

The writing of this book was made possible by the help of two institutes. The first part was written during my stay at the Max Planck Institute for Psycholinguistics in Nijmegen, The Netherlands, in 1980. I wish to thank them both for the excellent working conditions with which they provided me and for their help with the typing of the manuscript. The second part was supported by a grant from the Porter Institute for Poetics and Semiotics, Tel Aviv University. I owe particular thanks to Ruth Jacobson of the Porter Institute for her patient and careful editing of the manuscript.

1 STRUCTURAL RELATIONS AND RESTRICTIONS

Since the earliest stages of transformational grammar, it has been observed that certain semantic properties of sentences of natural language are sensitive to the structural relations between nodes in the syntactic tree. Within the interpretative framework that I am assuming in this work, this means that the operations interpreting surface structures, or translating them into semantic representations, are governed by syntactic conditions. The questions are, first, what are the syntactic relations that are relevant for the operation of such rules, and next, whether we can find general conditions restricting the operations of all interpretative rules (which may apply independently of each other).

The syntactic relations proposed in the earlier transformational work as relevant for the operation of interpretative rules (or transformations like 'pronominalisation') include 'command', 'in construction with', 'clause-mate' and the linear relation 'precede'. The relation found most useful at this stage was 'precede and command' which was introduced in Langacker (1966) to handle 'pronominalisation', and was later applied to the analysis of the scope of negation in Ross (1967) and of quantifier scope, in Jackendoff (1972). I argue in the following chapters that, in fact, his relation has no linguistic relevance. This chapter, however, is devoted first (in Section 1.1) to the general characterisation of structural relations in terms of the syntactic domains they define. Next, I define (in Section 1.2) the syntactic relation c-command, which will be assumed in the following chapters. In Section 1.2, I address the second question I posed above and state the general conditions on interpretative rules which this book attempts to establish.

1.1 Syntactic Domains

Although they have not been stated this way, structural relations such as 'precede', 'command' or 'precede and command' can be best understood as defining the syntactic domain of a given node — roughly, the portion of the tree consisting of those nodes which a given node bears the structural relation to. Such relations can be, then, characterised and compared in terms of the domains they define. Structural conditions on sentence-level rules, which are based on these relations, restrict such rules to operate on two nodes just in case one of them is in the domain of the other. In the case of semantic interpretation rules, the domain of a given node corresponds to the portion in the syntactic tree in which the given node can effect the interpretation of other nodes. In the case of anaphora interpretation, for example, such restrictions state the environment in which the referential interpretation of one NP may depend on that of the other. In the case of quantifiers' scope the syntactic domain of a given quantified NP determines its potential scope.

We may illustrate this characterisation of structural relations with the relation 'precede and command'. Following Langacker (1966), who introduced the relation of *command*, this relation is defined as in (1):

(1) a node A commands a node B if neither A nor B dominates the other and the S node most immediately dominating A also dominates B.

Jackendoff (1972, p. 140) and Lasnik (1976) suggested a modification of the definition so that it makes use of the notion *cyclic node* rather than S. Within the 'Extended Standard Theory', certain NPs are considered cyclic nodes, so this modification allows them to participate in the determination of command relations. In its most common use in linguistic theory, this relation is combined with linear relations into the more complex relation 'precede and command'. Thus, the restriction on anaphora which was suggested by Langacker, and which was adopted in most studies of anaphora restrictions, states, roughly, that the pronoun cannot both precede and command its antecedent, or that no coreference is possible between a pronoun and a full NP which follows and is commanded by this pronoun. This restriction captures the difference between (2) and (3):

(2) She denied that Rosa met the Shah.
(3) The man who travelled with her denied that Rosa met the Shah.

In (2) the pronoun precedes and commands the full NP, hence they cannot be coreferential. In (3) the pronoun precedes, but it does not command the full NP, and coreference is permitted.

Characterised in terms of syntactic domains, 'precede and command' defines the domains stated in (4).

(4) The domain of a node A consists of A together with all and only the nodes that A precedes and commands.

To exemplify some of the domain relations between nodes determined by (4), let us look at the abstract tree in (5). (Capital letters stand for any node; 'cy' stands for a cyclic node.)

(5)

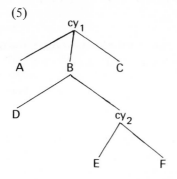

The domain of node A includes all the other nodes in cy_1, since A precedes and commands all these nodes. This will be represented in the following way:

(6) $A \: / \: B, C, D, cy_2, E \: F$

(6) is to be read: nodes B, C, D, etc. are in the domain of node A. Other domains in the tree (5) are given in (7).

(7) $B \: / \: C$
    $C \: / \: \emptyset$
    $D \: / \: cy_2, E, F, C$
    $E \: / \: F$

As we see, node C has nothing in its domain, since although, like A, it commands all the nodes in cy_1, it does not precede them. Node E has in its domain only the node F, since it does not command the nodes A, B, C, or D of cy_1. B has in its domain only C, since in Langacker's definition, in (1), the relation of command holds between two nodes only if neither of the nodes dominates the other. Since in (5), B dominated D and cy_2, by definition (1), it does not command these nodes. An alternative formulation of the command relation which does not have this requirement is also possible. See Jackendoff (1972, p.312) for discussion.

For the application of the coreference rule, the only domains which are relevant are those of NPs. Stated in terms of syntactic domains, the precede-and-command restriction is, roughly, the one given in (8). (We shall return to alternative formulations in Section 2.1.2 of Chapter 2.)

(8) A pronoun cannot be interpreted as coreferential with a non-pronoun in its domain.

We can examine now examples of domains of NPs, and the operation of (8) in some actual trees — those underlying the sentences (2) and (3)

(9a)

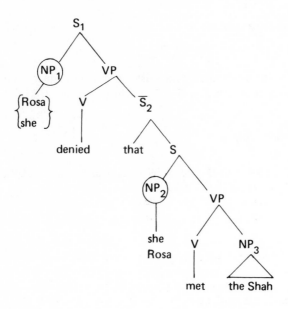

In (9a) the domain of the subject, NP_1, consists of all the nodes in S_1 (since NP_1 precedes and commands them), hence NP_2 is in the domain of NP_1. The coreference restriction (8) thus applies to these two NPs, and blocks coreference in the case where NP_1 is a pronoun and NP_2 is not (as in sentence (2)). If we check now the domain of NP_2, we see that it consists only of the VP of $\bar{S}_2$. NP_1 is not in the domain of NP_2 (since NP_2 neither commands nor precedes NP_1), hence the restriction (8) does not apply, and sentences in which NP_2 is a pronoun and NP_1 is not allow a coreference reading.

(9b)

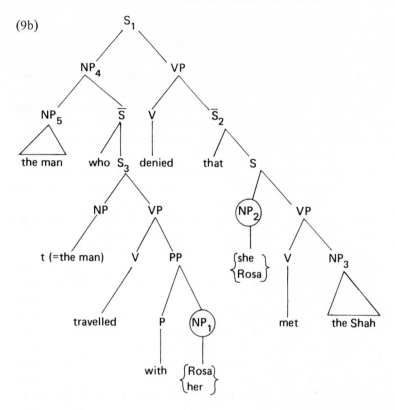

In (9b), on the other hand, neither of the nodes NP_1 and NP_2 is in the domain of the other: NP_1 has nothing in its domain and NP_2 has only the VP of $\bar{S}_2$ in its domain. Hence the restriction on coreference does not apply (coreference between NP_1 and NP_2 is not restricted) and we can get the coreference reading on either order of the pronoun and antecedent.

To summarise this concept of syntactic domain, we may look back at (6): the nodes (A, B, C, D, cy_2, E, F) constitute a domain; in other words (cy_1) is a domain – the domain of A. Thus, in tree (5), we have the domains (A, B, C, D, etc.); (B, C); (C); (D, cy_2, E, F, C), etc. In tree (9b), some of the domains defined are the nodes dominated by NP_4, which is the domain of NP_5, the nodes dominated by S_1 – the domain of NP_4, and the nodes dominated by the lower S_2 – the domain of NP_2.

The interest in this type of characterisation for structural relations lies in whether the domains defined this way have broader linguistic relevance, e.g. whether they correspond to indepently recognised syntactic units and whether there exist several linguistic rules that are constrained to operate within these domains. It takes little effort to see that the domains defined by (4) are quite arbitrary, and they may be chunks of the tree which are not constituents. Given a tree like (5), there is no intuitive sense in which B and C, for example, can be considered to constitute a domain. The reason why these domains are arbitrary is that their definition is sensitive to linear order. By this definition, given a sentence S, we can start at any arbitrary node and consider it together with all the nodes to its right which are dominated by S as constituting a domain. Given a sentence like *Ben introduced Max to Rosa in September*, for instance, the domains picked out are, first, the domain of the subject (the whole sentence) and secondly the domain of the verb (the VP, including the PPs). Since these domains are also constituents, their linguistic relevance is obvious. However, the same definition also yeields the domains [*Max to Rosa in September*] , [*to Rosa in September*] and [*Rosa in September*] . If such arbitrary chunks of the tree constitute a syntactic domain, it is hard to see what general content the notion of domain could have.

However, in the following chapters I will argue that the relation 'precede and command' — and, more generally, linear relations — in fact play no role in restricting the semantic interpretation of sentences, and that the structural restrictions on anaphora and quantification which are based on such relations are, independently, empirically incorrect. We can turn now to domains defined by an alternative structural relation.

1.2 C-Command

1.2.1. The structural relation for whose linguistic relevance I shall argue in the following chapters is *constituent command* (hereafter c-command), which was introduced in Reinhart (1976).[1] Its simplified definition is given in (10) and we shall return to its precise formulation in Section 1.2.2.

(10) Node A c (constituent)-commands node B iff the branching node most immediately dominating A also dominates B.

The linguistic need for a relation like (10) has been observed before for problems other than coreference: (10) is similar to (the converse of) the relation *in construction with* which was suggested by Klima (1964) to account for the scope of negation. (In (10), node B would be in construction with node A.) But by Klima's definition, *in construction with* holds only if neither A nor B dominates the other. The relevance of *in construction with* for the treatment of 'backward pronominalisation' has been observed by Culicover (1976).[2] The relation *c-command* is also close to the relation *superiority* suggested by Chomsky (1973), the difference being that *superiority* is asymmetric – nodes A and B cannot be superior to each other. Thus, sister nodes are excluded from the superiority relation, while definition (10) includes sister nodes (i.e. nodes that c-command each other).

The difference between the relations of command and of c-command is that while the first mentions cyclic nodes the second does not – all branching nodes can be relevant to the determination of c-command relations. Looking back at tree (5), repeated here as (11),

(11)

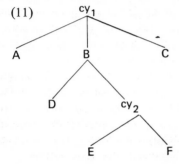

node A both commands and c-commands all the other nodes in (11) – as is also true for node C – but node D, while commanding node C (since it is dominated by cy_1 which dominates C) does not c-command node C, since the first branching node dominating D, namely B, does not dominate C.

The relation c-command defines the syntactic domain of a given node as follows:

(12)   The domain of a node A consists of all and only the nodes c-commanded by A.

The definition in (12) makes no mention of linear ordering (the relation 'precede'). All the nodes c-commanded by A are in the domain of A, whether they precede or follow it. The domains picked out by the two definitions are, thus, quite different: the domains defined by (12) for the tree in (11) are given in (13b), ignoring certain details which we shall return to directly. (13a) repeats the domains defined for this tree by the precede-and-command definition of domain (in (4)).

(13a) precede-and-command   (b) c-command
    A/B, C, D, cy_2, E, F   A/B, C, D, cy_2, E, F
    B/C   B/A, C
    C/∅   C/A, B
    D/cy_2, E, F, C   D/cy_2, E, F
    cy_2/C cy_2/D
    E/F   E/F
    F/∅   F/E

We see that node A has in its domain the same nodes by both definitions (since A happens both to precede-and-command, and to c-command, all the other nodes). Node E also has the same domain by either definition. In other words, for some nodes, the two definitions of domain give identical domains. In particular, this will be true for the subjects of simple sentences which have the whole sentence in their domain by either definition. The two definitions differ, however, with respect to the other nodes. While by the precede-and-command definition, C has nothing in its domain, by the c-command definition, the domain of C, just like the domain of A, is the whole clause (cy_1), since C c-commands all the other nodes in cy_1. The domain of D includes node C by the precede-and-command definition. But C is not in the domain of D by the c-command definition, since D does not c-command C. Similarly, by (12), C is not in the domain of cy_2, while D is, although D precedes cy_2.

It would be recalled that, unlike the definition of *command* the definition of *c-command* in (10) does not require that neither node dominate the other for the relation to hold. Therefore, c-command, unlike *command*, is reflexive; i.e. nodes c-command themselves. Consequently, by definition (12) the domain of a node A includes A. A further consequence of this formulation of c-command is that in a tree like (14a) node C is c-commanded by (and hence in the domain of) node B and, assuming that nodes dominate themselves, B is c-commanded by and is in the domain of C.

(14a)

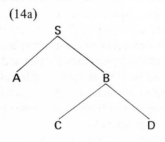

(14b)

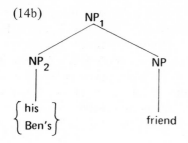

This means also that c-command is not transitive. In tree (14a) node C c-commands B, B c-commands A, but C does not c-command A. This, however, does not distinguish *c-command* from *command* since (as was pointed out in Cushing, 1978. for the similar relation *clause mate*), contrary to the common assumption, *command* is also non-transitive: in (14a), node C commands A, A commands B, but C does not command B (since the definition of command requires that neither of the relevant nodes dominate the other).

Although the result that C and B of (14a) c-command each other may seem unintuitive, this intuition stems from earlier beliefs in transformational grammar that relations like 'command' should be explicitly formulated to avoid such cases, and it does not have empirical support in the current picture of the coreference restrictions. The assumption underlying the notion 'the domain of a given node' is that this domain consists of nodes which the given node can be related to by a linguistic rule. A definition including a node a in the domain of node β can be proven wrong under this assumption if this definition allows a given rule to operate incorrectly on these two nodes, for example, if it allows the coreference rule incorrectly to block coreference of these two nodes. In tree (14b) the c-command definition of domain includes NP_1 in the domain of NP_2. Since NP_1 is not a pronoun, the coreference restriction (which will be formulated in Chapter 2) will block an interpretation of these two NPs (i.e. *his* and *his friend* or *Ben* and *Ben's friend*) as coreferential. This, however, is a correct result. The least we could conclude, therefore, is that there are no empirical results that prove wrong the inclusion of NP_1 in the domain of NP_2 (or of B in the domain of C). In fact this consequence of the definition of c-command may constitute one of its advantages over the relation 'precede-and-command': Coreference facts of the type illustrated in (14) cannot, in principle (and have not been intended to) be handled by 'precede-and-command', since, regardless of the definition of 'command', the relation 'precede' cannot allow NP_2 to precede NP_1. The c-command based restriction, on the other hand, may turn out to be sufficient to handle these cases, without using any additional principles.

In view of these details of the definition of c-command, it is easy to see that the domains defined by (12) will always be constituents. In fact, the definition (12) determines for any given node the minimal branching constituent which contains it. This can be checked with the list of domains in (13b), which are all constituents, but here we shall further illustrate it with tree (15).

(15)

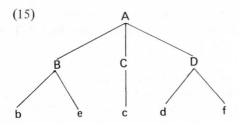

Node b in (15) c-commands nodes b (i.e. itself), e and B, which means that the domain of b consists only of these nodes, namely the constituent B, which is the minimal branching constituent containing b. This is also the domain defined for e. Similarly the domain of d, or f, is the constituent D. The domain of B, on the other hand, consists of all the nodes dominated by A, since B c-commands all these nodes. Node c is immediately dominated by C, which is not a branching node. The first branching node which dominates c is A, which means that the domain of c, like that of C, consists of the whole constituent dominated by A, which, again, is the minimal branching constituent containing c.

Applying the definition of domain to actual sentences, consider (16).

(16a) Lola met Max in the park.

   (b)

S
├── NP$_1$
└── VP
   ├── V
   ├── NP$_2$
   └── PP
      ├── P
      └── NP$_3$

The domain of the subject NP_1 is the whole sentence (namely the constituent dominated by S), since the subject c-commands all the nodes in S. The domain of the object, NP_2, consists of the nodes dominated by the VP, since the branching node most immediately dominating it is the VP. The domain of the 'object of the preposition' NP_3, on the other hand, consists of only the PP, since NP_3 c-commands nothing outside the PP. The domains which are defined by (12) are, thus, the S, the VP and the PP, which are all branching constituents.

We will define a given node A as *a D(omain) head* of a domain α iff A c-commands all and only the nodes in α. Examples for D-heads are the nodes to the left of the slash in (13b). Given this definition, there will always be more than one D-head per domain and D-heads are, thus, distinguished from 'heads' in the familiar use of the term, where a node is considered a head only if it is of the same category type as the branching node which dominates it (e.g. *the book* in *the book which Lola found*). This enables us to refer to the subject as an NP-D-head of the S domain, the object as an NP-D-head of the VP, and the oblique NP (or the object of a preposition) as an NP-D-head of the PP. This analysis, thus, correlates with Chomsky's (1965) treatment of grammatical relations: in languages with a VP, the distinction between grammatical relations in basic sentences corresponds, roughly, to structural distinctions.

1.2.2. While the formal properties of c-command which I surveyed above are the ones we shall assume here throughout, its definition as stated in (10) is simplified. In fact, the empirical examination of the operation of rules based on c-command, which we shall survey in the following chapters, reveals that in certain cases current syntactic theories assume branching nodes that do not correspond, empirically, to syntactic domains for interpretative rules. To handle such cases, the full definition of c-command I assume here (as in Reinhart, 1976) is the one in (17). (But in Chapter 8 we shall see that a further structure-specific modification is required.)

(17) Node A c(onstituent)-commands node B iff the branching node $α_1$ most immediately dominating A either dominates B or is immediately dominated by a node $α_2$ which dominates B, and $α_2$ is of the same category type as $α_1$.

(17) is needed to capture c-command relations in cases of $\bar{S}$ over S or $\overline{VP}$ over VP. In this version of the definition, the subject of S in (18b) c-commands the COMP of $\bar{S}$. Similarly, the object (NP_2 of (18b))

c-commands NPs in the PP (NP_3 of (18b)). In other words, (17) defines identical domains for the NP nodes of (18b) and (18c).

(18a) Lola found the book in the library.

(b)

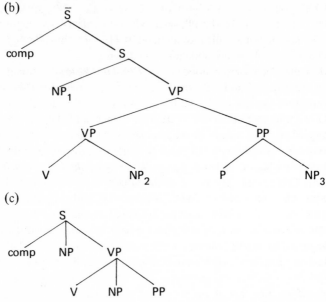

(c)

For ease of presentation only, I shall often use here the simplified definition (10), which requires using also simplified trees. Thus, throughout the presentation sentences like (18a) will be assigned the structure (18c) rather than (18b).

The relation c-command has been applied recently to the analysis of a wide range of phenomena (e.g. Chomsky and Lasnik, 1977; Chomsky, 1980). However, the definition of c-command used in these studies differs substantially from (17). It follows essentially the simplified definition given in (10), requiring further that A does not contain B, for the relation to hold. In Chomsky (1980), these details of the definition are crucial for the formulation of the opacity constraint. The assumption that the subject of a clause does not c-command itself and that it also does not c-command the COMP, provides, in this version of the opacity constraints, a unified analysis for the observation that non-nominative subjects and nodes in COMP are the only constituents that can 'escape' from a clause.

The major reason why I excluded the requirement that neither node dominates (or contains) the other from the definition of c-command has been to restrict the domains it defines to be constituents, which would not be the case otherwise. (e.g. the domains defined for tree (11) above will be the sets of nodes to the right of the slash in (13b), most of which are not constituents). It is not clear at the present stage whether there are obvious empirical consequences which depend on this difference between the two definitions, and therefore, this difference is not crucial, i.e. the interpretative rules we shall discuss will capture the same facts under both types of definition of c-command.

The other difference between the two definitions (in whether they allow for the α_1 over α_2 modification) is empirically crucial. As will be apparent in several of the cases in the following chapters the formulation in (17) is necessary to yield the right results. Given the analysis of opacity suggested in Chomsky (1980), then, there is no unified treatment of opacity and anaphora, since the domains defined for the opacity conditions are not the same as those required by the anaphora restrictions. Note, however, that in more recent formulations of the binding conditions (Chomsky, 1981) nothing hinges any more on this picture of the domain of the subject. These binding conditions are stated in terms of the relations of government and the crucial domains are those of the governing categories, which, although defined by c-command, are restricted to S's or NPs. Within this framework, therefore, the simplified definition, which is still assumed, is no longer crucial, and it can be replaced by (17).

1.3 Domain Restrictions on Interpretative Rules

The fact that the domains defined by c-command are always constituents makes these domains natural candidates for linguistic rules to operate on. In the following chapters I will argue that the interpretative rules are restricted to operating within these domains. (Of these rules, I shall pay most detailed attention to the rules governing the interpretation of pronouns.) I shall argue further that although the details of the different interpretative rules may differ, they all obey the same general conditions, which I shall outline now as the hypothesis that will be examined as we procede. The first is stated in (19).

(19) Sentence-level semantic interpretation rules may operate on two given nodes A and B only if one of these nodes is in the domain of the other (i.e. A is in the domain of B, or B is in the domain of A, or both).

(20)

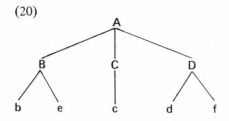

If (19) is correct, it means that given a tree like (15), repeated in (20), no sentence-level semantic interpretation rule can operate on nodes b and d, or e and d, since neither of these nodes is in the domain of the other. But such rules can operate, e.g. on c and d or on B and d since d is in the domain of c and of B. This condition constrains all sentence-level rules and not only interpretative rules. (In Chomsky's 1980, 1981 framework this is an automatic result of treating movement restrictions as a particular case of the anaphora restrictions.) We shall see some syntactic examples of this hypothesis in Chapter 10.

Note that (19) does not claim that if nodes do not meet the requirement that one is in the domain of the other they cannot possibly be related in any way. Various types of links between expressions are possible not only across domains, but also across sentences. Discourse conventions or pragmatic rules may obviously apply across sentences (and hence, across syntactic domains). (19) restricts only the operations of strictly sentence-level rules — more specifically, those rules which depend upon structural properties of the sentence (and not, say, upon its relation to the discourse).

A further domain-restriction on the operation of semantic rules applies only to a subset of such rules, those which assign some kind of prominence or primacy to a given node. The terms 'prominence' or 'primacy' have not been rigorously defined, but it has been supposed (e.g. Langacker, 1966, and Ross, 1967) that the antecedent has primacy over a (coreferential) pronoun. Following Keenan (1974), we may describe an expression α as having prominence over an expression β, if the assignment of reference to α is independent of the reference of β, but the assignment of reference to β may depend on that of α. Thus, the pronoun may depend for its reference on the antecedent, but not conversely. The hypothesis relevant to this type of case is stated in (21).

(21) If a rule assigns node A some kind of prominence over node B, A must be a D-head of the domain which contains B.

In Chapters 2-7 we will test this hypothesis in the case of the anaphora restrictions, and in Chapter 9, in the case of quantification. In the later chapter we shall see also that the assignment of function-argument representations to surface structure is statable in terms of c-command domain, obeying condition (19).

Notes

1. I would like to thank Nick Clements for suggesting to me the felicitious name 'c(onstituent)-command' for relation (10). Definition (10) differs slightly from the definition given in Reinhart (1976) which contained the condition that neither A nor B dominate the other.

2. Culicover's restriction states, roughly, that a pronoun can be coreferential with a full NP to its right only if the latter is not in construction with the pronoun (or, in our terms, only if the pronoun does not c-command the full NP). Culicover still assumes that the linear order of pronouns and antecedents matters, namely that 'forward pronominalisation' is free and what is needed is a special restriction on 'backward pronominalisation', an assumption I shall challenge in Chapter 2.

2 COREFERENCE OF DEFINITE NPs†

The problem of definite NP coreference is the one which originally motivated the relation 'precede and command' (in Langacker, 1966). It was introduced to account for a problem which is independent of the specific theory adopted concerning the status of anaphoric relations – a pronoun cannot be related arbitrarily to any full NP in a sentence. In other words, it is not sufficient that the context, the semantics of the sentence, or the situation in the world permit two NPs to be anaphorically related – certain structural properties of the two NPs impose further restrictions on their coreference options in a given sentence. As we put it in the previous chapter, the question is what is the domain in which one NP can restrict the referential interpretation of another NP, or what are the relevant domains for the application of the coreference restrictions. In this chapter I shall first argue that the precede-and-command restriction is irrelevant, and I shall introduce the c-command restriction.

Apart from the questions of the structural conditions on coreference, there are general theoretical questions to be asked, such as what is meant by 'coreference' and how are pronouns interpreted semantically. In this and the following chapter the discussion concentrates only on the structural properties of anaphora, and I will adopt, temporarily, the theoretical assumptions most commonly held in current anaphora studies, which I survey in Section 2.1. In Chapter 7, I will come back to these questions and argue that these theoretical assumptions should be abandoned. It is only in that chapter that we will consider the actual semantic interpretation of anaphora.

2.1. Theoretical Assumptions

2.1.1. Starting with the earliest analyses of anaphora in generative linguistics (e.g. Langacker, 1966; Ross, 1967), it was assumed that a crucial question is that of accounting for why coreference seems possible in, e.g. (1) and (2), but not in (3).[1]

(1) *Zelda* adores *her* teachers
(2) Those who know *her* adore *Zelda*
(3) **She* adores *Zelda's* teachers

The initial answer to this question was the assumption that the grammar contains some coindexing procedure, which determines coreference and that this procedure (or the transformation of pronominalisation in the earlier approach) is restricted so it can apply to structures like (1) and (2), but not to (3). It was later found out, however, in Lasnik (1976), that this mechanism is not sufficient to answer the question posed by (1)-(3). Since pronouns can select their reference outside the sentence (either deictically or from antecedents in previous discourse), the mere fact that a pronoun is not coindexed with a given NP in the sentence is not sufficient to prevent it from receiving the same referential interpretation from an extra sentential source. Lasnik argues, therefore, that to guarantee the correct application of the anaphora restrictions in such cases, we need to stipulate explicitly non-coreference. That rules assigning non-coreference might be needed has been, in fact, suggested before, in Chomsky (1973): in an environment which allows reflexivisation, such as (4), a non-reflexive pronoun or a full NP cannot corefer with the antecedent, as in (5).

(4)   *Zelda* bores *herself*
(5a) **Zelda* bores *her**
(5b) **Zelda* bores *Zelda**

Chomsky proposed that in such environments a rule of the grammar explicitly marks the NPs in (5) as disjoint in reference. What Lasnik suggests, then, is that the disjoint-reference rule should be extended also to non-reflexivisation environments such as (3). Lasnik argues, further, that no stipulated coreference or coindexing rules are needed for non-reflexive pronouns: if a pronoun is not marked as disjoint in reference from a given NP, its referential interpretation is free and whether it is assigned the same or different reference as the given NP is subject to pragmatic rather than syntactic considerations. The resulting picture is that there are three possible referential relations that can hold between two NPs, which are summarised in (6)

(6) A. *Obligatory (stipulated) coreference*, e.g.:
        (4) Zelda bores herself
    B. *Obligatory (stipulated) non-coreference*, e.g.:
        (5) Zelda bores her
            She adores Zelda's teachers
    C. *Optional (free) coreference*, e.g.:
        (1) Zelda adores her teachers
        (2) Those who know her adore Zelda

Correspondingly, assuming that we have asked the right question about anaphora, we end up assuming a 'three-valued' system of coindexing: NPs can be positively coindexed, negatively coindexed or neutrally indexed (i.e. neither positively nor negatively coindexed). In fact, as we shall see in Chapter 6, this three-valued indexing system is assumed, at least implicitly, in all current analyses of anaphora within interpretative semantics. Following this approach, I will state here the coreference restrictions on non-reflexive pronoun as non-coreference rules (i.e. rules assigning non-coreference to two NPs or contra-indexing them). In Chapter 7, I shall return to the details of a 'three-valued' indexing system, and point out its inadequacy, arguing for a different formulation of the anaphora questions.

2.1.2. We can turn now to the formulation of the structural restriction on anaphora. The original (Langacker's) restriction, determined by the relation 'precede and command', is given in (7). However, in Chapter 1 we stated the coreference rule in terms of syntactic domains, which, given the assumption that the rule determines non-coreference, is captured in (8). If the syntactic domains are defined by precede and command (as in (4) of Chapter 1), (7) and (8) are equivalent.

(7) A pronoun must be interpreted as non-coreferential with any non-pronoun NP that it precedes and commands.
(8) A pronoun must be interpreted as non-coreferential with any non-pronoun NP in its domain.

The rule (8) applies strictly to pairs consisting of a pronoun and a full NP (non-pronoun). However, an alternative formulation of this rule has been proposed by Lasnik (1976). Restating his 'precede and command' rule in terms of syntactic domains, it is given in (9).

(9) A given NP must be interpreted as non-coreferential with any non-pronoun in its domain.

The difference between (8) and (9) is that (9) applies to any given pair of NPs regardless of whether the D-head of the domain (the one that has the other in its domain) is a pronoun or not.

   Everything covered by (8) is covered by (9), but not conversely. This can be illustrated with the paradigm in (10)–(11). Within an interpretive approach to coreference, where pronouns are generated freely in the base, the following four sentences will be generated:

(10a) **Rosa* complained that *Rosa* had a headache.

  (b) **She* complained that *Rosa* had a headache.

(11a) *Rosa* complained that *she* had a headache.

  (b) *She* complained that *she* had a headache.

However, coreference is only possible in (11). Either restriction success-fully blocks coreference in (10b), where *Rosa* is in the domain of *she*. Either also permits coreference in (11). ((8) does not apply to (11), since in these sentences we do not have a full NP in the domain of a pronoun; (9) does not apply since the NP within the domain of the subject is a pronoun.) The two restrictions differ, however, in their application to (10a): (8) cannot block coreference in (10a), where, since there is no pronoun involved, the restriction as stated in (8) simply does not apply. The restriction (9), on the other hand, correctly blocks coreference here, since the embedded NP (*Rosa*) is in the domain of the matrix subject, and it is not a pronoun.

Since, prior to Lasnik, all discussions of coreference or pronominalis-ation have basically assumed the restriction (8), a special restriction was needed to limit coreference options between two full NPs in cases like (10a). Thus, Lakoff (1968) suggests a special output constraint for these cases, which, furthermore, assumes crucially that the notions *antecedent* and *anaphor* can hold for two full NPs. (In this view, the first *Rosa* in (10a) might count as the antecedent of the second *Rosa*.) Lasnik's ob-servation is that there is no need for two separate restrictions, and that a single condition can capture all the coreference options of two NPs.

The crucial test for this hypothesis is its prediction that given a sen-tence in which NP_1 does not both precede and command NP_2 (i.e. in our terms, NP_2 is not in the domain of NP_1), there is no restriction on their coreference options – we can find 'forward pronominalisation', 'backward pronominalisation' or no pronominalisation. The facts in (12) and (13) seem to support this prediction.

(12a) People who know *Nixon* hate *him*.

  (b) People who know *him* hate *Nixon*.

  (c) People who know *Nixon* hate *Nixon*.   (Lasnik, 1976, 5d)

(13a) The woman who marries *Ben* will marry *his* mother as well.

  (b) The woman who marries *him* will marry *Ben's* mother as well.

  (c) The woman who marries *Ben* will marry *Ben's* mother as well.

The sentences in (c) are perhaps less natural out of context than the sen-tences in (a). This is, partly, due to a general tendency to use a pronoun rather than a full NP, when the referent has already been mentioned in the discourse. The important point for Lasnik's argument, however, is that there is a substantial difference between the (c)-sentences in (12)–(13) and sentences like (10a), where one NP is in the domain of the other and where coreference seems impossible and not merely less natural. This difference can be seen as well in the following cases, when we reverse the order of the adverbial and main clauses:

> (14a) Whenever *Ben* comes to town, *Ben* gets arrested.
>   (b) **Ben* gets arrested whenever *Ben* comes to town.
> (15a) Although *McIntosh* isn't too smart, *McIntosh* is still one of our smartest leaders.
>   (b) **McIntosh* is still one of our smartest leaders, although *McIntosh* isn't too smart.

The (b)-sentences are worse than the (a)-sentences. In Lasnik's framework, the reason is that in the (b)-sentences, the first occurrences of the NP precedes and commands the other. Hence, one NP is in the domain of the other, and the restriction in (9) is violated. In the (a)-sentences, the preceding NP does not command the other. Thus, neither NP is in the domain of the other, and (9) does not apply.

Lasnik's observation had led, thus, to a restatement of the problem of coreference restriction: the problem is not specifying the conditions under which a pronoun can precede its antecedent or under which an NP cannot be coreferential with a pronoun to its left (as previous discussions assumed), but rather, specifying the conditions under which coreference between two definite NPs is not free. Stated in terms of syntactic domains, the resulting picture is that given any two NPs, the crucial question is whether either of them is in the domain of the other. If one of the two NPs in question is in the domain of the other, the co-reference restriction permits coreference only if this NP is a pronoun, regardless of whether the other NP, which is the head of the domain, is a pronoun or not.[2] I will assume here, until Chapter 7, this statement of the coreference rule, also when I introduce the alternative c-command rule. In Chapter 7, I will return to the difference between coreference of two full NPs and the anaphoric interpretation of pronouns, which will also explain why the judgments surveyed above are controversial for many speakers.

Although it is stated here as a rule of semantic interpretation, the generalisation in (9) is independent of any particular theory of anaphora, and one should be able to state it within non-interpretative frameworks.

Thus, in a theory like Montague's, where pronouns are generated as variables, (9) would be stated as a restriction on replacement of pronouns for variables. We should also note that (9) is not the actual coreference rule: it does not specify the indexing procedure and its interpretation, but rather its appropriate output. The way such conditions can be incorporated into the grammar depends upon the theoretical framework assumed. We postpone, again, the formal statement of the anaphora rule, until Chapter 6.

Apart from handling the facts in (10)–(15), the restriction (9) is sufficient to handle the non-coreference of (5b), repeated in (16a).

(16a) *Zelda* bores *Zelda*
  (b) *Zelda* bores *her*

In (16a), a non-pronoun is in the domain of a pronoun, so (9) blocks coreference. However, (9) says nothing about (5a), repeated in (16b), since here the NP in the domain of the other is, appropriately, a pronoun. However, as we mentioned, coreference is impossible in environments that allow reflexivisation, i.e. roughly, when the antecedent is in the same simplex S on NP as the pronoun.

To handle such cases we will assume the disjoint reference rule which was introduced in Chomsky (1973) and which may be stated roughly as in (17) which keeps the spirit (though not all the details) of its more recent formulation in Chomsky (1981).

(17) A given NP must be interpreted as non-coreferential with any non-R(eflexive or recripocal) pronoun in its domain if the NP is dominated by the minimal governing category dominating the pronoun (i.e. if the pronoun is in a reflexivisation environment).

The syntactic details of reflexivisation environments need not concern us here, and the notion 'minimal governing category' will be surveyed in Chapter 6. The anaphora options of R-pronouns are more restricted than those of regular pronouns, and, as we saw, they require, at the present stage of the theory, a coindexing (coreference) condition rather than a non-coreference condition. We shall return to such pronouns in Chapter 5, Section 5.2.

To conclude, then, we assume two non-coreference rules: the one in (9) is the general condition on anaphora and it applies to any pair of NPs. The one in (17) is specific to non-R-pronouns occurring in reflexivisation environments. Both rules are stated in terms of syntactic domains, but the crucial question that we shall turn to now is which syntactic domains they are sensitive to, i.e. what are the structural relations that govern the coreference options restricted by these rules.

2.2 The Non-relevance of 'Precede-and-Command'

As we saw in Chapter 1, the domains defined by 'precede-and-command' are quite arbitrary, since the chunks of the tree preceded and commanded by a given node do not correspond to independent syntactic units like constituents. It should be quite puzzling, in fact, if it turns out that the coreference rule (or any linguistic rule) operates in such arbitrary domains. However, we will see now that in the case of coreference, this puzzling situation does not arise and that the relation of precede-and-command is not what determines the coreference options of NPs.

There are several counterexamples to the precede-and-command rule, many of which were noted by Lakoff (1968). First, the range of backward pronominalisation is much wider than the rule predicts. In all the following cases, the pronoun precedes and commands its antecedent (or a non-pronoun is in the domain of a pronoun, if the domain is defined in terms of precede-and-command) but coreference is still possible.[3]

(18a) Near *him, Dan* saw a snake.

  (b) In *her* bed, *Zelda* spent her sweetest hours.

  (c) For *his* wife, *Ben* would give his life.

  (d) How obnoxious to *his* friends *Ben* is.

  (e) Fond of *his* wife though *Ben* is, I like her even more.

(19a) The chairman hit *him* on the head before *the lecturer* had a chance to say anything.

  (b) We finally had to fire *him* since McIntosh's weird habits had finally reached an intolerable stage.

  (c) Rosa won't like *him* any more, with *Ben's* mother hanging around all the time.

  (d) We'll just have to fire *him*, whether *McIntosh* likes it or not.

  (e) Believe it or not, people consider *him* a genius in *Ford's* home town.

  (f) 'I watched *him* as you fondled *the child* just now' (*The Complete Sherlock Holmes*, p. 1043).

Furthermore, cases like (18), with preposed constituents, provide a counterexample to the contention that coreference is always possible

when the antecedent precedes the pronoun (or that forward 'pronominalisation' is free). In these cases, forward pronominalisation is impossible,
as can be seen in (20).

(20a) *Near *Dan*, *he* saw a snake.
 (b) *In *Zelda's* bed, *she* spent her sweetest hours.
 (c) *For *Ben's* wife, *he* would give his life.
 (d) *How obnoxious to *Ben's* friends *he* is.
 (e) *Fond of *Ben's* wife though *he* is, I like her even more.
 (f) *(I predicted that Rosa would quit her job and) quit *Rosa's*
   job *she* finally did.

There is nothing in the existing restriction on coreference to block these
sentences – the pronoun is properly in the domain of the antecedent,
given the precede-and-command definition of domain. (Or, in other
words, the full NP is not in the domain of the pronoun, since the pronoun does not precede it.) Looking at (18) and (20) alone, one might
be tempted to attempt a solution by means of ordering the coreference
rule, or pronominalisation, before the application of preposing rules,
since in all these cases, the coreference options seem to be identical to
those which exist before preposing occurs. (Thus, parallel to (18a) and
(20a) we find *Dan saw a snake near him* but not **He saw a snake near
Dan*.)

Although arguments against any ordering solution to the problems
of coreference have been widely discussed (e.g. in Lakoff, 1968; Postal,
1970; Jackendoff, 1972; and Wasow, 1972), let us briefly see why no
such solution is available even in the case of preposed constituents. (It
should also be noted that even if such a solution were to exist for the
cases in (18) and (20), the problem for the precede-and-command rule
of coreference still persists in the cases of (19), since in these cases no
transformation has applied, but the pronoun nevertheless precedes the
antecedent.) First, observe that not always is forward anaphora impossible from a preposed constituent. In the following pair (noted in Jackendoff, 1975), coreference is possible in (b):

(21a) *In John's picture of *Mary*, she found a scratch.
 (b) In John's picture of *Mary*, *she* looks sick.

However, in the pre-preposed versions of these sentences, coreference is
equally impossible in both sentences.

(22a) **She* found a scratch in John's picture of *Mary*.
   (b) **She* looks sick in John's picture of *Mary*.

Hence, no ordering solution can account for the difference between (21a) and (21b), and the coreference rule must be able to apply to their surface structure.[4]

The most crucial point against ordering solutions is that, as was pointed out in Lakoff (1968), there is an asymmetry between coreference options of subjects and those of objects (or non-subjects) in cases with preposed constituents. Thus, while 'forward' pronominalisation is impossible in (20), where the pronoun is the subject, it is possible in (24) and (25), where the pronoun is not the subject.

(23a) Near *Dan*, I saw *his* snake.
   (b) In *Dan's* apartment, Rosa showed *him* her new tricks.
(24)   How obnoxious to *Ben's* friends I found *him* to be!

And compare as well the following pairs:

(25a) **Ben's* problems, *he* won't talk about.
   (b) *Ben's* problems, you can't talke to *him* about.
(26a) **For *Ben's* car, *he's* asking 3 grand.
   (b) For *Ben's* car, I'm willing to give *him* 2 grand.

But, as illustrated in (27), the source of the acceptable sentences in (23)–(26) is just as bad as the source of the unacceptable sentences in (20), (25a) and (26a):

(27a) **I found *him* to be obnoxious to *Ben's* friends.
   (b) **You can't talk to *him* about *Ben's* problems.
   (c) **I'm willing to give *him* 2 grand for *Ben's* car.

No ordering solution, therefore, can distinguish between the acceptable and unacceptable cases of 'forward' pronominalisation in sentences with preposed constituents. These cases suggest that there must be some structural properties of the surface structure of these sentences which determine their coreference options. These properties cannot be captured by the relation of precede-and-command, which would equally allow all the sentences in (20)–(26) to have the coreference reading.

The problem presented by sentences with preposed constituents (which are in any case stylistically marked for some speakers) could perhaps be dismissed as marginal or faced with some *ad hoc* constraints (some such constraints will be mentioned below). But as we saw in (19), the problem for the precede-and-command rule is not restricted to preposed constituents. The asymmetry of subjects and objects (or non-subjects in general) is even clearer in these areas. No coreference is possible in the sentences in (28), in which the pronoun is a subject.

(28a) **He* was hit on the head before *the lecturer* had a chance to say anything.
  (b) **He* was fired since *McIntosh's* weird habits had finally reached an intolerable stage.
  (c) **He* won't like Rosa any more, with *Ben's* mother hanging around all the time.
  (d) *Believe it or not, *he* is considered a genius in *Ford's* home town.

It is possible that, given out of context, some speakers will hesitate to accept the judgments in (19) and will claim that there is no substantial difference between (19) and (28). In fact, sentences like (19) were judged in Langacker (1966) to be ungrammatical, a judgment later challenged in Lakoff (1968). Such disagreements seem to be due to discourse constraints on backward anaphora: in general even in the cases where the grammar clearly permits both forward and backward anaphora, the actual choice of the second in discourse is less natural than the choice of the first. While, as I shall argue, the linear order of constituents plays no role in grammatical theory, it plays a crucial role in pragmatic theory: the natural tendency of a coherent discourse is first to establish a new referent (introducing it by its name or description) and then to refer back to it anaphorically. The alternative order requires some discourse motivation, or justification. It is significant that we can find disagreement in judgments concerning the sentences in (19), but not concerning the sentences in (18), which also involve backward anaphora. The reason is that in (18), backward anaphora is the only grammatical option (since coreference in (20) is impossible), while in the case of (19), forward anaphora is obviously permitted. Hence, a decision between the two options is required, and the choice of backward anaphora must be prag- matically motivated.

A way to test whether backward-anaphora interpretation in a given sentence is grammatically impossible or pragmatically awkward is by placing the sentence in a context which generally facilitates the use of backward anaphora. One such context is provided by embedding the sentence in subordinate clauses, as in (29). While (19a) will improve, (28a) is still impossible.

> (29a) Since the chairman hit *him* on the head before *the lecturer* had a chance to say anything, we'll never know what the lecture was supposed to be about.
>
> (b) *Since *he* was hit on the head before *the lecturer* had a chance to say anything, we'll never know what the lecture was supposed to be about.

What constitutes a 'reason', or an 'appropriate context' for using backward anaphora in a discourse still awaits much further study. Kuno (1972a) has argued that backward anaphora is possible only when the referent is a topic of the previous discourse (or old information). This has been challenged by Carden (1978), who cites many counterexamples from actual texts. A generalisation which may turn out to capture both Kuno's and Carden's facts is that backward anaphora is possible only when the clause containing the pronoun is not 'dominant', in the sense of Erteschick-Shir (1973) and Erteschick-Shir and Lapin (1979). This would explain also why such anaphora seems more acceptable when the whole sentence containing it is embedded in a subordinate clause as in (29).

However, it is sufficient that there exist contexts in which the sentences in (19) are appropriate (while such contexts are much harder to find for (28)), since I am dealing here only with the grammatical constraints on coreference, which should block only those sentences which are not permitted in a standard discourse.

The asymmetry between subjects and non-subjects is a crucial problem for the precede-and-command rule. The relation of command by definition cannot distinguish between subjects and objects of the same S. (Everything commanded by the subject is commanded by the object, etc.). A desperate proposal to have different rules for subjects and objects will also fail because it is obviously not the case that object pronouns can always precede and command their antecedents. They clearly cannot in (27).

What determines the possibility of coreference in (19) is not just the fact that the pronoun is an object, but rather the fact that the antecedent is not in the VP, since the PP containing the antecedent is sentential. When the PP is in the VP, as in (27), coreference is impossible. Thus, a mere distinction between grammatical relations (subject, object, etc.) is not sufficient. In Chapter 4 we shall see in more detail that a 'relational' solution for these problems is impossible.

There have been several attempts to treat the problems posed here. Lakoff (1968) believed that the problems he raised should be handled by output constraints (without touching the pronominalisation rule itself). However, he provides only the constraints needed to block forward pronominalisation in cases like (20). His conditions and his remarks about them can be collapsed into the constraint stated in (30) (excluding his discussion of stress behaviour).

(30) When NP_1 precedes and commands NP_2, and NP_1 is [-pro], NP_2 is [+pro], NP_1 cannot be coreferential with NP_2 (or: the sentence is unacceptable when NP_1 and NP_2 are coreferential) if NP_2 is immediately dominated by an S-node which also dominates NP_1. (Lakoff, 1968)

This *ad hoc* constraint successfully blocks the sentences in (20), while permitting, correctly, the sentences in (23), which do not meet the conditions of (30), since objects (at least in theories of the 1968 vintage) are not immediately dominated by an S-node. However, this constraint has nothing to say about all the cases of unexpectedly good backward pronominalisation.

An alternative *ad hoc* performance constraint for the same problem was suggested by Wasow (1972) (attributed to Chomsky):

(31) [Wasow, 1972, p. 61] : If a preposed NP serves as the antecedent for a pronoun in the same clause which is too close to it, the sentence is unacceptable.

That the distance between the antecedent and the pronoun is not what determines the acceptability of the sentence can be shown by pairs as in (32). In (32b) the antecedent is closer to the pronoun than in (32a); still, only (32b) is good.

(32a) *In *Zelda's* kitchen *she* spoke about butterflies.
   (b) In the letter Dr Levin got from *Zelda, she* spoke about butterflies.

Note also that a sentence like (20a) is not improved if the distance between the antecedent and the pronoun is lengthened:

(33) *Near *Dan,* $\left\{ \begin{array}{l} \text{who is my best friend,} \\ \text{who's been living in the jungle for 20 years,} \end{array} \right\}$ *he* saw a snake.

Wasow has also attempted a solution to the problem of backward anaphora. He introduces the relation *more deeply embedded than* to substitute for *(not) command*. He suggests that the coreference rule be changed so that it blocks coreference if the pronoun both precedes the NP and is not more deeply embedded than the NP. This new relation will capture, by convention, all the relevant cases captured by *command*, since, if A does not command B, A is, by convention, more deeply embedded than B. The advantage of this relation is that it can also range over cases where A and B are dominated by the same cyclic node. For example, Wasow suggests the following convention:

(34)   If A is part of the prepositional phrase, B is not, and B commands A, then A is more deeply embedded than B.

Given (34) and the reformulated coreference rule, sentences like (18a) – *Near* him, Dan *saw a snake* – are no longer a problem, since the pronoun *him* is more deeply embedded than the NP *Dan*.

But, though more adequate than the others, Wasow's rule is not yet sufficient to solve the problems of backward pronominalisation. By definition (34), the pronouns in the sentences of (19) are less deeply embedded than the antecedents (since the antecedent is in a PP, the pronoun is not, and the pronoun commands the antecedent). Wasow's rule, therefore, incorrectly blocks backward pronominalisation in these sentences.

In many good cases of backward pronominalisation, it is counter-intuitive even to try to find a proper way to define the pronoun as more deeply embedded than its antecedent, e.g.:

(35)   In *his* village, everybody believes that the queen has announced (that . . .) that *Bill* is a genius.

Wasow's intuitive notion of 'depth of embedding' was, however, the first step toward freeing the rule of coreference (or the definition of syntactic domains) from the relation *command*. As he himself noted in a footnote, the formal relation which can capture intuitions about 'depth of embedding' is *superiority* (which is partly similar to c-command). Wasow's difficulties are due to the fact that he follows his predecessors in the assumption that the coreference restriction must mention the relation of *precede*. The crucial step which remains to be taken is dispensing with this assumption.

An alternative framework which has been proposed to face difficulties of the type mentioned above is couched in purely semantic or pragmatic terms. Within this approach the structural properties of NPs have no relevance to their coreference options, and coreference options are determined solely by presupposition relations in the sentence (Bickerton, 1975) or theme-rheme relations (Hinds, 1973, and Kuno, 1972a, 1975b, although the latter does incorporate the syntactic restriction of precede-and-command). This approach will be discussed in Chapter 4, where we will see that although semantic or discourse considerations may impose further restrictions on coreference options, it is impossible to state the restriction on coreference in purely semantic or discourse terms. To the extent that such proposals seem to work it is precisely because there is a significant correlation between syntactic relations and semantic properties.

2.3 The C-Command Rule

We will now see that if the syntactic domains for the application of the coreference rule are determined by c-command, all the problems we observed in the previous section can be handled. For convenience, I repeat here the definitions of c-command and the domains it defines, which were given in (17) and (12) of Chapter 1.

(36) A node A c-commands node B if the branching node α_1 most immediately dominating A either dominates B or is immediately dominated by a node α_2 which dominates B, and α_2 is of the same category type as α_1.

(37) The domain of a node A consists of all and only the nodes c-commanded by A.

(36) is the full definition of c-command. However, for ease of presentation, we may consider at times simplified trees that collapse the S and the $\bar{S}$ nodes or the two VP nodes, so that the simplified definition (A c-commands B if the branching node most immediately dominating A dominates B) can apply to them.

In Chapter 1, I also proposed the two hypotheses, repeated in (38) and (39), which I assume to be the general conditions which all sentence-level interpretative rules conform to.

(38) Sentence-level rules may operate on two given nodes only in the case that one of these nodes is in the domain of the other.

(39) If a rule assigns node A some kind of prominence over node B,
A must be a D(omain)-head of the domain containing B.

In the case of the coreference restrictions, conforming to (38) should
mean that there are no sentence-level restrictions on the coreference
interpretation of two NPs when neither is in the domain of the other.
In such cases, coreference should always be permitted syntactically,
regardless of whether one of the NPs in question is a pronoun. Whether
the two NPs are assigned the same or different references in such cases
depends on pragmatic, rather than sentence-level considerations. In
other words, the referential interpretation of a given NP may affect only
the referential interpretations of NPs in its domain, since two nodes not
conforming to the condition (38) cannot be related by a sentence-level
rule. This is in fact consistent with the general formulation of the anaphora condition proposed in Section 2.1, where it was assumed that
the anaphora restrictions assign non-coreference and that they apply
only if one NP is in the domain of the other, but what this domain is,
remains to be shown.

The second condition (39), determines that if one NP is in the domain
of the other, the 'prominent', or the referentially independent, node
should be the D-head node. In the case of coreference between a full NP
and a pronoun (which meets condition (38)), this entails that the antecedent must be the D-head, so if the pronoun is the head, no coreference
can be obtained. However, the picture of anaphora I outlined in Section
2.1.2 has broader applications, blocking coreference also between two
full NPs. Given this picture (which will be radically revised in Chapter 7),
the way the coreference rule conforms to (39) may be described as
follows: Once a reference has been assigned to a D-head NP_1 of a given
domain, all other NPs in the domain of NP_1 must be marked by pronouns
as anaphoric, in order to be assigned the same reference – i.e. their referential dependency upon the D-head, which is required by (39) for coreference to hold, should be marked linguistically. Since as we defined D-heads
there can also be more than one NP D-head per domain (if the NPs are
sisters), this description entails that no coreference should be possible in
such cases, since in such cases condition (39) requires that each of them
be 'prominent' or referentially independent of the other. In Section 3.3
of Chapter 3 we shall see that this is the correct prediction.

Once the relevant domains are defined by c-command, as made explicit in (40), this description of the entailments of condition (39) for
anaphora will be captured by the anaphora condition we have already
stated in general terms of syntactic domains in (9) of Section 2.1.2.[5]

(40) A given NP must be interpreted as non-coreferential with any distinct non-pronoun in its c-command domain.

Our definition of D-head in Section 1.2 of Chapter 1 entails that if B is in the domain of A, A is a D-head of a domain containing B. So, in conformity with (39), (40) assigns prominence to the D-head.

As I mentioned in Section 2.1.2, restrictions like (40) specify the appropriate output of the coindexing procedure, rather than the procedure itself. The way this condition has been incorporated into the coindexing system of the interpretative semantic in Chomsky (1980, 1981) will be surveyed in Chapter 6.

The coreference condition (40), then, is the one we assume, and we shall examine now the empirical motivation for it. It would be recalled, however, that (40) cannot handle the non-coreference of sentences like *Rosa punished her*; for these cases we still assume the disjoint-reference rule as stated in (17).

2.4 A Comparison Between the C-Command and the Precede-and-Command Rules

2.4.1. Let us see first how (40) captures the problems for the precede-and-command rule which we discussed in Section 2.2. The problems arose typically in two types of structures, illustrated in (41) and (42). It would be recalled that I am using here, for the ease of presentation only, simplified syntactic trees, such as (41) (where the PP should, in fact, be attached to $\bar{S}$).

(41)   (42)

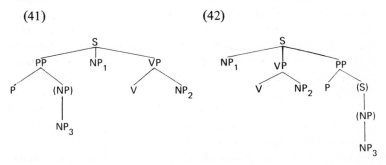

Once we get over the habit of looking at trees from left to right, we can see that the structural relations between the NPs in the two trees are identical. Let us check first the domain relations of NP_1 and NP_3: in both trees NP_1 c-commands (and commands) NP_3, the only difference being that in (41) NP_3 precedes NP_1, while in (42) NP_3 follows NP_1. Therefore, by the c-command definition of domain, NP_3 is in the domain of NP_1 in both trees (in other words, all the nodes in S (or $\bar{S}$) are in the domain of the subject, regardless of whether they precede or follow it). Hence, the coreference rule (40) requires that in both trees NP_3 must be a pronoun in order to be coreferential with NP_1. Applied to sentences with the structure of (41), this restriction blocks coreference in (43),

> (43a) *Near *Dan*, *he* saw a snake.
> (b) *Near *Dan*, *Dan* saw a snake.

in which the first *Dan* is NP_3 of tree (41). In the same way, 'forward pronominalisation' is blocked in all the other cases of (20) above. Applied to sentences with the structure (42), the restriction blocks the 'backward pronominalisation' in the sentences of (28), e.g.,

> (44a) **He* was fired since *McIntosh*'s weird habits had finally reached an intolerable stage.
> (b) **McIntosh* was fired since *McIntosh*'s weird habits had finally reached an intolerable stage.

For the precede-and-command definition of domain, NP_3 is in the domain of NP_1 in tree (42) but not in (41), where NP_1 does not precede NP_3. Hence, as we saw in Section 2.2, the sentences in (43) and in (20) cannot be blocked. The c-command domain, on the other hand, provides an identical account for (43) and (44).

We saw that NP_3 in both trees is in the domain of NP_1. The next question is whether NP_1 is in the domain of NP_3. By the precede-and-command definition it is not in (42), but it is in (41). Hence, as we saw, 'backward pronominalisation' is blocked incorrectly in the sentences in (18), one of which is repeated in (45).

> (45) Near *him*, *Dan* saw a snake.

However, given the c-command definition of domain, NP_1 is in the domain of NP_3 in neither tree, since the first branching node dominating NP_3 is PP, which does not dominate NP_1, and therefore nothing blocks coreference in (45). (The same is trivially true for sentences like (44a) with 'forward' rather than 'backward' pronominalisation.)

Next, let us consider the relations of NP_3 and the object NP_2, in trees

(41) and (42). This relation is, again, identical in both trees – NP$_2$ does not c-command NP$_3$, since it is immediately dominated by the VP, which does not dominate NP$_3$. Hence NP$_3$ is not in the domain of NP$_2$, the coreference restriction does not apply, and coreference is possible, even if NP$_3$ is a full NP (and NP$_2$ is a pronoun). This means that 'backward pronominalisation' is permitted in the sentences of (19), which have the structure (42), e.g.:

(46)   We had to fire *him* since *McIntosh*'s weird habits had reached an intolerable stage.

(*McIntosh* (NP$_3$) is not in the domain of the pronoun (NP$_2$); hence coreference is not blocked.)

In structures like (41), this means that 'forward pronominalisation', which is not permitted with subjects, is permitted with non-subjects, as in the cases of (23)-(26), e.g.:

(47)   For *Ben*'s car I'm willing to give *him* 2 grand.

We saw that the asymmetry between subjects and objects with respect to coreference – the difference between (44a) and (46) and between (43a) and (47) – was a major problem for the precede-and-command domain. For the c-command domain, this is just the predicted result of the fact that subjects have the whole sentence in their domain while objects have only the VP in their domain. The c-command domain, thus, naturally distinguishes between subjects and objects. We saw, further, that there is no way simply to mention the grammatical relations of the NP in the coreference restriction, so that it will apply differently to subjects and objects, since the mere fact that a given NP is an object does not permit free coreference between that NP and any NP to its right, as can be seen in the comparison between (19), or (46), above, and (48). (And compare also (48) with (47).)

(48)   *I'm willing to give *him* 2 grand for *Ben*'s car.
(49)   *See diagram on next page.*

This again indicates that what really determines coreference is the c-command domains of NPs. In (48), the noun *Ben* is NP$_3$ of tree (49), which is in a verb-phrasal PP (unlike NP$_3$ in structures like (42) which is in a sentential PP). Hence, *Ben*, in (48), is in the domain of *him* and the coreference restriction blocks the sentence.[6]

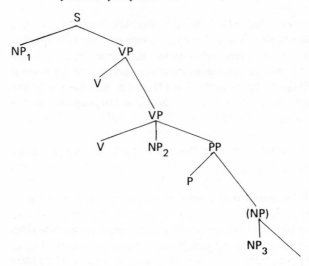

2.4.2. A systematic empirical evaluation of the two alternative definitions of domain depends on noting that c-command entails command, i.e. if node A c-commands node B, then A also commands B and if A does not command B, then A also does not c-command B. When the linear order is also taken into consideration, the relations between the two definitions are as illustrated in (50):

(50)   B is in the domain of A by   B is in the domain of A by the
       the c-command definition   precede-and-command definition:

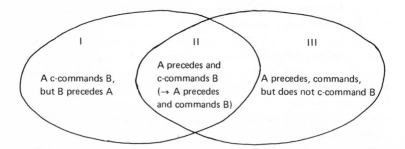

In a right-branching language it is often the case that the c-commanding node precedes the c-commanded node. The intersection, in which both definitions include B in the domain of A, is, therefore, quite large. This may account for how it has been possible for the precede-and-command rule to yield the right prediction in such an amazing number of cases and nevertheless be the wrong rule. It may also help explain why the relation of precede is believed to play such a crucial role in the grammatical restrictions on coreference. Obviously, in an overwhelmingly large body of the language, forward pronominalisation is the only grammatical option. Given the c-command relation, this fact is just an obvious result of the application of the coreference rule to right-branching trees. This is not true for the relation *command*, where all the nodes dominated by the same S equally command each other. A rule stated in terms of command must therefore introduce the relation *precede* into the rule of coreference. The failure to distinguish between grammatical and pragmatic constraints has also contributed to the belief that *precede* is a major factor in the grammar of coreference.

It is clear that the large correlation between the domains defined by precede-and-command and by c-command holds only for right-branching languages. The sharpest discrepancy between the domains picked up by the two definitions will show up in VOS languages (assuming that these languages have a VP). In such languages a preceding node would often be in the domain of a following node. I have not studied cross-language restrictions on anaphora, and, consequently, I cannot argue for the hypothesis that the c-command restriction on anaphora is universal. However, the following examples from Malagasy (a VOS language with some evidence for a VP) suggest that this hypothesis should be considered. (The examples are from Ed Keenan, personal communication.)

(51a) namono   *azy* ny anadahin-d*Rakoto*
      hit/killed *him* the sister-of-*Rakoto*
      Rakoto's sister killed *him*.

(b) *namono ny anadahin-d*Rakoto* izy
     hit/killed the sister-of-*Rakoto* he
     he killed *Rakoto*'s sister.

In (51a) the pronoun precedes and commands the antecedent, hence, by the precede-and-command restriction, the sentence should have been blocked. However, since the pronoun is in the VP, and, thus, does not c-command the antecedent (i.e. it is not in the c-command domain of the pronoun), the c-command restriction correctly permits coreference. The sentence in (51b), on the other hand, does not violate the requirement of precede-and-command (since the antecedent precedes the pronoun), but coreference is, nevertheless, blocked. This is precisely the prediction of the c-command restriction, since the pronoun c-commands the antecedent, although the antecedent precedes.

Since the two definitions of the domain differ empirically only in the relatively small number of structures of the types I and III mentioned in (50), all that is left for the evaluation of the predictions made by the two definitions is to check structures of these types. It is not an accident that problems for the precede-and-command rule arose in trees like (41) and (42). The structure in (41) is an example of type I, since the subject c-commands but follows the NP in the PP; the structure in (42) is an example of type III — the object precedes and commands but does not c-command the NP in the PP. In fact, structures with PPs attached to S like (41) and (42) provide a major source for types I and III, and I will, therefore, devote the next chapter to a more detailed study of such cases.

In a right-branching language there are almost no further examples (apart from the cases with preposed PPs) of the type I situation in (50), namely cases where the antecedent precedes the pronoun, but the pronoun c-commands the antecedent.[7] The situation of type III is more common, and I will, therefore, continue to exemplify further this type of case.

2.5 Coreference in Sentences with Extraposed Clauses

Sentences with extraposed clauses provide another test for the alternative definitions of syntactic domain discussed above. Suppose we have a pronoun in object position and an antecedent in the extraposed clause to its right. If the extraposed clause is attached to the VP, it is in the domain of the pronoun by both definitions of domain and coreference should be blocked. If, on the other hand, the extraposed clause is attached to S, we have an example of type III in (50) where the pronoun precedes and commands but does not c-command the antecedent. Hence, by the precede-and-command definition the antecedent is in the domain of the pronoun and coreference should be blocked, while by the c-command definition the antecedent is not in the domain of the pronoun and coreference is permitted.

Starting with Rosenbaum (1967) it has often been argued that the transformation of extraposition which derives sentences like (52b) from the structure underlying (52a) moves the that-clause in (52a) to the VP-final position, yeilding the (simplified) structure (52c)[8] (which can be, alternatively, base-generated).

(52a) That *Rosa* has failed (should have) bothered *her*.[9]
  (b) *It (should have) bothered *her* that *Rosa* has failed.

(c)

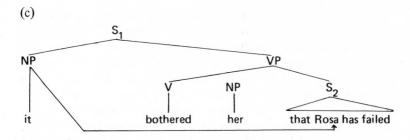

Given this analysis of the position of extraposed clauses, the c-command definition of domain yields the right coreference result: in sentence (52b) coreference between *her* and *Rosa* is correctly blocked since *Rosa*, in S_2, is in the domain of the pronoun *her* (the pronoun is immediately dominated by the VP, which dominates S_2). However, if we look now at other types of extraposition we see that the situation is different. Thus (53b) is derived from (53a) by extraposition from NP (namely, extraposition of S_2) but, unlike (52b), the sentence in (53b) permits 'backward pronominalisation'.

(53a) $[_{S_1}$ Nobody $[_{S_2}$ who knows anything about *Rosa*'s weird sleep-ing habits] would ever call *her* before noon]

(b) $[_{S_1}$ Nobody would ever call *her* before noon $[_{S_2}$ who knows anything about *Rosa*'s weird sleeping habits]]

(c) $[_{S_1}$ So many people wrote to *him* $[_{S_2}$ that *Brando* couldn't answer them all]]

Similarly 'backward pronominalisation' is permitted in (53c) which, as argued in Williams (1974), is derived by extraposition of the result clause (S_2) from its initial position in the Determiner of the subject NP.[10]

If all extraposed clauses are attached to the VP-final position, then the objects in (52b), (53b) and (53c) have identical domains, and there is no way to account for the difference in their coreference options. (Coreference in (53b) and in (53c) would be equally blocked in this case by the precede-and-command rule and by the c-command rule.) An alternative analysis for extraposition was suggested in Williams (1974, 1975). He argued that all extraposed clauses are attached to the matrix S node, rather than to the VP. Under this analysis the acceptability of coreference in (53b) and (53c) would be accounted for by the c-command rule, since the object in this case does not c-command S_2. However, for the same reason coreference should be permitted in (52b) as well. The precede-and-command rule will still successfully block coreference in

(52b), but it would also incorrectly block coreference in (53b) and (53c).

In view of this difficulty, it is appropriate to check the common assumption that extraposition is a unified phenomenon and all extraposed clauses are attached to the same position. We saw that there are two views: one, that all extraposed clauses are attached to the VP, and the other, that all such clauses are attached to S. Emonds (1976), who elaborates the first view (arguing, further, that extraposition is structure-preserving, namely that the extraposed clause is moved into the S position that is independently present in the VP) supports his proposal with the fact that extraposition is impossible when the VP contains a filled S position, as in (54).

(54a) That she smokes proves (that) she is nervous
   (b) *It proves (that) she is nervous that she smokes

However, the same test does not hold for extraposition from NP, as indicated in the following sentences from Williams (1975).[11]

(55) Many people said they were sick who weren't sick.

Extraposition of result clauses is also possible in such contexts, as seen in (56).

(56) So many people told him he is a genius that he started believing it.

So, in fact, Emonds's strongest argument for his analysis of extraposition holds only for the extraposition of 'sentential subject' of the type illustrated in (52), but not for all types of extraposition.

A similar difficulty shows up in Williams's (1975) argument for the alternative view that all extraposed clauses are attached to the S position. In fact, his arguments hold only for extraposition from NP and Result-clause extraposition. His main argument is that extraposed clauses cannot show up before sentential prepositional clauses (if they were to be attached to the VP, they should have been permitted in this position). As we see in (57), this is indeed true for the two types of extraposition in (57b) and (57c), where the *although* clause cannot be construed as modifying the matrix S, but the sentence in (57a) is perfect, in violation of Williams's prediction.[12]

(57a) It shocked Rosa that she lost the case, although she had no reason to believe she would win.

(b) *A man came in who looked very threatening, although the office was officially closed.

(c) *So many people wrote to Brando that he couldn't answer them all, although they did not know him.

These facts suggest that regardless of whether they are derived transformationally or not, extraposed clauses are not always attached to the same position. Further, there is also a more decisive argument which shows that this is indeed true: if the extraposed clause is attached to the VP it should be possible to prepose it along with the VP, when the VP is preposed. This is indeed true for extraposition of sentential subjects, as illustrated in (58a). However, the same movement in the case of the other two types results in the nonsensical (58b) and (58c). (The sentence (58a) is perhaps not a most natural one, but it is obviously grammatical.)[13]

(58a) I warned you that it would upset Rosa that you smoke, and upset her that you smoked it certainly did.

(b) It was predicted that many people would resign who disagreed with the management's policy,
*and resign who disagreed with the management's policy many people did.

(c) I was afraid that so many people would show up that we wouldn't have enough room
*and show up that we didn't have enough room so many people did.

The same point can be illustrated by 'though movement' (which derives the (b) sentences below from the structures underlying the (a) sentences): the extraposed S_2 in (59) can be dragged along with the VP, as in (59b), but the extraposed $\dot{S}_2$ in (60) cannot.

(59a) Though it was unlikely [$_{S_2}$ that she would pass], she still decided to take the exam.

(b) Unlikely that she would pass though it was, she still decided to take the exam.

(60a) Though many people are unhappy [S_2 who live in New York], nobody thinks of moving.

(b) *Unhappy who live in New York though many people are, nobody thinks of moving.

We can conclude, therefore, that while extraposed 'sentential subjects' are attached to the VP, the other types of extraposed clauses are attached to S (hence they cannot be preposed with the VP). Consequently the coreference facts in (52)–(53), repeated in (61)–(63), are no longer a mystery.

(61)   *[$_{S_1}$ It should have [$_{VP}$ bothered *her* [$_{S_2}$ that *Rosa* has failed]]]

(62)   [$_{S_1}$ Nobody would ever [$_{VP}$ call *her* before noon] [$_{S_2}$ who knows anything about *Rosa*'s weird sleeping habits]]

(63)   [So many people [$_{VP}$ wrote to *him*] [$_{S_2}$ that *Brando* couldn't answer them all]]

Given the c-command definition of domain, *Rosa* is in the domain of the pronoun in (61), hence coreference is blocked. In (62) and (63), on the other hand, the antecedents (*Rosa* and *Brando*) are not in the domain of the pronoun since their clauses are outside the VP. Hence the restriction on coreference does not apply to block coreference in these cases. By the precede-and-command definition of domain the object pronouns have identical domains in (61)–(63) since in all three cases the pronoun precedes and commands the antecedent. Hence the precede-and-command restriction blocks coreference in all three sentences. It could perhaps have been argued that coreference in (62)–(63) would be permitted by the precede-and-command rule if the extraposed clauses are attached to a higher S (S̄), and, thus, are not commanded by the objects. Note, however, that the same subject-object asymmetry which posed a problem to the precede-and-command rule in the examples discussed in Section 1.4 shows up in the case of extraposition: coreference is impossible in (64) and (65).

(64)   **He* met a woman in Chicago who went to school with *Dan*'s mother.

(65)   **She* was approached by so many people in Rome that *Rosa* couldn't do any work.

If the object does not command the extraposed clause, the subject does not either. Hence if the suggested solution could be true, coreference should have been permitted in (64) and (65). The c-command restriction correctly blocks coreference in these sentences, since, given the full definition of c-command, in (36), the subject, unlike the object, c-commands nodes which are attached either to S or S̄. Extraposition from NP and extraposition of result clauses thus provide one more argument for the preference of the c-command definition of domain.

2.6 PPs and Indirect Objects

Another instance of type III in (50) above arises whenever an NP dominated by a PP (or a branching NP) precedes another NP. The examples
in (66) illustrate such cases, where the c-command condition yields the
right results: coreference is possible although the antecedent precedes
and commands the pronoun. While (66c–e) can be handled by a modified
definition of command that considers NPs as the relevant cyclic nodes,
(66a–b) cannot.

> (66a) You won't believe who I saw near *him* in *Ben*'s car.
> (b) Rosa never fails to think about *them* on *her lover*'s birthday.
> (c) Rumours about *her* please *Rosa*.
> (d) Details of *her* death fill the day for family of the *latest victim*
>   (Headline in NYT, quoted in Carden, 1978).
> (e) . . . and father Wolf taught him his business . . . till every rattle
>   in the grass . . . meant just as much to him as the work of *his*
>   office means to *a businessman* (Kipling, 'Mowgli brothers',
>   quoted in Carden, 1978).

However, problems for the c-command restriction on anaphora arise
when we consider anaphora options of indirect objects. If indirect objects are dominated by a PP, the c-command definition of domain
assigns different domains to direct and indirect objects, since, in this
case, the domain of indirect objects consists of the PP alone. However,
the following examples show that there is no difference in anaphora
options of direct and indirect objects:

> (67a) *It didn't surprise *her* that *Rosa* has failed the exam.
> (b) *It didn't occur to *her* that *Rosa* has failed the exam.
> (68a) *I met *him* in *Ben*'s office.
> (b) *I spoke to *him* in *Ben*'s office.
> (69a) *Someone should tell *her* that *Rosa*'s driving is dangerous.
> (b) *Someone should point out to *her* that *Rosa*'s driving is dan-
>   gerous.

Coreference in the (a) sentences above is blocked since the pronoun c-
commands the antecedent. But coreference in the (b) sentences is just
as impossible although, by the formal defintion, the indirect-object pronoun does not c-command the antecedent. Note, further, that the similarity between anaphora options of direct and indirect objects is preserved

when they are preposed (topicalised). Thus, coreference is equally blocked in the (a) and (b) sentences of (70) and (71).

(70a) *Him, I met in *Ben*'s office.
  (b) *To *him*, I spoke in *Ben*'s office.
(71a) *Him, *Max*'s mother gave a book.
  (b) *To *him*, *Max*'s mother gave a book.
(72a) *Him, *Don*'s mother found a gun near.
  (b) Near *him*, *Don*'s mother found a gun.

The c-command restriction has no problems in blocking the (a) sentences, where the pronoun c-commands the antecedent. It also, correctly, permits coreference in (72b), since the pronoun is dominated by a (locative) PP, and, therefore, it does not c-command the antecedent. The problem is, however, the (b) sentences in (70) and (71). If the indirect object in these sentences is dominated by a PP, the c-command restriction predicts that they should behave like the PP in (72b), and coreference should be permitted.

To handle these cases we may assume that indirect objects are distinguished syntactically from such PPs as locative and instrumentals. Rather than being dominated by a PP they are dominated by an NP with a case marker which is lexically realised in English with a preposition, but it can be realised by other means in case-marked languages. If this is assumed, indirect objects c-command everything in the VP, and when they are preposed they c-command everything in S, which will capture the facts in (70) and (71).[14] However, the problems for c-command arise in a few other PP types as well, which suggests that this solution might not be sufficient and I shall return to these problems in Chapter 8.

2.7 Coordinate Structures

I have argued that the linear order of a pronoun and a full NP plays no role in the sentence-level restrictions on coreference, which are sensitive only to properties of constituent structure. One case where the linear order may seem to play a role is coordinate structures, such as (73), where anaphora seems impossible.

(73) She entered the room and Rosa collapsed.

It is not clear that the precede-and-command restriction on anaphora can handle such cases, since, given the standard definition, the preceding pronoun does not command the antecedent. In any case, the c-command restriction clearly does not apply in such cases. In fact, however, there is no reason to expect that the unavailability of anaphora in such cases should be attributed to sentence-level consideration. The same problem arises 'across sentences' as in (74) where, excluding literary narrative contexts, anaphora is unlikely to be obtained and where, obviously, no sentence-level account is possible.

(74) She entered the room proudly with her new hat on. A few minutes later Rosa collapsed.

The linear order requirement on anaphora in such cases is attributed to discourse considerations. In normal, rational discourse, new referents are first introduced by their proper name or by a description which enables the hearer to identify them, and once a reference is unmistakably established, it may be referred back to with a pronoun. It is the same standard communication norm that explains the difficulties in obtaining coreference in (73).

As we noted already in Section 2.2, the use of backward anaphora, when the grammar permits it, is in any case restricted by various discourse and stylistic considerations. Although the precise conditions permitting such use are not fully understood, it is sufficient to note here that (as observed, e.g. in Bolinger, 1979; McCray, 1980; and Mittwoch, 1979) when they are met, backward anaphora in conjoined sentences is possible as in (75). Usually it is easy to get coreference if the first conjunct is pragmatically subordinated (Mittwoch, 1979) to the second.

(75a) *She* has the whole city at her disposal and *Rosa* just sits at home.[15]
   (b) *He* has sent Melinda dozens of roses as testaments of his love, and yet never has *Walter* been so absolutely sure of failure. (McCray, 1980)
   (c) *He* hasn't contacted me, but I'm sure *John* is back. (Mittwoch, 1979)

Obviously, the linear order of the pronoun and the full NP may affect the actual referential choice for the pronoun in a given context, just as many other discourse considerations may. Our task here, however, is not to account for this actual choice of reference, but rather to determine under what conditions the choice is restricted by purely sentence-level considerations. If the grammar allows a pronoun to corefer with a given NP, this of course, does not mean that they would actually corefer in a given discourse.

Notes

† Section 2.5 of this chapter was published in part in Reinhart (1980) and is reprinted with permission of MIT press. A summary version of the material of Chapters 2 and 3 was published in Reinhart (1981a).

1. Following the conventional notation in studies of anaphora, marking two NPs with italics means that the sentence is considered under its coreference interpretation only. A star before such sentences means that the sentence is considered ungrammatical in this interpretation.

2. One consequence of this statement of the coreference restriction is that the terms antecedent and anaphor are superfluous. As we have seen, the problem is not defining the required structural relations between antecedents and anaphors, but rather defining the structural conditions which affect the coreference options of any two NPs.

3. Given Jackendoff and Lasnik's modification of the definition of command which we observed in Chapter 1 – namely, that it mentions cyclic nodes rather than just S-nodes – the sentences in (18b–e) are not counterexamples to the precede-and-command relation, since the pronoun does not command the antecedent by this definition of command. However, this modification does not help to account for (18a), nor does it have anything to say about the sentences in (19) where the pronoun is not in a possessive NP, and, thus, commands the antecedent under this definition as well.

4. It could, perhaps, be argued, as proposed in Kuno (1971, 1975b), that in (21b), unlike (21a), there is no preposing and that the PP originates in initial position. Thus, since the sentence is not derived from (22b), 'forward pronominalisation' is not blocked. But the question will then be, what permits backward pronominalisation in a case such as (i).

(i) In John's picture of *her*, *Mary* looks sick.

since the acceptability of (i) cannot, in this case, be explained by the ordering of coreference prior to the preposing of the PP. This solution will also fail to hold in the next example, (23), where there is no reason to argue that the PP originates in initial position.

5. We also have to add to (40) the requirement that the non-pronoun be distinct, since by the definition of c-command, nodes c-command themselves, so without this addition (40) would have the contradictory effect of requiring all full NPs to be non-coreferential with themselves.

6. Of the examples mentioned in Section 2.2, I have not accounted yet for the pairs in (21) and (22) and for the difference between the (a) and (b) sentences in (32). These cases will be discussed in Chapter 3.

7. A possible example of a situation of type I is provided by coordinate NPs. For many speakers, coreference is impossible in sentences like (ia) and (ib).

(ia) ?*Cavallo's* wife and *he* are getting on my nerves.
(b) ?I met *Cavallo's* wife and *him* in the office.

(c)

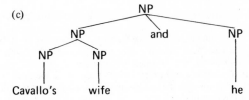

If the coordinate NPs in (a) and (b) have the structure in (c), the impossibility of coreference is due to the fact that the pronoun c-commands the antecedent, although the pronoun follows it. However, it is not clear that the NPs in (i) have the structure in (i). Alternatively *and* might be attached to a higher NP dominating *he*, in which case *he* does not c-command *Cavallo*. Furthermore, the awkwardness of these sentences seems to have an independent semantic (or pragmatic) account in terms of 'empathy' (a notion developed in Kuno, 1975b, and Kuno and Kaburaki, 1975): Cavallo is the center of empathy in these sentences (which is indicated by the fact that his wife is not introduced independently, but rather identified as a function of Cavallo). Their rule stating that the center of empathy should not be pronominalised intra-sententially accounts, therefore, for the inappropriateness of (ia) and (ib).

Another potential example of a situation of type I is a double object construction as in (ii).

(ii)   *I sent *the book*'s owner *it*.

In (ii), the pronoun *it* c-commands the antecedent *the book* and coreference is indeed blocked. However, this type of example carries only little force, since for most dialects of English a pronoun cannot occur in this position anyway, as illustrated in (iii).

(iii)   ??I sent Bill it.

After the revision of the coreference restriction I propose in Chapter 7, it would turn out that in neither of the last two cases should non-coreference be expected.

8. In fact, as argued, e.g. in Chomsky and Lasnik (1977), it is more likely that the extraposed clause is attached to a VP higher than the one dominating the object. Such structural differences do not affect my subsequent argument, since given the full definition of c-command, as e.g. in (36), the object nevertheless c-commands nodes dominated by the higher VP. Note, incidentally, that such cases serve as an argument for preferring this definition of c-command. Under the simplified definition adopted in Chomsky and Lasnik (1977), or Chomsky (1980) (which we surveyed in Section 1.2.2 of Chapter 1), the coreference facts in this section cannot be handled, assuming this position of the extraposed clauses.

9. I included the modal *should have* in (52) to assure that the inappropriateness of coreference is not merely due to a conflict in point of view. It was argued in Kuno (1972b) and in Reinhart (1975a) that when an embedded clause can be interpreted as representing the point of view of a person designated by a noun in the matrix sentence, a noun in the embedded clause can refer to this person only if this noun is a pronoun. However, this restriction does not apply in cases involving a modal like *should have*, as indicated by the fact that (52a) is acceptable. (The point-of-view convention applies equally forwards and backwards, and would have otherwise blocked coreference in (52a) as well).

10. It is likely that sentences like (53c), just as (52b), are not, in fact, derived transformationally. This, however, is irrelevant for the present discussion. My

question is where the *that* clause attached, regardless of whether it originates in this position or moved into it.

11. Emonds (1976, n. 19, p. 146) is aware of the fact that judgments concerning extraposition from NP in the case where the S position in the VP is filled do not support his analysis of extraposition, and he suggests some performance account for this fact. However, this account is based on the assumption that a judgment of such cases as acceptable is only possible if the extraposed clause is exceptionally long, which is certainly not the case in (55).

12. In his dissertation, Williams (1974) is aware of such difficulties and he concludes that 'sentential subject' extraposed clauses are attached to S while the other types are attached to S̄. The arguments below will show that this solution is not sufficient and extraposed sentential subjects are attached to the VP.

13. In Emonds's (1976) framework, VP preposing is a root transformation, hence it should be possible to apply it to the output of the structure-preserving transformation of extraposition. Extraposition should in any case be ordered before VP-preposing to allow for sentences like (58a).

14. A possible argument for this proposal is the fact that the indirect object marker *to* cannot have an independent stress while locative prepositions can. Thus, in (i) the normal intonation would put the stress on *near*, while this is impossible in (ii).

(i) Nea̅r him, Rosa found a book.
(ii) *To̅ him, Rosa gave a book.

On the other hand, if this solution is adopted, a substantial problem to be solved is the fact that, in English, unlike in the languages with clearer case marking, the *to* marker can be left behind while the indirect object is preposed, as in (iiib).

(iiia) To Bill, Rosa gave a book.
  (b) Bill, Rosa gave a book to.

15. This example is from Mark Liberman, personal communication.

3 PREPOSITIONAL PHRASES AND PREPOSED CONSTITUENTS

Sentences with prepositional phrases (hereafter PPs) provide several tests for the coreference restriction I proposed in Chapter 2 and for the relevance of c-command syntactic domains in general. We saw that in these cases, the precede-and-command definition of domain has failed most impressively, precisely because in these structures the domains defined by the alternative definitions (precede-and-command vs. c-command) are clearly distinct. In the previous chapter, I mentioned some clear examples of sentential and verb-phrasal PPs. However, sentences with PPs are particularly interesting, since many of them provide what looks like coreference mysteries: sentences which look identical syntactically differ in their coreference options, and, furthermore, the same PP in the same sentence may behave differently with respect to coreference if it is lengthened. Such mysteries have led several scholars to believe that there can be no grammatical account of coreference in sentences with PPs (or in general), and that they should be faced with performance constraints (Wasow, 1972) or purely semantic restrictions in terms of presuppositions (Bickerton, 1975).

We will see that, in fact, all these seemingly mysterious coreference differences correlate with syntactic differences among sentences with PPs which are captured naturally by the c-command definition of domain. Thus, these cases provide further support for this notion of domain. A partial functional (theme-rheme) account for these cases may seem possible because, as we will see, there are certain correlations between syntactic domains and functional relations in these cases. In fact, in many cases the syntactic position of a PP depends crucially upon the interpretation given to the sentence, and it may vary from speaker to speaker. This provides a systematic way of accounting for disagreement on judgments among speakers. The point is that there should be a correlation between the interpretation given to the sentence by a given speaker and his judgments concerning both coreference and the syntactic tests which distinguish the PPs structurally.

The main purpose of this chapter is to make clearer the notion of domain and to establish the correlation between the coreference options of NPs and their syntactic domains. However, the further striking correlations between syntactic domain and semantic or functional relations in sentences with PPs also provide an example of the potential power of the notion of syntactic domain, and thus anticipate the discussion of Chapter 9, which deals with other interpretative rules restricted by c-command domains. I will therefore include some detailed examples of such correlations.

3.1 Sentential and Verb-phrasal Prepositional Phrases

Like adverbs, certain PPs are inherently sentential or verb-phrasal, i.e. their position in the tree is fixed. Thus, as Williams (1974) points out, *in order to*-phrases can only be attached to S, while infinitive *to*-phrases, as in *We sent Rosa home to please her father*, can be attached either to S or to VP.[1] Other sentential PPs discussed by Williams (1974, 1975) are *although . . .* , (causal) *since . . .* , *whether or not . . .* , and *with*-phrases of the type illustrated in (1c).[2] (I am following Emonds, 1976, in his analysis of *although* clauses etc. as PPs.) PPs which are always verb-phrasal (according to Williams and many others) are instrumental (*with . . .*) and manner (*by . . .*) PPs. In certain other cases, the PP itself is not inherently marked as to its position, yet its occurrence in a sentence with a verb which is strictly subcategorised to require a PP determines its obligatory position in the VP. Thus, locatives (e.g. *in NP*) are obligatory verb-phrasal following verbs like *dwell, reside*, or *put*. Similarly the verb *flirt* requires a *with*-phrase, which will then be verb-phrasal.

In cases where the position of the PP is clear-cut, we get clear coreference judgments. While the sentences of (1a)–(1e), some of which were mentioned in section 2.2, are possible in a proper discourse, no discourse will permit coreference in sentences like (2a)–(2e).

(1a) We sent *him* to West Point in order to please *Ben*'s mother.
  (b) We'll just have to fire *him* whether *McIntosh* likes it or not.
  (c) Rosa won't like *him* anymore, with *Ben*'s mother hanging around all the time.
  (d) *Rosa tickled *him* with *Ben*'s feather.
  (e) *It's time to put *him* in *the baby*'s bed.

As we saw, given the c-command definition of domain, sentential PPs are not in the domain of the object. Hence the coreference restriction does not apply to block coreference in (1). Verb-phrasal PPs, on the other hand, are in the domain of the object (c-commanded by the object). In the sentences in (2), then, the antecedent is in the domain of the pronoun, which violates the coreference requirement.

However, in many cases, the PP itself is not inherently marked (nor do selectional restrictions force its occurrence in only one position) and, as was first observed in Kuno (1975a), its position in the sentence seems to depend upon subtle semantic and discourse considerations.[3] I will illustrate this situation with the following pairs of sentences with locatives in (2)-(4).[4]

(2a) *Ben* is an absolute dictator in *his* office.
(b) *Ben* placed his new brass bed in *his* office.
(3a) Rosa $\begin{cases} \text{looks sick} \\ \text{is riding a horse} \end{cases}$ in Ben's picture.
(b) Rosa found a scratch in Ben's picture.
(4a) People worship Kissinger in Washington.
(b) The gangsters killed Hoffa in Detroit.

Several syntactic tests indicate that the same PP is sentential in the (a)-sentences and verb-phrasal in the (b)-sentences. It should be kept in mind, however, that the position of the PP is dependent upon various aspects of the interpretation of the sentence, and thus it can be relative to speakers and to contexts. In particular, I have found several speakers who can interpret the PP in (4b) as sentential. What I want to illustrate is the correlation between the semantic interpretation of the PP, judgments of the tests indicating its syntactic position, and judgments of its coreference options. If the interpretation given to the PP is different from mine (which would be indicated by a disagreement in judgments concerning the syntactic tests), so should the coreference judgments be.[5]

3.1.1 Syntactic Tests

a. Two Tests with Pseudo-clefts (from Ross, 1973). The predicate part of pseudo-cleft sentences can contain only VP material. The *what*-clause, on the other hand, can contain only non-VP material. We thus get the following two tests, where the subscript indicates the node that immediately dominates the PP:

(5) I (a) *[what . . . did] is $VP + PP_s$
    (b) [what . . . did] is $[. . . + PP_{vp}. . .]_{VP}$
   II (a) [what . . . did + PP_s] is . . .
      (b) *[what . . . did + PP_{vp}] is . . .

Subjecting the sentences in (2)-(4) to these two tests shows that the PP in the (b)-sentences is part of the VP. Therefore, its occurrence is permitted in constructions like (5) I (b) and is blocked in (5) II (b). But the PP in the (a)-sentences is not in the VP. Hence its occurrence is permitted in the complementary environment. (In judging the sentences below, their intended reading should be kept in mind. For example (6) II (b) is acceptable if Rosa is depicted in Ben's picture as finding a scratch, which is not the intended reading.)

(6) I (a)   *What Rosa did was ride a horse in Ben's picture.
    (b)   What Rosa did was find a scratch in Ben's picture.
  II (a)   What Rosa did in Ben's picture was ride a horse.
    (b)   *What Rosa did in Ben's picture was find a scratch.
(7) I (a)   *What Ben is is an absolute dictator in his office.
    (b)   What Ben did is place his new brass bed in his office.
  II (a)   What Ben is in his office is an absolute dictator.
    (b)   *What Ben did in his office is place his new brass bed.

b. VP Preposing (from Ross, 1973). The various types of VP fronting operations must apply to the whole VP. For example, such transformations can operate on the VP in (8), but not on parts of the VP, as in (9). As we see in (10)–(12) such operations can 'leave behind' the PP of the (a)-sentences in (2)–(4), which indicates that it is not part of the VP, but the same is impossible for the (b)-sentences.

(8) $\ldots$ NP [$_{VP}$ V NP] PP $\ldots$

(9) $\ldots$ NP [$_{VP}$ V NP PP] $\ldots$

'Though' movement:
(10a) An absolute dictator though Ben is in his office, he is a sweetheart at home.
  (b) *Place his new brass bed though Ben did in his office, he is not always so whimsical.
VP preposing:
(11a) I wanted Rosa to ride a horse in Ben's picture, and ride a horse she did, in Ben's picture.
  (b) They wanted Rosa to find a scratch in Ben's picture,
    *and find a scratch she did in Ben's picture.
(12a) It was predicted that people would worship Kissinger in Washington, and worship Kissinger they did in Washington.
  (b) It was predicted that the gangsters would attack Hoffa in Detroit, *and attack Hoffa they did in Detroit.

c. PP Preposing. Jackendoff (1972) noted that there is a difference in the preposing options of sentential and verb-phrasal adverbs. Verb-phrasal adverbs cannot be attached to S inside the sentence, e.g. between the subject and the VP, while sentential adverbs can, e.g.

(13) John $\begin{Bmatrix} \text{probably} \\ \text{*slowly} \end{Bmatrix}$ was eating a carrot.

The same difference holds for sentential and verb-phrasal PPs, and it clearly distinguishes the (a)- and (b)-sentences of (2)-(4). (To avoid the reading on which *people in Washington* in (15a) is a constituent, I have added *anyway* to the PPs in these examples.)

(14a) Rosa, in Ben's picture (anyway), looks sick.
  (b) *Rosa, in Ben's picture (anyway), found a scratch.
(15a) People, in Washington anyway, worship Kissinger.
  (b) *The gangsters, in Detroit (anyway), killed Hoffa.

3.1.2. *Some Semantic and Pragmatic Differences between Sentential and Verb-phrasal PPs*

An ordinary intuitive description of the semantic difference between sentential and verb-phrasal adverbs which can be extended to the two types of PPs, is that the first modifies the sentence, while the second modifies only the VP. However, what this means exactly, or what could count as semantic indications of this difference in the range of 'modification', needs clarification. It should be noted that the relevance of this question to the notion of syntactic domain goes beyond the establishment of the coreference options in the pairs under consideration. So far, we have concentrated on the domain relations of NPs (questions like is the NP in a PP in the domain of the object, etc.). However, the definition of the c-command domains (in (12) of Chapter 1) does not mention NPs. It defines the domains of all the nodes in a sentence, stating that the domain of a given node is everything c-commanded by it. If we check now the domains of PPs (or adverbs), it is obvious that sentential PPs (as in (16a)) and verb-phrasal PPs (as in (16b)) have different domains. (Again, I use, for simplicity, the trees of (16), rather than the precise trees, containing two VPs.) The PP in (16a) c-commands all the nodes dominated by S (since it is immediately dominated by S). Hence the domain of a sentential PP (or adverb) consists of all the nodes in S or of the whole sentence. The PP in (16b) c-commands only (and all) the nodes in the VP; hence the domain of a verb-phrasal PP (or

(16a)   (16b)

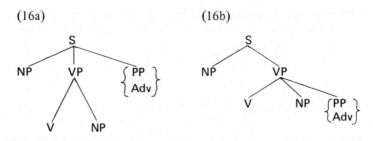

adverb) consists only of the VP. Once the correspondence between domain relations and semantic relations is established, the difference in the semantics of the two types of PP will be merely a consequence of these general correspondence rules. I will return to these rules in Section 9.1, and here I will only list some of the semantic indications for a PPs being sentential or verb-phrasal, and show that they apply to the pairs in (2)-(4).

a. Quantifier Scope. Ioup (1975) has observed that a quantifier in a PP cannot have a wider scope than a quantifier in subject position. Although she does not distinguish between sentential and verb-phrasal PPs, all her examples are from verb-phrasal PPs. In accordance with this observation, in the pairs under consideration here, the (b)-sentences (with verb-phrasal PPs) have only one possible scope reading, namely the one in which the quantifier in the PP is in the scope of the subject quantifier. Thus, the sentence in (17b) has only the reading in which there is someone such that he found a scratch in all of Ben's pictures, and similarly, (18b) does not have the reading on which *some* is inside the scope of *all*.

    (17a) Someone is riding a horse in all of Ben's pictures.
      (b) Someone found a scratch in all of Ben's pictures.
    (18a) Some reporters worship Kissinger in every capital he visits.
      (b) Some gangsters ambushed Marcello in every town he visited.

The (a)-sentences (with sentential PPs), on the other hand, are ambiguous with respect to quantifier scope. (17a) can have, like (17b), the reading in which the PP quantifier is inside the scope of the subject quantifier, but also the reading in which the subject quantifier is inside the scope of the PP quantifier, namely that all the paintings of Ben are such that someone is riding a horse in them (not necessarily the same person). The same is true for (18a). (The reading with wider scope for the subject quantifier requires imagining a situation in which a certain group of reporters follow Kissinger from capital to capital and worship him wherever he is.) This situation is consistent with Ioup's framework, since she observed also that topics have scope options similar to subjects, and, as we will see shortly, sentential PPs, but not verb-phrasal PPs, can be considered to be topics.

b. Entailments. It has been observed in semantic studies of adverbs (e.g., Bartsch and Vennemann, 1972, and Cooper, 1974) that an affirmative sentence with a manner (VP) adverb always entails the same sentence without the adverb. But a negative sentence with a manner adverb does not have such an entailment. The same holds, in the pairs under consideration, for the sentences with verb-phrasal PPs:

(19a) Rosa found a scratch in Ben's picture.
　　　→ Rosa found a scratch.
　(b) Rosa didn't find a scratch in Ben's picture.
　　　~ → Rosa didn't find a scratch.
(20a) The gangsters killed Hoffa in Detroit.
　　　→ The gangsters killed Hoffa.
　(b) The gangsters didn't kill Hoffa in Detroit.
　　　~ → The gangsters didn't kill Hoffa.

In sentences with sentential adverbs or PP, no predictable entailments hold (though entailment may be forced by particular adverbs). In our pairs, *Rosa rides a horse in Ben's picture* does not entail *Rosa rides a horse*, nor does the negation of this sentence entail *Rosa doesn't ride a horse.*[6]

c. Theme-rheme Relations. The two types of PPs differ also in their thematic (theme-rheme) functions in the sentence. Kuno (1975a) has argued that while sentential PPs are part of the old information of a sentence, verb-phrasal PPs usually provide new information. As suggested by Kuno and many others, this difference in function can be checked with questions. A questions (with 'normal' question intonation) usually questions only the new information part of the sentence. (Below, the symbol '#' stands for pragmatic or semantic awkwardness.)

(21a) A: Is Rosa riding a horse in Ben's picture?
　　　B: #No, in Max's picture.
　(b) A: Did Rosa find a scratch in Ben's picture?
　　　B: No, in Max's picture.

(22a) A: Is Ben an absolute dictator in his office?
      B: #No, in his kitchen.
   (b) A: Did Ben place his new brass bed in his office?
      B: No, in his kitchen.

In the (b)-sentences, a response denying the PP is appropriate, which indicates that it is the PP which is questioned in this case (or that the PP is the new information); in the (a)-sentences, such a response is inappropriate, indicating that the PP is not new information.

Another test that can be suggested for the theme-rheme distinction is the occurrence of expressions like *anyway* or *at least*. Such expressions indicate topichood, or afterthought, and they cannot modify new information. (Thus, they can never occur in clefted phrases, which always convey new information; compare *Ben's father, anyway, will never allow it* to # *It's Ben's father, anyway, who will never allow it*.) Consequently, *anyway* can occur in our examples only with the sentential PPs as in (a) of (23) and (24).

(23a) Rosa looks sick, in Ben's picture anyway.
   (b) #Rosa found a scratch, in Ben's picture anyway.
(24a) People worship Kissinger, in Washington anyway.
   (b) #The gangsters killed Hoffa, in Detroit anyway.

3.1.3 Coreference facts

The discussion above has established the differences in the status of the PP in the pairs under consideration. The structure of the (a)-sentences in (2)–(4) is the one given in (16a), while the (b)-sentences have the structure (16b). If we focus now on the domain relations of the NPs involved in these structures, we see first that the NP in the PP is in the domain of the subject in both cases. The coreference restriction ((40) of Chapter 2) requires therefore that the NP in the PP must be a pronoun in order for coreference to hold. It correctly predicts, then, that there will be no difference in the coreference options of the subjects and the NP in the PP in the two types of sentences, and indeed, the (a)- and (b)-sentences in (25) and (26) are equally impossible.

(25a) *He* is an absolute dictator in *Ben*'s office.
   (b) *He* placed his new brass *bed* in Ben's office.
(26a) *He* is considered a genius in *Kissinger*'s home town.
   (b) *He* was killed in *Hoffa*'s home town.

However, the two types of sentences differ in the domain relations of the objects. While the verb-phrasal PP is in the domain of the object, the sentential PP is not. The coreference restriction, therefore, puts restrictions only on the coreference options of the object and the NP in the verb-phrasal PP, while in the case of sentential PP, coreference is free (which means that coreference is possible even if the object is a pronoun and the NP in the PP is not). Thus we get the following differences in coreference options:

(27a) Rosa is kissing *him* passionately in *Ben*'s high school picture.
  (b) *I can't even find *him* in your picture of *Ben*.
(28a) People worship *him* in *Kissinger*'s native country.
  (b) *The gangsters killed *him* in *Hoffa*'s home town.

The (a)-sentences have the same status as the sentences in (1a–c) (and in (19) of Chapter 2): they may need some discourse justification for their usage, due to discourse constraints on backward anaphora. ((28a), for example, would seem more natural in a discourse like: *Although people still worship* him *in* Kissinger's *native country, I can assure you that his glory won't last for long*.) But (for speakers who agreed to the judgments in the tests mentioned above), the (b)-sentences are ungrammatical even in a proper context. ((28b) is still bad in a discourse like: *Although the gangsters killed* him *in* Hoffa's *hometown. I can assure you that he won't be forgotten for some time*.)

3.2 Preposed PPs

In Section 2.2 of Chapter 2 we saw that pairs like those in (29) show that the coreference restriction cannot apply to deep structure, before preposing the PP.

(29a) *She* is riding a horse in Ben's picture of *Rosa*.
  (b) *She* found a scratch in Ben's picture of *Rosa*.
  (c) In Ben's picture of *Rosa, she* is riding a horse.
  (d) *In Ben's picture of *Rosa, she* found a scratch.

Although the sources (29a and b) of sentences (29c and d) are equally bad, when the PP is preposed, (29c) is possible, but (29d) is still bad. At the same time, the examples in (29) show that marking the grammatical relations will not help, since in both cases the pronoun is the subject and the antecedent is in a PP. Obviously, the linear order does not matter either, since the antecedent precedes the pronoun in both (29c) and (29d). Jackendoff (1975) attempted a semantic account for these pairs which has to do with the fact that the sentences involve pictures (or images). However, as observed in Kuno (1975b), this fact is accidental, since as we see in (30)–(31), the same distinction appears in the other pairs, which were discussed here (as well as in pairs like (32) and (33)) which do not involve images. Sentences like (33a) were noted in Koster (1979).

(30a) In *Kissinger's* home town, *he* is considered a genius.

  (b) *In *Hoffa's* home town, *he* was killed by the gangsters.

(31a) In *Ben's* office, *he* is an absolute dictator.

  (b) *In *Ben's* office, *he* placed his new brass bed.

(32a) With *Rosa's* new job, *she'll* end up in the hospital.

  (b) *With *Rosa's* new boss, *she* doesn't argue.

(33a) According to *Felix, he* won the race.

  (b) *In front of *Felix, he* held a candle.

In all these cases, the PP in the (a)-sentences originates as a sentential PP, while in the (b)-sentences, it originates as a verb-phrasal PP. (If the PP is not preposed, coreference is equally blocked in the (a)- and the (b)-sentences.) If sentential and verb-phrasal PPs are preposed to the same position, the (a)- and (b)-sentences in (30)–(33) have identical surface structures, and hence identical domain relations, and the difference in their coreference options remains a mystery.[7] However, we will see now that there are syntactic differences between the (a)- and (b)-sentences, which suggests that they do not have the same surface structure.[8]

3.2.1 The Syntax of Preposed PPs

Within the COMP theory it would be assumed that if there is a transformation of PP-preposing, the PP is moved into COMP position. (This analysis of PP preposing is developed in Emonds, 1976.) Since it is currently believed that there is only one COMP position in the sentence, this means that if a PP is preposed, the COMP is filled and no other constituent, such as a *wh*-word, can be moved into it, or, alternatively, that if the COMP position is filled either by a moved *wh*-word, or by a Q(uestion) or Imp(erative) marker, PP-preposing cannot take place. If we look now at the sentences below, we will see that this is indeed true in the case of preposed verb-phrasal PPs, but the sentential PPs do not obey any such restrictions. Thus, *wh*-questions are possible after the sentential PP in (34a), though not after the verb-phrasal PP in (34b).

(34a) In Ben's picture of her, how does she look?
  (b) *In Ben's picture of her, what did she find?
(35a) In Washington, who do they worship?
  (b) *In Detroit, who did the gangsters kill?
(36a) According to Felix, who won the race?
  (b) *In front of Felix, who holds a candle?
(37a) With her new job, why can't Rosa be more cheerful?
  (b) *With her new boss, why does(n't) Rosa argue?

Yes/no questions are also possible in the case of preposed sentential PPs, as in (38a) and (39a), but not in the case of preposed verb-phrasal PPs, as in (38b) and (39b).

(38a) In Ben's picture, does Rosa look her best?
  (b) *In Ben's picture, did Rosa find a scratch?
(39a) With her new job, can she spend more money?
  (b) *With her boss, does she argue?

The same is true for imperatives:

(40a) In my next picture, look more cheerful, please!
  (b) *In my next picture, find a scratch, if you can!
(41a) With your new job, go spend more money!
  (b) *With your boss, stop arguing!

These facts show that preposed verb-phrasal PPs are indeed moved into COMP position, but that sentential PPs require different treatment. They occur in a position preceding the COMP, and since COMP is the leftmost constituent of a sentence, this suggests that they are attached to a higher node than the one dominating COMP. (Alternatively it is possible that these PPs are not moved at all and that they can be generated both in final and in higher initial positions.) Banfield (1973) has suggested that certain presentential elements like exclamations or conjoined predicates or NPs (e.g. the first conjunct in the sentence *One more glass of beer and/or I'm leaving*) are to be generated under a higher category E(xpression), which can expand to a presentential constituent and S̄. This proposal was adopted in van Riemsdijk and Zwartz (1974) for the analysis of left-dislocated (as opposed to topicalised) constituents.

Preposed sentential PPs share some properties with left-dislocated and presentential constituents – they are not semantically dependent on the sentence (as we saw in Section 3.1.2), and they can be described as 'setting the scene' (in Kuno's, 1975b, terminology) for the rest of the sentence. (I will return to their semantic function in the sentence in Section 3.2.3.) They seem, therefore, possible candidates for generation under E. This decision, however, is not crucial, and I will not elaborate on it.[9] What is crucial, though, is that there is a syntactic difference between the two types of sentence, which is illustrated in (42).

(42a) (preposed) sentential PPs   (b) preposed verb-phrasal PPs

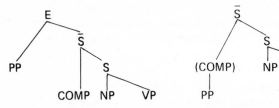

Another possible indication of the structural difference is provided by quantified sentences of the two types. We saw in (17), repeated here as (43), that there are scope differences between the two types when the PP appears S-finally:

(43a) Someone is riding a horse in all of Ben's pictures.
   (b) Someone found scratches in all of Ben's pictures.

Roughly, the difference was that in (43a) it can be either the same person in all of Ben's pictures or a different person, while in (43b) it must be the same person who found scratches in all the pictures (which means that *someone* must have wider scope). Now let us see what happens if we prepose the PP:

(44a) In all of Ben's pictures someone is riding a horse.
   (b) In all of Ben's pictures someone found scratches.

The (a)-sentence loses its ambiguity: (44a) has only the reading with wider scope for *all* (i.e. it need not be the same rider in each picture). The (b)-sentence, on the other hand, becomes ambiguous. Some speakers cannot assign any reading to (44b), probably, for pragmatic reasons that will be discussed in Section 3.2.3, but those who get the sentence (and a stress on *all* should help) agree that it is ambiguous: it can be one person or different people who found scratches in all the pictures. These facts do not yet supply us with evidence for the structural differences between (44a) and (44b), since I have not yet established the correlation between domain relations of quantifiers and their scope, which I will do in Chapter 9. However, note that there is very little hope of finding a non-syntactic account of this difference. Ioup (1975) has argued that topics and subjects have identical status with respect to scope (with a slight preference for a wide scope for topics). However, the major function of preposing is to make the preposed constituent a topic (which means that preposed constituents are always topics, unless they have a special intonation marking). Consequently, in (44), both PPs are topics, so by this criterion they should have identical scope options.

If we look now at the syntax of the sentences, we will see that when the verb-phrasal PP of (43b) is preposed, its domain relations become identical to those in (43a), with a sentential PP in final position – the only difference being in linear order of the quantifiers. A comparison of (45b) and (45c) makes this clear. It would be recalled that for the full definition of c-command in (17) of Chapter 1, there is no difference between the domains of nodes dominated by S and $\bar{S}$.

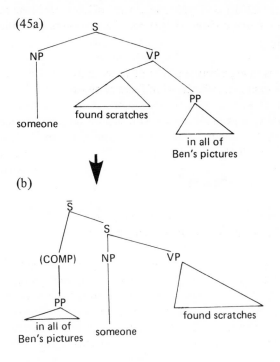

(c)

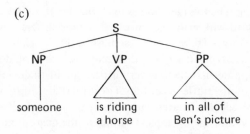

In both (45b) and (45c), the NP and the PP are in each other's domain. In both of these cases, we get scope ambiguity. Other things being equal, if the sentence in (44a) had a structure identical with that of (44b) – namely (45b) – the two sentences would have identical scope options. It is plausible, therefore, to conclude that they do not have identical structures.

3.2.2 Coreference in Preposed PPs

Given the structures in (42), the coreference difference between the (a)- and (b)-sentences in (30)–(33) is no longer a mystery. The (a)-sentences (one of which is repeated in (47)) have the structure of (42a), repeated in (46), in which the subject NP_2 does not c-command NP_1 in the PP, since the definition of c-command in (17) of Chapter 1 allows it to c-command only nodes dominated by $\bar{S}$ – see footnote 9. In other words, NP_1 in the PP is not in the domain of the subject NP_2. Also, the subject NP_2 is not in the domain of NP_1 (since the latter c-commands only the nodes in the PP). The coreference rule, therefore, puts no restrictions on the coreference options of these two NPs, and we can get 'forward pronominalisation', as in (47a), 'backward pronominalisation', as in (47b), or no pronominalisation at all, as in (47c).

(46)

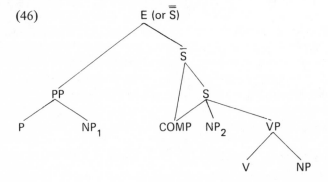

(47a) In *Ben*'s office, *he* is an absolute dictator.
  (b) In *his* office, *Ben* is an absolute dictator.
  (c) In *Ben*'s office, *Ben* is an absolute dictator.

The (b)-sentences of (30)–(33), one of which is repeated in (49a), have the structure (42b), repeated in (48). In this structure, the subject NP_2 does c-command the PP (by (17) of Chapter 1), which means that NP_1 in the PP is in the domain of the subject. The coreference restriction, therefore, requires that NP_1 must be a pronoun in order to be coreferential with NP_2, hence blocking coreference in (49a) and (49c). As in tree (46), however, the subject is not in the domain of NP_1 (whose domain is only the PP). Hence the rule does not block (49b). In sentences with the structure (48), then, the only grammatical way to express coreference is as in (49b) (unless, of course, both NP_1 and NP_2 are pronouns).

(48)

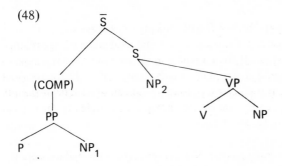

(49a) *In *Ben*'s office, *he* placed his new brass bed.
  (b) In *his* office, *Ben* placed his new brass bed.
  (c) *In *Ben*'s office, *Ben* placed his new brass bed.

It should be mentioned that the decision concerning where the PP is attached, when preposed, does not depend on any semantic properties of the PP itself. The rule is purely structural: constituents preposed from the VP are attached to the COMP of $\bar{S}$, while sentential PPs are attached to a higher node if they are preposed, or, more plausibly, they can be generated both in final position under S and in initial position higher than $\bar{S}$. For example, in sentence (50), the PP *in his next picture* is sentential in its own clause ($\bar{S}_2$).

(50) $[_{\bar{S}_1}$ Ben promised Rosa $[_{\bar{S}_2}$ that she would look more attractive in his next picture$]]$

However, $\bar{S}_2$ itself is in the VP of $\bar{S}_1$; hence when the PP is preposed, it behaves like a VP constituent and is attached to COMP of $\bar{S}_1$. This is confirmed by the fact that the COMP position in this case cannot be filled by a *wh*-word, as in (51).

(51) *In his next picture, how did he promise Rosa that she would look?

Consequently, the preposed PP in such cases is in the domain of the subject; hence the NP in the PP must be a pronoun, and (52a) is blocked.

(52a) *In *Ben*'s next picture, *he* promised Rosa that she would look more attractive.
 (b) In *his* next picture, *Ben* promised Rosa that she would look more attractive.

The last point is, perhaps, not too convincing since preposing a PP out of an embedded clause is not free, and, for some speakers, it is impossible.[10] Hence, for these speakers the sentences in (52) are unacceptable regardless of coreference. The argument holds, therefore, only for speakers who can prepose in such cases. Speakers who can get the (a)-sentences below (which do not involve coreference problems) clearly distinguish between the (b)- and (c)-sentences.

(53a) In her wedding picture, she   [hopes [that she will look attractive.]]
          tive.]]   VP $\bar{S}_2$
 (b) In *her* wedding picture, *Rosa* hopes that she will look attractive.
 (c) *In Rosa's wedding picture, *she* hopes that *she* will look attractive.
 (d) In *Rosa*'s wedding picture, *she* looks attractive.
(54a) In his family, he   [told me [that he is considered a genius.]]
                          VP $\bar{S}_2$
 (b) In *his* family, *Ben* told me that he is considered a genius.
 (c) *In *Ben*'s family, *he* told me that he is considered a genius.
 (d) In *Ben*'s family *he* is considered a genius.

The PP in (53) and (54) is sentential in its clause (and consequently, if this clause is not embedded, 'forward pronominalisation' is possible when the PP is preposed, as in the (d)-sentences). However, since in the (a)-(c)-sentences the $\bar{S}$ node which dominated the PP before preposing ($\bar{S}_2$) is dominated by the VP, the PP behaves as a V-phrasal PP when it is preposed, and 'forward pronominalisation' as in (53c) and (54c) is impossible.

PPs that consist of P and S (such as *after-*, *when-* or *because*-clauses) are always sentential (see Williams, 1974, 1975), which explains why coreference can go both ways when they are in initial position (as in (55)). However, in cases where it is clear that these PPs must have originated in a clause inside the VP, no 'forward pronominalisation' is possible, as illustrated in (56).

(55a) When *Rosa* finishes school, *she* will go to London.
  (b) When *she* finishes school, *Rosa* will go to London.
(56a) *When *Rosa* finishes school, *she* has promised Ben that *she* will go to London.
  (b) When *she* finishes school, *Rosa* has promised Ben that *she* will to to London.

Here again, questions are possible after the PP in (55), as in (57a), but not after the one in (56) (as in (57b)), which indicates that only the PP in (56) is in COMP position, or, in other words, that in (56), but not in (55), the PP is in the domain of the subject.

(57a) When *she* finishes school, will *Rosa* go to London?
  (b) *When *she* finishes schook, has *Rosa* promised Ben that *she* will go to London?

These facts further support the claim made here to the effect that the coreference options of NPs are determined on the basis of their surface structure domains. Needless to say, neither the relation of precede-and-command nor the distinction between grammatical relations (subject, object, etc.) provides an adequate account of these facts.

Preposed PPs still provide other coreference mysteries, such as the change in coreference options when the PP is lengthened. Since such cases depend even more crucially on the interpretation given to the sentence, before attempting an account of them, we should have a brief look into the interpretation of preposed PPs.

3.2.3 Some Aspects of the Semantics and Pragmatics of Preposed PPs

The semantics of preposed PPs is quite puzzling. Of the semantic criteria that distinguished the two types of PPs in final position (see Section 2.1.2), only the one concerning entailments still distinguishes them in initial position: the sentence *In Ben's picture Rosa found scratches*, still entails *Rosa found scratches*, and its negation still does not entail *Rosa didn't find scratches*. Similarly, the sentence *In Ben's picture, Rosa looks attractive* behaves with respect to entailment in the same way that it did with the PP in final position: namely, there is no entailment. We have already seen, in Section 3.2.1, that quantifier scope does change with preposing, and we will see now that theme-rheme relations change as well. Preposed (or topicalised) constituents are known to be the topics of the sentence – or to express old information.[11] (This holds for 'normal intonation': as noted by Gundel, 1974, topicalised constituents can also serve as contrastive focus with the proper contrastive intonation.) So, when verb-phrasal PPs are preposed, they function as themes (or topics), and theme-rheme tests no longer distinguish them from sentential PPs. Thus, *anyway*, which is impossible in final verb-phrasal PPs, as in (c) below, is possible both in the case of (a) and of (b).

    (58a) In Ben's picture anyway, Rosa looks sick.
      (b) In Ben's picture anyway, Rosa found a scratch.
      (c) *Rosa found a scratch, in Ben's picture anyway.
      [construe *anyway* in (c) as attaching to the PP]
    (59a) In his office anyway, Ben is an absolute dictator.
      (b) In his office anyway, Ben placed his new brass bed.
      (c) *Ben placed his new brass bed, in his office anyway.
      [construe *anyway* in (c) as attaching to the PP]

So, a PP in initial position is a thematic element, or a topic, regardless of whether it originates as sentential or verb-phrasal. Still, intuitively, we feel that there is some difference in the function of the two types of PP in these sentences. Kuno (1975b) has described, without much detail, sentential PPs like those in the (a)-sentences above as 'setting the scene' for the rest of the sentence. This correlates also to Dik's (1978) distinction between topics and themes. Although this seems intuitively right, it is worthwhile to try and make somewhat more explicit the intuitions which underlie such descriptions as 'setting the scene'.

    We have already seen that the explanation for the different functions of the two PPs in the sentence cannot come from examining the information status of the PPs themselves, since both are topics. The answer must lie, therefore, in the information status of the rest of the sentence, or in the exact relation of the PP to the sentence. To see this, let us focus on the subjects of sentences with preposed PPs. As we see in (60), sentential PPs can be followed by indefinite subjects. But indefinite subjects are much worse in sentences with preposed verb-phrasal PPs, as in the sentences of (61). (Contrastive intonation of the subject, or a 'list reading', in the sentences of (61) should be excluded.)[12]

(60a) In Ben's picture, a fat woman is riding a horse.
  (b) In Ben's family, a cousin always did the dishes.
  (c) With such poor security arrangements, a thief managed to walk off with the office football pool.
  (d) In spite of the efforts of the police, a bomb exploded yesterday in the courthouse.
(61a) #In Ben's picture, a fat woman found a scratch.
  (b) #In Ben's office, a stranger spent the night.
  (c) #With the boss, a client has been arguing bitterly.
  (d) #With a loud noise, a bomb exploded yesterday in the courthouse.
  (e) #In a great huff, someone just left the boss's office.

Since indefinite nouns carry no existential presupposition, they usually convey new information and they cannot easily serve as topics. The fact that their occurrence in subject position in the sentences of (61) results in somewhat awkward sentences suggests, therefore, that constituents in this position tend to be interpreted as old information. In other words, it is not only the preposed PP which must be the theme in such structures, but the subject as well. The function of PP-preposing in the case of verb-phrasal PPs is not just to make the PP a theme, but mainly to make the VP the rheme (new information). Hence, given some notion of pragmatic 'aboutness' (see e.g. Reinhart, 1981b) sentences with preposed verb-phrasal PPs state something 'about' the PP and 'about' the subject. The fact that, as we saw in the sentences of (60), subjects in sentences with initial sentential PPs do not have to be definite, suggests that they do not function as topics. In these cases, the whole main clause is the new information, and the PP alone is the topic.

The sentence *In Ben's picture, Rosa is riding a horse* can be interpreted as stating that Rosa's riding a horse is a member of the set of things that took place in Ben's picture (or the set of properties of Ben's picture). The sentence with the verb-phrasal PP — *In Ben's picture, Rosa found a scratch* — on the other hand, is interpreted as stating that finding a scratch is a member of the intersection of the set of the properties of Ben's picture (things that happened in or to it) and Rosa's properties (things that Rosa did), or, in other words, that it is a member of the set of things that Rosa did to Ben's picture.[13]

The difference in the information (theme-rheme) relations in sentences with preposed sentential and V-phrasal PPs suggests another type of correlation between syntactic domains and semantic properties. The structures underlying the two types of sentences are repeated in (62b) and (63b), where the constituents which serve as topics are circled.

(62) *Preposed V-phrasal PPs*
      (a) In Ben's picture, Rosa found a scratch.
      (b)

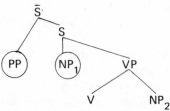

(63) *Preposed Sentential PPs*
      (a) In Ben's picture, Rosa is riding a horse.
      (b)

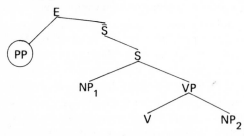

Roughly stated, the generalisation which is suggested is that (in 'normal' or intonationally unmarked situations) only constituents which are D-heads of a given domain can function as topics of this domain. The term D-head of a domain α is used as defined in Section 1.2 of Chapter 1, namely it would be a node which c-commands all the other nodes in the domain α (note that defined this way there can be more than one D-head per domain since sister nodes c-command each other). Thus in (63b) the PP is a head of the domain E, but the subject, NP_1, is not. Hence the PP, but not the NP, is the topic of E. In (62b), on the other hand, both the PP and the NP are heads of the $\bar{S}$ domain, hence both can serve as topics. Obviously this generalisation is not sufficient, since given the definition of D-head, there are, in (62b) for example, three D-heads of the $\bar{S}$ domain: the PP, the subject NP_1, and the VP. Still only the first two are topics. The specification of the complete conditions for topic-hood goes well beyond the present discussion. The point here, however, is that whatever further specification may be needed, in unmarked cases, only D-heads of sentences serve as topics. This generalisation provides also an account for the difference in the information status of non-preposed PPs. In Section 3.1.2 we saw that while V-phrasal PPs in final position always carry new information (i.e. with normal sentence intonation they cannot serve as topics), sentential PPs in final position tend to be part of the old information (or topics). This was illustrated, for example, with the occurrence of *anyway* in (23a) and (23b), repeated in (64) and (65) below.

(64)   # Rosa found a scratch, in Ben's picture anyway.
(65)   Rosa is riding a horse, in Ben's picture anyway.

The two types of structures which are involved are repeated in (66) and (67).

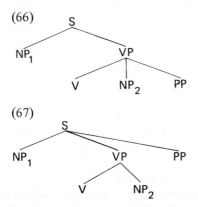

(66)

(67)

The V-phrasal PP in (66) is not a D-head of the S-domain (since it c-commands only nodes in the VP). Hence this PP cannot be a topic of the sentence. The sentential PP in (67), on the other hand, is a D-head in the S domain, hence it can serve as a topic.

The correlation between domain relations and theme-rheme relations may account for the partial success of non-syntactic accounts of co-reference. Bickerton (1975) and Kuno (1972) have argued in different ways that the topic (or Kuno's predictable theme) of a sentence cannot be pronominalised intrasententially. We saw that usually the topic of the sentence will also be a D-head of the S-domain, hence it cannot be a pronoun coreferential with a non-pronoun in its domain. In the case of a preposed sentential PP (i.e. structures like (63b)) where the subject is not a D-head of the E-domain, it is also not a theme in that domain, and hence both the syntactic (c-command) restriction, and the functional restriction on topics permit the subject to be 'pronominalised' as in (30a) or (31a), repeated as (68) and (69) below.

(68) In Ben's picture of *Rosa, she* is riding a horse.

(69) In *Ford*'s home town *he* is considered a genius.

In Chapter 4, Section 4.1, we will see why the coreference rule cannot, nevertheless, apply directly to representations involving theme-rheme distinctions, and where the thematic oriented approach consequently fails.

3.2.4 Further Coreference Mysteries

Lakoff (1968), Akmajian and Jackendoff (1970) and Wasow (1972) all noted that in certain cases, if the preposed PPs are lengthened, 'forward pronominalisation' becomes acceptable. Thus, while in Lakoff's famous sentence in (70a) coreference is impossible, for many speakers it improves in (70b). The same is true for pairs like those in (71)–(73).

(70a) *In *John*'s apartment, *he* smoked pot.

   (b) In *John*'s newly renovated apartment on 5th Avenue, *he* smoked pot.

(71a) *For *John*'s car, he managed to get over two grand.

   (b) ?For *John*'s badly battered old jalopy, *he* managed to get over two grand.

(72a) ?In *Zelda*'s letter, *she* speaks about butterflies.

   (b) In *Zelda*'s latest letter, *she* speaks about butterflies.

(73a) *In Ben's picture of *Rosa, she* found a scratch.

   (b) ?In Ben's most recent picture of *Rosa, she* found a scratch.

Wasow (1972) suggested that these facts indicate that 'forward pronominalisation' is, in fact, permitted by the grammar, but some performance constraint prohibits a preposed antecedent from being too close to a coreferential pronoun in surface structure. Arguments as to why such a constraint cannot be right were mentioned in Section 2.2 of Chapter 2. Note also that for some speakers, (73b) is much better than (73a), despite the fact that the distance between the antecedent and the pronoun is identical. ((73b) is not as good as, say, (72b) for some speakers, but as we will see, this is not due to the antecedent's distance from the pronoun.)[14]

Given all we have seen above concerning the syntax and semantics of PPs, it can be argued now that the explanation for the differences between the (a)- and (b)-sentences lies in the function of the PP in the sentence, namely that in the (b)-sentences, but not in the (a)-sentences, the PP is sentential. So far I have concentrated mainly on cases where the decision as to whether the PP was sentential or verb-phrasal was clear-cut: the sentences behaved the same way with respect to all the tests. However, as we saw in the last section, the relations of a preposed PP in a sentence are very subtle, since they are dependent basically upon the information relations in the sentence. In cases where the PP does not obligatorily have to be verb-phrasal, its interpretation as sentential or verb-phrasal in initial position may depend on complex considerations.

Let us see first some syntactic support for my claim that those who accept the (b)-sentences in (70)–(73) interpret the PP of these sentences as sentential (i.e. as attached to a position higher than COMP). After the PPs in the (b)-sentences, questions are possible (while they are not possible after the (a)-sentences). Again, this holds for speakers who agree to the coreference judgments in these sentences: the (a)-sentences are not all equally bad. Thus, for many speakers (72a) is, in itself, much better than (73a) and, consequently, for these speakers (75a) will be better than (76a).

(74a) *In his apartment, does he smoke pot?
  (b) In his newly renovated apartment on 5th Avenue, does he smoke pot?
(75a) *In her letter, what does she talk about?
  (b) In her latest letter, what does she talk about?
(76a) *In Ben's picture of her, did she find any scratches?
  (b) In Ben's most recent picture of her, did she find any scratches?

We saw that in the case of initial sentential PPs, the whole main clause is a statement 'about' the PP. And, intuitively, we could, perhaps, explain the difference between the (a)- and (b)-sentences in (70)–(73) by saying that the 'lengthened' PP in the (b)-sentences is becoming relatively more important, or more independent of the rest of the sentence. Hence the rest of the sentence can be more easily interpreted as a statement about this PP.

We noted in Section 3.2.2 that in cases where the PP could only have originated in the VP, for the sentence to make sense, its attachment to COMP is obligatory (namely, it obeys purely structural restrictions). Consequently, in these cases, 'forward pronominalisation' will not improve with lengthening. Thus the (b)-sentence in (77) is not better than the (a)-sentence (which was discussed in Section 3.2.2, example (52)).

(77a) *In *Ben's* picture, *he* promised Rosa that she would look attractive.

(b) *In *Ben*'s next picture for Vogue magazine, *he* promised Rosa that he would make her look attractive.

In these cases, the PP must be interpreted as being in COMP, which guarantees its semantic association with the VP. Otherwise, the sentence would not make sense. The PP, therefore, is obligatorily in the domain of the subject, and coreference is blocked if an NP in the PP is not a pronoun.

For the same reason, PPs which can be only verb-phrasal, like instrumental PPs, are not improved when lengthened:

(78a) *With *Rosa*'s feather, *she* tickled Dan.
   (b) *With *Rosa*'s most magnificent peacock feather, *she* tickled Dan.

In the sentences of (73), there is a strong association between the locative and the verb (much stronger, say, than in (70) or (72)). However, the verb *find* is not strictly subcategorised to require a PP. Therefore, it is still possible for some speakers to interpret the PP in initial position as sentential, though it is harder than in (70b) and (72b). With a verb like *put*, which is strictly subcategorised for a locative, the PP can only be attached to COMP position and hence coreference will not be improved.[15]

(79a) *In *Ben*'s box, *he* put his cigars.
   (b)*In *Ben*'s most precious Chinese box, *he* put his cigars.

In sum, unless the PP must obligatorily be attached to COMP (for the sentence to make sense), its position in front of the sentence may vary with speakers and with sentences. If a given sentence makes sense (for a given speaker in a given context) when the PP is interpreted as sentential, in applying the coreference restriction this PP will be treated as sentential and as being outside the domain of the subject. The fact that the position of the PP depends so crucially in these cases upon the interpretation of the sentence, explains also why we find such a variety of judgments concerning coreference acceptability.[16]

3.3 Topicalisation and Left-dislocation

Sentences with topicalisation provide further support to the c-command definition of domain. Consider, first, paradigms of the following type, which were noted in Postal (1971).

(80) (Postal, 1971, p. 197)

   (a)*John* keeps a snake near *him*.

   (b) **Him, John* keeps a snake near.

   (c) Near *him John* keeps a snake.

(81a) *Sonya*'s husband would give his life for *her*.

   (b) **Her, Sonya*'s husband would give his life for.

   (c) For *her, Sonya*'s husband would give his life.

In both (b) and (c) of (80)–(81), the pronoun precedes and commands the antecedent. Still, the sentences differ in acceptability. For the c-command restriction on anaphora this is precisely the predicted result. In the (c)-sentences of (80)–(81), where the whole PP is preposed, coreference is not blocked, since the pronoun is dominated by the PP and, thus, does not c-command the antecedent (i.e. the antecedent is not in the domain of the pronoun). In the (b)-sentences of (80)–(81), on the other hand, the pronoun is dominated directly by S̄. Hence it c-commands the antecedent, and the sentence is correctly blocked.

Next, let us check cases of 'forward pronominalisation', which are always permitted by the precede-and-command rule. The c-command restriction correctly predicts that 'forward pronominalisation' is blocked in topicalisation-sentences when the pronoun is the subject, as in (82), but it is permitted in (83), where the pronoun is not immediately dominated by S and, therefore, does not c-command the topicalised NP:[17]

(82a) **Sonya, she* denies that Hirschel admires.

   (b) **Sonya*'s recipes, *she* will never give you.

(83a) *Sonya*'s rcipes, you'll never get from *her*.

   (b) *Sonya, her* husband would give his life for.

It is interesting to observe, now, that coreference options in left-dislocation (henceforward *LD*) sentences differ from those in topicalisation sentences. Compare, for example, the sentences in (82) with those in (84):

(84a) (As for) *Sonya, she* denies that Hirschel admires *her*.

   (b) (As for) *Sonya*'s recipes, *she* will never give them to you.

The difference between coreference options in topicalisation and in LD sentences is, thus, parallel to the difference we observed between sentences with preposed V-phrasal PPs and those with preposed sentential PPs. In fact, this difference in coreference options is due to the fact that topicalised and left-dislocated NPs differ structurally in precisely the same way that the two types of preposed PP do. Van Riemsdijk and Zwartz (1974) offer several strong arguments to the effect that LD cannot be a transformation. (Their discussion concerns the analogue of LD in Dutch, but most of their arguments hold for English as well.) Although space prevents a recapitulation of all their arguments here, they suggest that 'left-dislocated' elements are generated in the initial position under a category higher than the $\bar{S}$ which dominates the rest of the sentence, which is, under their analysis, the Category E. Within this analysis LD sentences will have the structure in (86) (i.e. a structure identical to that of preposed sentential PPs). While topicalisation sentences may have the structure in (85), or an equivalent structure (with respect to domain relations), which is consistent with Chomsky's (1977) hypothesis that topicalisation involves *wh*-movement.[18]

(85)   Topicalisation sentences:

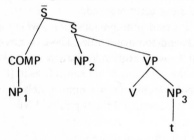

(86)   LD sentences:

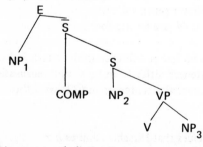

This structural distinction is supported by the same type of fact that supported the distinction between preposed V-phrasal and sentential PPs. Thus, in structures like (86) the COMP position is free, hence it can be filled by a *wh*-word as in the (b)-sentences of (87)–(88). But, as indicated by the (a)-sentences of (87)–(88), this is impossible in sentences with the structure (85), since the COMP position is filled.

(87a) *Rosa, when did you last see?

　(b) (As for) Rosa, when did you last see her?

(88a) *Rosa, who can stand, anyway!

　(b) (As for) Rosa, who can stand her, anyway!

(Further syntactic differences between these two types of sentences are surveyed in detail in van Riemsdijk and Zwartz, 1974.)

Given this structural difference between topicalisation and LD sentences, the difference in their coreference options has a straightforward account in terms of c-command domains. In (85), the topicalised NP_1 is in the domain of the subject, NP_2 (by the full definition of c-command in (17) of Chapter 1). Consequently coreference is blocked if the topicalised NP_1 is not a pronoun, as in (82b) (**Sonya's** *recipes,* **she** *will never give you*). In (86), on the other hand, the left-dislocated NP_1 is not in the domain of the subject, NP_2, hence the coreference restriction does not apply and coreference is possible, e.g. in (84b) (**Sonya's** *recipes,* **she** *will never give them to you*). However, the subject in (86), *is* in the domain of the left-dislocated NP_1, hence coreference is blocked in case the subject is not a pronoun, as in (89). (In other words, coreference in (89) is blocked, since the pronoun c-commands the antecedent.)

(89)　*(As for) *her, Sonya* denies that Hirschel admires *her.*

It would be observed, further, that the structural difference between topicalisation and LD sentences correlates with pragmatic differences identical to those we noted between preposed v-phrasal and sentential PPs. We saw in Section 3.2.3 that subjects of sentences with preposed v-phrasal PPs are still topics in their sentences (e.g. they cannot be indefinite NPs). Precisely the same difference holds between LD and topicalisation: while in LD sentences the left-dislocated NP is the only topic, in topicalisation sentences both the topicalised NP and the subject are topics. This is illustrated by the fact that the subject can be indefinite in the (b)-, but not in the (a)-sentences below:

(90a) #Sonya, a gangster attacked yesterday.

　(b) (As for) Sonya, a gangster attacked her yesterday.

(91a) #Sonya's recipes an expert has praised in the contest.

　(b) (As for) Sonya's recipes, an expert has praised them in the contest.

Topicalisation and left-dislocation, thus, provide a further example of the correlation between c-command domains, coreference options and other aspects of the interpretation of sentences.[19]

3.4 Summary

The discussion in this chapter has shown that independent syntactic tests distinguish between four structures with PPs, two of which (in (93)) are identical with respect to domain relations. For ease of presentation, I will use in the summary simplified trees, rather than the precise ones we examined throughout the chapter.

(92)   verb-phrasal PPs in final position

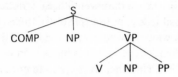

(93a) sentential PPs in   (b) verb-phrasal PPs in
       final position   initial position

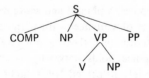 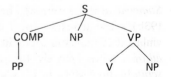

(94)   sentential PPs in initial position

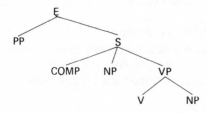

Thus, with respect to domain relations, there are only three cases of sentences with PPs: those of (92), (93) and (94). We found that these cases are distinguished typically with respect to coreference, theme-rheme relations and quantifier scope. All three of these criteria seem to correspond with the domain relations. Topicalised NPs pattern with preposed v-phrasal PPs as in (93b), and left-dislocated NPs pattern with preposed sentential PPs, as in (94), and they exhibit the same type of correlation between syntactic domains, coreference and semantic properties.

a. Theme-rheme Relations. In (92) the PP cannot be the theme (cf. examples like (24b) #*The gangsters killed Hoffa, in Detroit, anyway*). The normal reading is the one where the subject, which is a D-head of the S domain, is the theme, and the VP is the new information part (although other arrangements are possible). In (93) there is a tendency for both D-heads of the S domain — the subject and the PP — to function as themes. Although this tendency is clearer in the structure (93b), it shows up in (93a) as well. (A fuller account will be needed here, since the VP can also be considered as the D-head of the domain — so the decision as to what is theme and what is rheme is not only structural.) In (94), where there is only one D-head of the E domain, this D-head is the only theme and the rest of the sentence ($\bar{\text{S}}$) is the new information.

b. Scope. In (92), where the PP is in the domain of the subject, but the subject is not in the domain of the PP, there is no scope ambiguity — the quantified subject must have wide scope (cf. sentences like (17b) *Someone found a scratch in all of Ben's pictures*). In both (93a) and (93b), where the subject and the PP are in each other's domains, scope ambiguity is possible (cf. sentences (17a) *Someone is riding a horse in all of Ben's pictures* and (44b) *In all of Ben's pictures someone found a scratch*). In (94), where the subject is in the domain of the PP, but the PP is not in the domain of the subject, there is no scope ambiguity — the quantified subject is within the scope of the quantified PP (cf. sentence (44a) *In all of Ben's pictures someone is riding a horse*).

c. Coreference. In (92), the PP is in the domain of the object. Hence sentences like (95) are impossible.

(95) *Rosa tickled *him* with *Ben*'s feather.

In both (93a) and (93b), the PP is not in the domain of the object. Hence, we can get (96) for (93a) and (97) for (93b):

(96)   Rosa is kissing *him* passionately in *Ben's* high school picture.
(97)   For *Ben's* car, I'm willing to give *him* two grand.

In the three structures (92), (93a) and (93b), the PP is in the domain of
the subject. Hence we do not get (98)-(100), respectively.

(98)   **She* tickled Ben with *Rosa's* feather.
(99)   **She* is kissing Ben passionately in *Rosa's* high school picture.
(100) **For *Ben's* car, *he* is asking two grand.

In (94), on the other hand, the PP is not in the domain of the subject.
Hence we can get (101):

(101) In *Rosa's* high school picture, *she* is kissing Ben passionately.

In Chapters 9 and 10, I will suggest an explanation for the correlations
which were observed in this chapter.

Notes

1. Faraci (1974), who was the first to study in detail the distinction between
in order to- and *to-*phrases, suggested that *in order to-*phrases are attached to the
node Predicate Phrase, while *to-*phrases can be attached either to PredP or to the
VP. However, this is not crucial to his analysis. Following Faraci's basic distinctions,
Williams (1974) has shown that the relevant structural distinction is between sentential and verb-phrasal positions.

2. Williams distinguishes, in fact, between four positions into which PPs can be
inserted: VP, PredP, S and S̄. In this discussion, I will collapse the first two as verb-
phrasal PPs and the second two as sentential PPs. Williams also lists *during, before,
after, while* and *because* phrases as sentential (attached to S).

3. This is, perhaps, true for many adverbs as well. Heny (1973) has argued
against the common assumption that the distinction between sentential and verb-
phrasal adverbs is inherent in the adverbs themselves. In many cases, the same adverb can be sentential or verb-phrasal, depending upon the semantics of the sentence.
His example is the occurrence of *lavishly* in (i) and (ii)

(ia)   John furnished all the rooms of his house lavishly.
(b)   *John lavishly furnished all the rooms of his house.
(ii)   John lavishly filled all his bathtubs with beer.

In (i), *lavishly* functions like a verp-phrasal PP (and cannot have wider scope than
all); in (ii) it functions like a sentential PP (and does have wider scope).

4. Pairs like (2) were observed in Kuno (1975b); examples of the type of (3)
(with the PP preposed) were noted by Jackendoff (1975); their relevance to the
distinction between verb-phrasal and sentential PPs was noted by Kuno (1975a, b).

5. The reason why most disagreements show up in the sentences of (4) is that
in the other sentences the verbs *find* and *place* are strongly linked to the PP (where

place is even subcategorised to require a PP), while in (4b) the PP is strictly optional, so it is easier to interpret it as sentential. As was argued by Kuno (1975a), sentences like (4b) can always be interpreted either way, given the right context.

6. Several other semantic tests that distinguish sentential and verb-phrasal adverbs were suggested in Thomason and Stalnaker (1973). Some of their tests are controversial (see Heny, 1973, and Lakoff, 1970) or do not apply at all to PPs. However, at least one of their tests clearly applies to the pairs under consideration here. Only sentential adverbs or PPs can be paraphrased by sentences in which the adverb or PP modifies the matrix *it is true*. Accordingly, the (a)- but not the (b)-sentences below are possible (the mark # stands for semantic anomaly).

(ia) It's true in Washington that people worship Kissinger.
(b) # It is true in Detroit that the gangsters killed Hoffa.
(iia) It's true in Ben's picture that Rosa looks sick.
(b) # It's true in Ben's picture that Rosa has found a scratch.

7. Kuno (1975b) attempted to solve this problem by arguing that sentential PPs originate in initial position, while verb-phrasal PPs originate in final position. The verb-phrasal PPs in final position meet the conditions for reflexivisation (which applies prior to PP-preposing) and, thus, the NP in the PP is marked [+reflexive], while the sentential PP (in initial position) does not meet these conditions. Since an NP which is marked [+reflexive] must be a pronoun, forward pronominalisation is still impossible when the verb-phrasal PP is preposed. The problem with this solution is that the sentential PP can be postposed to final position, and since they are not marked [+reflexive], what would prevent the sentence* She *looks sick in Ben's picture of* Rosa? Kuno assumes also the regular precede-and-command constraints, which, supposedly, could still block this sentence, but they would equally block backward pronominalisation to objects, as in: *Rosa is kissing* him *passionately in* Ben's *high school picture*. If, in order to distinguish between the last two sentences, we establish the c-command definition of domain, there is no need for Kuno's reflexivisation and ordering solution, since, as we shall see directly, this general coreference restriction is sufficient to take care of the pairs with preposed constituents in (30)–(33) as well.

8. Similar facts were noted in van Riemsdijk and Zwartz (1974), for the case of Topicalisation and Left Dislocation.

9. Alternatively, such PPs can be dominated by $\bar{\bar{S}}$, as in (ia).

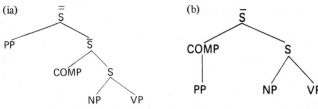

Note that the full definition of c-command in (17) of Chapter 1 allows the relation to consider only 'one node up' in case the first branching node dominating a given node is dominated by a node of the same category type. In (ib), where there is only one $\bar{S}$ node, the subject NP c-commands the PP by this definition, but in (ia) it does not, which is precisely the result we need here.

10. This was argued, for example, in Lakoff (1972). Still, such preposing is not always blocked, though the conditions which affect its acceptability are not too well understood. For some examples, see Postal and Ross (1970).

11. In Reinhart (1981b) I argue that topics do not necessarily represent old information, but such details are not crucial to the present discussion.

12. It should be noted that we are dealing here with tendencies, rather than strict rules. The theory of theme-rheme (or focus-presupposition) relations is, in any case, far from being formal enough to state any rigorous restrictions.

13. A possible line for formalising this distinction using lambda abstraction is illustrated below. It follows in principle (though not in detail) Jackendoff's (1972) treatment of focus and presupposition, in which abstraction is applied to the new information (focus) expression of the sentence. First, we assume that the logical (function-argument) structure of the (a)-sentences of (i)–(ii) is represented (at least in part) by the (b)-sentences (namely, that in (i) *in Ben's picture* is a function from VP to VP, i.e. from a function to a function, and that in (ii), it is a function from S to S).

(ia)   Rosa found a scratch in Ben's picture.
(b)   (in Ben's picture (find a scratch)) (Rosa)
(iia)   Rosa is riding a horse in Ben's picture.
(b)   in Ben's picture (rides a horse (Rosa))

We can represent the theme-rheme relations of the sentences involved as follows, where the argument (the italicized expression) represents the new information of the sentence.

(iiia)   Rosa found a scratch in Ben's picture.
(b)   [λF(F(Rosa))] *find a scratch in Ben's picture*
(c)

The reading (iiib) assumes 'normal intonation', whereby Rosa is topic. It further assumes that the whole VP is the new information. Other analyses are possible (e.g. abstraction of *in Ben's picture* alone).

(iva)   In Ben's picture Rosa found a scratch.
(b)   [λF((in Ben's picture(F))(Rosa))] *find a scratch*
(c)

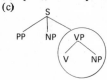

(va)   Rosa is riding a horse in Ben's picture.
(b)   [λF(in Ben's picture(F(Rosa)))] *ride a horse*
(c)

(via) In Ben's picture Rosa is riding a horse.
  (b) [λx(in Ben's picture (x))] *Rosa is riding a horse*
  (c)

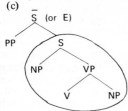

The advantage of this analysis is that it captures simultaneously thematic properties (new and old information) of the sentences and logical properties which determine entailments. This is crucially illustrated in (iv) and (v). The sentences in (iva) and (va) have an identical distribution of thematic material. However, they still differ in their entailments. In other words, while the thematic relations in sentences like (iiia) change when the PP is preposed, their entailments do not change. The analysis in (ivb) and (vb) gives precisely this result. In both formulas the VP (*find a scratch, ride a horse*) is the focus (which, in this analysis, is indicated by being the major argument expression in the formula). However, the internal analyses of the predicates differ in (ivb) and (vb). These analyses still follow the distinction between (ib) and (iib), which, as was mentioned above, assures the correct entailments of (ia) and (iia). Thus, in (ivb) the PP *in Ben's picture* is a function on F (namely, a function from functions to functions), while in (vb) the PP *in Ben's picture* is a function applied to the formula *F(Rosa)*, to yield a formula. Consequently (ivb) entails correctly λF(f(Rosa)) *find a scratch* (which would be a representation for *Rosa found a scratch*), but (vb), correctly, does not entail λF(F(Rosa)) *ride a horse*. This captures simultaneously properties that seem to be determined by the deep structure (the entailments) and surface structure (theme-rheme relations). Within the interpretive approach this is possible since constituents in COMP positions (or any constituent which leaves traces) are interpreted in logical form as being in the position marked by the trace.

The particular second-order logical notation which I have used is not crucial and is used only for its convenience. It is possible that the focus can be represented (in a more cumbersome way) within first-order logic.

14. Another indication that surface distance is not what matters can be observed in Hebrew, where the possessor occurs in final position in a noun phrase. Thus, the only way to express *Zelda's latest letter* is the equivalent of *the latest letter of Zelda* (*hamixtav haaxaron šel Zelda*). Still, the Hebrew translation of (72b) is better than that of (72a), though in both cases the pronoun immediately follows the antecedent.

15. In fact, the (b)-sentences in (77)–(79) are somewhat funny even with the right (i.e. 'backward') order or pronominalisation, since all the additional information in the PP pushes it toward sentence-topichood, while its syntactic position in COMP forces its association with the VP.

16. Another puzzling fact which has been observed with preposed PPs is the improvement of 'forward pronominalisation' when *only* or *even* are involved, e.g.:

  (i)   In *John's* apartment, only *he* smokes pot.
  (ii) In *Zelda's* letter, even *she* speaks about inflation.

Although I do not sufficiently understand the semantics of *even* and *only* to account for these facts, it has been observed, at least for *even* (in Jackendoff,

1972), that *even* always introduces new information, or focus. Hence, by the pragmatic criterion of Section 3.2.3, the main clause in (ii) represents new information, which means that the PP is sentential.

17. (83b) would not be acceptable in some dialect (the one which blocks co-reference in sentences like His *mother loves* Dan). These dialectical differences will be discussed in Section 8.2.

18. Chomsky (1977) has suggested that topicalisation is an instance of *wh*-movement. Thus, the sentence in (ia) is derived from the (simplified) underlying structure in (ib).

(ia)   Rosa Dan hates.
(b)

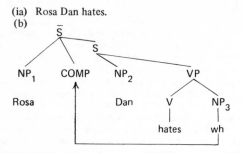

The *wh* is later obligatorily deleted by a surface filter rule. (In Chomsky's analysis, NP$_1$ is dominated by a category E which is, however, distinct from Banfield's E which we have been considering here, and which is attached to $\bar{S}$ rather than $\bar{\bar{S}}$. Chomsky assumes, further, that LD sentences have an identical structure to that in (ib), except that in these cases no *wh*-movement has applied.

Note, however, that if we accept the analysis of topicalisation as *wh*-movement it does not necessarily follow that LD sentences have identical structures. We still can assume the structure in (ib) for topicalisation sentences and the one in (86) for LD sentences. The examples which follow in the text ((87)–(88)) do not decide between these two hypotheses, since it can be argued that the COMP position in the case of topicalisation is marked as filled (although the *wh*-word is deleted) hence no further *wh*-movement is possible. However, there exists at least one argument which suggests that a structural distinction between LD and topicalisation sentences is required: we can find topicalised NPs following left dislocated NPs as in (ii), but not conversely, as in (iii).

(ii)   (As for) Rosa, my next book I will dedicate (t) to her.
(iii)   *My next book, Rosa, I will dedicate (t) to her.

If LD and topicalisation sentences have identical structures, in order to derive (ii) we have either to permit two NPs in pre-COMP position or to assume a structure with two COMP positions, like: [$\bar{S}$ NP [$_S$ COMP NP VP]]. But, then, what prevents *wh*-movement from yielding (iii) as well? In the alternative analysis which I proposed, on the other hand, the difference between (ii) and (iii) is the predicted result: since left-dislocated constituents are attached to a higher S than the one dominating COMP (i.e. [$\bar{\bar{S}}$ NP [$\bar{S}$ (NP) COMP NP VP]]), *wh*-movement is possible only into the COMP position controlled by the 'topicalised' NP, as in (ii).

19. The difference in relative scope that we observed between preposed v-phrasal and sentential PPs is inapplicable to topicalisation and LD. The pattern established by preposed constituents suggests that LD sentences should allow wide scope only to the left-dislocated NP. However, the relevant sentences with LD, e.g. (i), are

unacceptable regardless of relative scope, since, as observed in Gundel (1974), left-dislocated NPs can never be indefinite or quantified.

(i)   # Two languages, everybody speaks them.

(The parallel topicalisation sentence *Two languages, everybody speaks* is ambiguous, as predicted.)

4 A SURVEY OF FUNCTIONAL APPROACHES TO DEFINITE NP ANAPHORA

There are certain alternative approaches to definite NP anaphora which I have ignored so far. For these approaches, the failure of the precede-and-command restriction on anaphora, as well as independent beliefs about the nature of language, indicate that coreference is not dependent at all on properties of the syntactic tree.

We have noted earlier (primarily in Chapter 3) that there are many striking correlations between coreference options and non-configurational properties of sentences: grammatical relations may seem to play a role here, in view of the subject-object asymmetries which we observed; discourse properties (theme-rheme relations) interact with the coreference options of pronouns as well as semantic considerations such as quantifier scope or function argument representations. In the syntactic, or interpretative approach which I have taken here, such correlations are explained by independent interaction of each of the aspects of the interpretation of sentences (coreference, grammatical relations, 'topic' relations and semantic relations) with syntactic properties of their surface structures. Thus all these independent aspects are sensitive to the same syntactic restrictions. (The way this works will be discussed in Chapters 9 and 10.) Alternative approaches, however, may consider what I have called here 'interpretative aspects' as more 'basic' and attempt to derive from them the restrictions on coreference.

In Sections 4.1 and 4.2, I consider possible attempts to define the coreference restrictions in functional or relational terms and argue that despite the observed correlations, such restrictions cannot be sufficient. Recent semantic approaches that are surveyed briefly in Section 4.3 are argued to be empirically equivalent to the syntactic approach.

4.1 Discourse-oriented Approaches

Obviously the actual selection of a reference for a pronoun in a given discourse is a pragmatic procedure which is effected by considerations such as the previous context, pragmatic inferences, or the identification of the topic of the given discourse. It might be in place, therefore, to check whether, as several scholars have proposed, the conditions restricting the set of available options for coreference interpretation cannot be stated in pragmatic terms which are altogether independent of structural properties. The correlation we observed in Chapter 3 between coreference options and information (theme-rheme) relations may seem to support further such a move. So we may examine now potential ways to account for coreference in these terms.

Hinds (1973, p. 33) suggests that the principle in (1) governs generally the acceptability of pronominalisation:

(1) A function of pronominalisation is to indicate that the referent of the pronoun is marked as thematic material.

Combined with the assumption that 'all grammatical devices used in a single sentence must be compatible in terms of their functions . . .' (ibid., p. 40), the generalisation in (1) predicts, for example, that if a certain transformation results in marking a given NP as the rheme, the NP cannot be a pronoun. The awkwardness of 'forward pronominalisation' in sentences like (2b) (which Kuno, 1972b, has attributed to a conflict in point of view) is due, according to Hinds, to the fact that the passive transformation marks the matrix deep-structure subject rheme, but the pronominalisation marks it as theme.

(2a) That *he* would be a candidate was announced by *McIntosh* yesterday.
 (b) ?That *McIntosh* would be a candidate was announced by *him* yesterday.

Although the generalisation in (1) may seem commonsensical (since pronouns tend to be introduced in the discourse when the referent is already known) it is nevertheless incorrect when intrasentential coreference options are considered. The most acknowledged thematic element in the sentence — the subject — can never be a pronoun coreferential with any other non-pronoun in the sentence. Thus, basic facts like those in (3) violate Hinds's principle in two ways: in the grammatical sentence (3a) the pronoun is part of the rheme, and not the theme of the sentence. Furthermore, if the function of pronominalisation is to mark the theme, the matrix subject should be a pronoun, as in (3b).

(3a) *Ben* said that Rosa likes *him*.
 (b) **He* said that Rosa likes *Ben*.

Hinds does not suggest that the principle in (1) alone determines co-reference options and he also assumes the rules of precede-and-command, but it is still unreasonable to adopt as a general rule a principle which would be systematically violated in the most common cases (due to the operation of other linguistic rules). While it is often true that a pronoun would be introduced into the discourse only when the referent is some-how known, if there is any potential functional explanation for intra-sentential coreference restrictions, it goes in the opposite direction from Hinds's principle: a major function of 'pronominalisation' within a sentence is to indicate that the pronoun is *not* the topic (theme) of the sentence. (More precisely, that it is not in topic position, since, obviously, if the pronoun is coreferential with the topic, its referent is the topic of the proposition expressed by the sentence.)[1]

Although no existing functional treatment of coreference has stated this last principle precisely in this way, several proposals follow it essentially. Thus Bickerton (1975) states that pronominalisation flows from presupposed NPs to NPs in the asserted part of the sentence (but not conversely), and it can go either way when the two NPs are pre-supposed. This means that coreference is impossible when the topic (or, the presupposed NP in Bickerton's framework) is the pronoun and the non-pronoun is (part of) the rheme (which, in Bickerton's framework, is the asserted NP). But otherwise coreference is free. Kuno's (1972a, 1975b) relevant restriction is that the predictable topic (i.e. a sentence topic which is also a discourse topic) cannot be pronominalised intra-sententially. Both writers assume that these restrictions alone cannot account for all coreference facts. Kuno assumes, in addition, the syntactic restrictions of precede-and-command (along with several other discourse restrictions). Bickerton, on the other hand, claims that syntax plays no role in determining coreference options, and he adds further conditions stated in terms of assertion and presupposition.

From a different perspective, Bolinger's (1979) thematic principle reaches a very similar result. Bolinger's point of departure is that the anaphora conditions can be reduced to the question when can a reference be 'reidentified', or reintroduced with a full name after it has already been introduced into the discourse. Among several other pragmatic principles he proposes the principle that 'the topic may be reidentified easily in the theme, but in the rheme only if the theme lacks a normally topical form (Bolinger, 1979; (Principle 180), p. 306). What this principle states, in effect, is that if a pronoun occurs in topic position, its ante-cedent cannot be reintroduced in rhematic position, which yields the result that topics cannot generally be 'pronominalised' intrasententially.

In fact, a restriction along these lines captures many of the facts we observed in the previous chapters (and, perhaps even more than their authors have assumed.) To see this, let us assume that coreference is free except for cases where a noun in topic position has been pronominalised intrasententially. The way the restriction works is illustrated in (4).

(4a) **She* wears the dress that *Rosa*'s mother bought.
  (b) *Her* mother wears the dress that *Rosa* bought.
  (c) The dress *she* bought is too big for *Rosa*.
  (d) With *her* new dress on, *Rosa* did the dishes.

In the acceptable sentences (b)–(d), the pronoun is not the topic (although it may be a part of the topic NP). But in (4a), where the pronoun is the topic, coreference is correctly blocked. The restriction on topic pronominalisation can, furthermore, account for the problematic cases in (5) and (6).

(5a) In Ben's picture of *her, Rosa* found a scratch.
  (b) **In Ben's picture of *Rosa, she* found a scratch.
(6a) In Ben's picture of *her, Rosa* is riding a horse.
  (b) In Ben's picture of *Rosa, she* is riding a horse.

We saw in Chapter 3 that the sentences in (5) and (6) differ in their theme-rheme relations. (I will not repeat the arguments here; see Section 3.2.3.) The subject in sentences with preposed verb-phrasal PPs, as in (5), is still the topic. The restriction on topic pronominalisation, therefore, blocks the subject from being a pronoun, as in (5b). (The whole NP in the PP is also a topic. However, *her* in (5a) is only part of the topic, and not a topic in itself. Hence the restriction permits it to be a pronoun.) In the case of preposed sentential PPs, on the other hand, the subject is not a topic for the whole S, hence the restriction on topics does not apply to it, and both (6a) and (6b) are possible.

However, it is easy to see that the restriction, as stated, has very little to say about NPs which are not subjects, since these NPs are normally not the topics of their sentences. What blocks, then, coreference in (7)?

(7a) **Rosa locked *him* in *Ben*'s room.
  (b) **I told *him* that *Dan* is crazy.

An answer will have to examine the relative information status of the two NPs. Thus, although the objects in (7) are not, under standard conditions, the topics of their sentences, the information they represent is still older, or more thematic relative to that represented in the PP, or in the embedded *that* clause.[2] Here we are already reaching an area that is not fully formalisable. However, an alternative functional framework which might be helpful here is that of Firbas (e.g., 1975). Instead of just dividing the sentence into thematic and rhematic material, Firbas assumes a hierarchy of 'Communicative Dynamism' − CD − which is determined by three parameters: linear order, semantic considerations (e.g. the type of the verb) and the degree of context dependency (e.g. whether the given expression represents old or new information). Expressions with a low degree of CD are thematic and those with a high degree are rhematic. Assuming such an hierarchical analysis of the information relations in the sentence, we may attempt to define the anaphora restriction as in (8).

(8) The pronoun cannot be lower in its degree of CD than the antecedent (i.e. if a given full NP is higher on the hierarchy of CD than a given pronoun, they are interpreted as non-coreferential).

Principle (8) correctly blocks coreference in the sentences of (7), where the pronoun's position is relatively more 'thematic' than that of the antecedent. Furthermore, it captures the difference between (7a) and (9).

(9) Rosa is kissing *him* passionately in *Ben*'s picture.

The PP in (9) is sentential and, as we saw in Chapter 3, sentential PPs represent thematic information. Hence there is no reason to assume that the antecedent in this PP has a higher degree of CD than the pronoun.

Despite its vagueness, principle (8) seems to capture many of the anaphora facts captured by the c-command restriction. This, in fact, is not an accident. As we shall see in more detail in Chapter 9 (Section 9.3), there is some correlation between domain-relations and the positions in the sentence which are easiest to be interpreted as thematic. Unless special intonational (or other) cues are used, it is easiest to identify NP D-heads as topics or as more thematic than NPs c-commanded by them. So, in the unmarked case, if a given NP c-commands the other, it is also lower in its degree of CD than the other. That some correlation between preferred thematic interpretations and structural properties of sentences exists should not be surprising: all functional analyses assume some structural parameters such as linear order or grammatical relations.

In Chapter 10, I attempt a processing explanation for why it is easier to place topical or thematic information (among other things) in c-commanding, or D-heads, positions.

The question which arises now is which of the two accounts for anaphora is more 'basic'. Could it be the case that coreference options are in fact determined directly by discourse considerations like those approximated in (8)? In this case, the apparent success of the structural restriction would turn out to be an accidental result of the interaction between theme-rheme structures and syntactic structures, but there will be no reason to assume that syntactic considerations play any role in determining coreference.

The crucial point for answering this question is that, as is well known, the correlations between structural properties and functional (theme-rheme) relations is just a matter of the preferred strategy. The context or the intonation of the sentence may force alternative functional assignments. Thus, although it is easiest to use subjects as topics, with proper intonation, they can also be used as foci. For example, the stressed ROSA in (10a) is the focus, and not the topic, as indicated by the question-answer sequence, in (10b). Similarly, the context may select the object rather than the subject as the topic even without drastic intonational clues, as in (11B).

 (10a) ROSA suggested that we invite her brother.
  (b) A: Did ROSA suggest that we invite her brother?
    B: No, MAX did.
 (11) A: What's Rosa doing tonight?
   B: Ben invited her to his party.

Obviously, the syntactic tree is not affected by such intonational or contextual considerations, and the question would be, then, whether the anaphora options change in such cases. It seems clear that they do not, and coreference is still impossible in the sentences of (12) and (13).

 (12) *SHE* suggested that we invite *Rosa*'s brother.
 (13) A: What's Rosa doing tonight?
    B: *He* invited her to *Ben*'s party.

Since in these cases the subject-pronoun is not lower in its CD-degree than the antecedent, restriction (8) does not apply and coreference should be, incorrectly, permitted.[3]

More generally, the point here is that (except for the cases we observed in Section 3.2.2) subject usually cannot be pronominalised intrasententially. For the c-command restriction this follows from the fact that the subject c-commands everything in the sentence. The discourse-oriented approach explains the same fact by the tendency of subjects to function as topics. However, since this is only a matter of tendency, in the cases where the subject does not function as topic this approach systematically fails to capture the facts.[4]

This point is not restricted to subjects. Thus, no intonation would permit coreference in sentences like those in (7) (*Rosa locked **him** in **Ben**'s room, *I told **him** that **Dan** is crazy) although in the appropriate context and intonation the pronouns in these sentences can easily function as foci and have higher CD than the antecedent.

I should add that even among cases of normal intonation, where there is usually a correlation between the thematic function and the position in the syntactic tree, we can find certain sentence-structures that indicate that coreference is restricted by the syntactic properties and not directly by the functional properties of sentences. As we saw in Chapter 3, all the sentences below involve two topics, i.e. both the preposed constituent and the subject are topics.

> (14a) *Her, Zelda* says that Zalman would give his life for.
> (b) *Zelda, she* says that Zalman would give his life for.
> (15a) *For Zelda, she* says that Zalman would give his life.
> (b) For *her, Zelda* says that Zalman would give his life.
> (16) Near *him, Dan* keeps his gun.

Since all the italicised NPs have identical thematic status, restriction (8) cannot distinguish between these cases. Nevertheless, coreference is possible only in (15b) and in (16). In terms of c-command domains this difference between these sentences is due to the fact that although the NP in the PP is a topic, its syntactic domain still does not extend beyond the PP, since it does not c-command anything else in the sentence. (The subjects in (15) and (16) on the other hand, do c-command the PP, which means that the PP is in their domain, hence coreference in (15a) is still blocked.)

In summary, then, the large correlation between the predictions of the syntactic restriction on anaphora and those of functional restrictions like (8) is due to the fact that usually there is a correlation between domain relations and functional (theme-rheme) relations. However, the fact that when there is a discrepancy between domain relations and functional relations coreference options follow the syntactic requirements, indicates that coreference restrictions are determined by syntactic properties.

Nevertheless, the question I posed in the beginning of this section still holds: it is still appropriate to wonder why the pragmatic procedure of identifying the reference of a pronoun should be restricted by syntactic rules. In Chapter 7, I distinguish between pragmatic coreference (definite NP anaphora) and bound anaphora, and argue that what we have stated so far as the c-command restriction on coreference does not, in fact, apply directly, but follows via pragmatic inference from the operation of the syntactic rules of bound anaphora. Once the restriction is stated this way, there is more room to account for apparent 'violations' of the structural conditions in actual discourse, and such cases are discussed in Section 7.4.

4.2 Relational-grammar Approaches

The assymetry in the anaphora options of subjects and objects has provided a major support for the c-command restriction in the previous chapters. However, this asymmetry may appear to suggest that perhaps the crucial factors governing coreference are relational rather than configurational. We should check, therefore, whether the coreference restriction can be stated in terms of grammatical relations. Although no analysis of the restrictions on coreference within the framework of relational grammar has appeared in print,[5] I will attempt first to show what such an analysis might look like and then proceed to show that it cannot handle most of the problems discussed in the previous section.

A first approximation of what a relational restriction on coreference would state is given in (17). (The relational hierarchy assumed here is that of Perlmutter and Postal, 1974, by which the nodes bearing a relation to the clause are the subject, the direct object, the indirect object, the obliques and the chomeures, in that order.)

(17) An NP lower in the relational hierarchy cannot control pro-
     nominalisation of NPs higher in the hierarchy (or: coreference
     is impossible if the pronoun is higher in the relational hierarchy
     than the antecedent).

(18a) **He* keeps a gun near *John.*
  (b) *Near *John, he* keeps a gun.
  (c) Near *him, John* keeps a gun.

This restriction is sufficient to block cases in which the subject has been pronominalised intrasententially, as in (18a), where an oblique NP controls pronominalisation of the subject. It works also in some of the cases where the precede-and-command restriction fails: coreference in (18b) is blocked, although the antecedent precedes the pronoun, since as in (18a) the antecedent is oblique, while the pronoun is the subject, in violation of (17). In (18c), on the other hand, coreference is permitted by (17), although the pronoun precedes and commands the antecedent, since in this case the antecedent is the subject, which is higher in the hierarchy than the oblique pronoun. However, as stated, restriction (17) can do very little beyond the cases cited. The relational hierarchy is designed to capture only the relations of nodes to the same clause. As stated, therefore, (17) cannot apply to pairs like (19) where the antecedent does not bear a relation to the clause that the pronoun bears a relation to. Hence, it fails to distinguish between (19a) and (19b).

(19a) **She* admires the people who work with *Lola*.
  (b) The people who work with *Lola* admire *her*.

If we assume a more general notion of 'outrank', which allows NPs on the hierarchy within a clause to outrank those not on the hierarchy, (19a) will be correctly blocked, since the pronoun outranks the antecedent. However, the same principle will also incorrectly block coreference in (19b). It is clear, therefore, that (17) should be modified.

The generalisation which is suggested by the facts in (19) is that when the full NP does not itself bear a hierarchy relation to the pronoun (i.e. it is neither lower nor higher in this hierarchy), it still cannot control the pronoun if any of the nodes dominating this full NP (in the syntactic tree) is lower in the hierarchy than the pronoun. Thus, in (19a), although the full NP *Lola* bears no hierarchy relation to the pronoun, it is dominated by the object of the matrix clause, which is lower on the hierarchy than the subject pronoun, and it cannot control this pronoun. In (19b), on the other hand, the node dominating the NP *Lola* in the matrix clause (namely the subject of the matrix clause) is not lower in the hierarchy than the pronoun, and coreference is permitted.

The coreference restriction which captures this generalisation is stated in (20). The restriction mentions the notion 'dominate' which is not a notion of relational grammar proper. However, I assume that this notion can be defined appropriately in relational terms (with a recursive definition using the notion 'bear a relation to a phrase α').

(20) NP_1 cannot control pronominalisation of NP_2 iff either NP_1 or
     any node α dominating NP_1 (under an appropriate definition

of 'dominate') is lower in the relational hierarchy than NP_2. In such a case NP_2 will be said to *outrank* NP_1 (*with respect to coreference*).

For ease of presentation, I will use here the notion 'outrank (with respect to coreference)' rather than repeating the more cumbersome iff clause of (20). This notion should be understood only as defined in (20) and whether this definition of 'outrank' holds more generally (i.e. for cases other than coreference) need not concern us here. We will say, thus, that restriction (20) prohibits the pronoun from outranking the antecedent.

The way (20) is stated, it applies only in a case where one NP outranks the other. This means that if neither NP outranks the other, co-reference is free (regardless of which NP is the pronoun). This, for example, was the case in (19b), repeated in (21a). Since neither NP in this structure outranks the other, (20) allows also the alternative 'order of pronominalisation' as in (21b).

(21a) The people who work with *Lola* admire *her*.
  (b) The people who work with *her* admire *Lola*.

Restriction (20) captures most of the facts captured correctly by the restriction in terms of precede-and-command, and it fares better than the latter in the cases with preposed PP s mentioned in (18b, c). How-ever, we will see now that it yields several incorrect results: restriction (20) cannot block coreference in sentences like (22).

(22) *We should point out to *him* that *Ben* is getting on everyone's nerves.

In (22), there is no reason to assume that the object *that*-clause has been demoted (since there are no signs of the indirect object's being promoted into object); hence, the pronoun in this sentence does not outrank the antecedent. The antecedent is dominated by the direct ob-ject node which is higher in the hierarchy than the indirect object pronoun. So coreference should be permitted by (20).

Next, observe that (20) faces problems in the case of topicalisation. Topicalisation, like PP preposing, does not, presumably, change the grammatical relation of the preposed node. In the case of PP preposing as in the (a) sentences of (23), this fact seems to provide support for the relational restriction (20), since coreference options do not, indeed, change with preposing. However, in the case of topicalisation, coreference options do change, as we see in the (b) sentences of (23) and in (24).

(23) I (a) Near *him, Ben* always keeps a gun.
    (b) **Him, Ben* always keeps a gun near.
  II (a) For *her, Zelda's* husband would give his life.
    (b) **Her, Zelda's* husband would give his life for.
(24)   **Him, John's* father likes.

In the (b)-sentences above, just like in the (a)-sentences, the pronoun does not outrank the antecedent, since, while the pronoun is the object, the antecedent is either the subject or is dominated by the subject. But coreference is, nevertheless, blocked.

These two counterexamples to (20) could perhaps be dismissed with some *ad hoc* constraints. However, I will proceed to show that this restriction cannot handle the problem that seems to provide the strongest motivation for the relational approach, namely the asymmetry in co-reference options of subjects and objects (or non-subjects in general). This problem has shown up in three types of cases:

a. The Difference between the Relation of the Subject and of the Object to a Sentential PP (or a PP Clause). We saw in Chapter 2 that when the antecedent is in a final sentential PP (or PP clause) coreference is impossible if the preceding pronoun is the subject, as in the (a)-sentences below, but if it is not the subject, as in the (b)-sentences, coreference is possible, given the appropriate context.

(25) I (a) **She* doesn't visit us any more, since *Rosa* is always so busy.
    (b) We don't see *her* much any more, since *Rosa* is always so busy.
  II (a) **She* was last seen when *Lola* graduated from high school.
    (b) I saw *her* last when *Lola* graduated from high school.

It is not clear, to begin with, what relation the PP clauses in these sentences should bear to the matrix clause within relational grammar. In any case, to yield the right coreference results, the position of these PPs in the relational hierarchy should be lower than that of the subject, but higher than that of the object (so that it will be outranked by the subject but not by the object), which is an unmotivated and implausible solution, given what we know about the relational hierarchy.

b. The Difference in the Relation of Objects to Verb-phrasal and to Sentential PPs. We also saw in Chapter 2 that it is not the case that object pronouns can freely corefer with an antecedent to their right. While such coreference is possible in the (b)-sentences of (25) above, it is impossible in (26) and in (27b), where the PP is verb-phrasal, rather than sentential.

(26a) *It's time to put *him* back in *the baby's* crib.
   (b) *Rosa tickled *him* with *Ben's* feather.
(27a) People still regard *him* highly in *Carter's* home town.
   (b) *Rosalin met *him* in *Carter's* home town.
   (c) *He* is still regarded highly in *Carter's* home town.

The sentences in (26) differ from those in (25) not just in the syntactic position of the PP, but also in the fact that in (25), but not in (26), the PP is clausal (i.e. contains a clause). This fact, however, is not what accounts for the coreference difference, since the coreference options of the object vary in the (a)- and (b)-sentences of (27) as well, where neither PP is clausal, but while in (27b) the PP is in the VP, in (27a) it originates outside the VP under S. (The arguments for this syntactic distinction were given in Section 3.1.)

This distinction between verb-phrasal and sentential constituents cannot be captured within (existing) relational grammars. The object pronoun outranks the antecedent, which is in the PP, in both cases, so restriction (20) should block coreference equally in both sentences. If it could somehow be postulated that the object pronoun in (27a) does not outrank the sentential PP (say, because this PP is attached to a higher clause and, thus, bears no relation to the clause containing the object pronoun), the subject of such sentences will also fail to outrank the PP and (20) will incorrectly permit coreference in (27c).

c. The Difference between the Relation of the Subject and of the Object to a Preposed PP. As was mentioned above, the transformation of PP preposing does not change grammatical relations, which accounts for the partial success of restriction (20) in handling coreference in this case. However, we noted in Section 2.2 that the coreference options of the object do change when the PP is preposed. Thus, coreference is possible in the (b)-sentences below where the pronoun is the object, though it was impossible before the preposing of the PP, as in the (c)-sentences. However, when the pronoun is the subject, as in (a), coreference is impossible.

(28a) *With *Ben's* peacock feather *he* tickled Rosa gently.
   (b) With *Ben's* peacock feather, Rosa tickled *him* gently.
   (c) *Rosa tickled *him* gently with *Ben's* peacock feather.

(29a) *For *Ben's* car *he's* asking two grand.
  (b) For *Ben's* car I'll give *him* at most two grand.
  (c) *I'll give *him* at most two grand for *Ben's* car.

The subject pronoun in the (a)-sentences and the object pronouns in the (b)-sentences equally outrank the antecedents, which are dominated by an oblique NP. Hence, restriction (20) cannot capture the differences in coreference options between these sentences.

In sum, we saw that the particular type of subject-object asymmetry which is handled by the c-command restriction cannot be handled by a relational restriction. This is due, mainly, to two reasons. First, coreference options may depend upon the syntactic position of the antecedent, e.g. whether it is inside or outside the VP. This information cannot be captured naturally within existing relational grammars. Next, there exist movement rules which do not change grammatical relations, but they do, nevertheless, change the tree-structure of sentences, and also the coreference options of NPs. The fact that in these cases the relational restriction fails, suggests that the restriction on coreference is configurational (i.e. it applies to surface-structure trees) rather than relational.[6]

4.3 Semantic Approaches

Keenan (1974) suggested an outline for an analysis in which coreference options of NPs (as well as quantifier-scope) are determined on the basis of the logical (i.e. function-argument) structures of their sentences. The major part of the general principle he suggests is given in (30). (The use of the term 'functional' here is different from that in the previous sections. It means simply that the principle applies to function-argument expressions.)

(30) *The Functional Principle*
  (i) The reference of the argument expression (in a function-argument expression) must be determinable *independently* of the meaning or reference of the function symbol. (Keenan, 1974, §1)

From (the full formulation of) the Functional Principle it follows that if there are any dependency relations between expressions in argument position and expressions in the function position, the latter may depend upon the former, but not conversely. Two examples of dependency relations are 'pronominalisation' and relative scope. Pronouns may be viewed as dependent upon their antecedents for determining their reference, and somewhat similarly, when a quantified NP, α, is in the scope of a quantified NP, β, α depends on β but not conversely. The functional principle, thus, is an attempt at a unified account for anaphora and for quantifier scope. Such an account, if correct, could explain the correlation we observed in Chapter 3 between anaphora options and the scope-interpretation of sentences. The restrictions which are derived from the functional principle (30) are stated in (31) and (32).

> (31) NPs in function symbols cannot control the pronominalisation of their arguments. (Keenan, 1974, §3.1)
> (32) Quantified NPs in argument position generally have wider logical scope than NPs in the function symbol. (ibid., §3.2)

Within a non-transformational approach to coreference, a rule equivalent to (31) will block coreference in semantic representations where the pronoun is in an argument position and the full NP is in the function expression.

Since the restrictions in (31) and (32) operate on semantic (logical) representations, their application depends crucially upon the precise assignment of function-argument analyses to sentences of natural languages. Keenan argues that in basic (simplex) sentences like *Ben hit Rosa* the subject occupies the argument position and the VP (*hit Rosa*) is the function symbol. (Arguments for this and the following function-argument assignments are developed extensively in Keenan and Faltz, 1978.) Given this analysis, the restriction on coreference in (31) will block coreference in (33b) (where the argument is a pronoun) but not in (33a).

> (33a) (*Ben*) (hit *his* friend)
>   (b) *(*He*) (hit *Ben*'s friend)

This analysis can be extended to more complex sentences as in (34), where the *that* clause, which is in the VP, is part of the function expression. Hence (34b), in which the argument is a pronoun, violates the requirement in (31).

> (34a) (*Rosa*) (denied that *she* hit Ben)
>   (b) *(*She*) (denied that *Rosa* hit Ben)

When scope assignment applies to semantic representations of this type, the principle (32) will assign sentence (35a) the quantified structure in (35b) — namely, it would give wider scope to the universal quantifier.

(35a) (Every girl) (kissed some boy)
   (b) ($\forall$x) ($\exists$y) (kissed x,y))

(The interpretation of 'wider scope' means that in the interpretation of (35a), the choice of a girl, is independent of the choice of a boy, while the choice of a boy may depend on the choice of a girl.)

Another example of the constructions which Keenan discusses is that of possessive NPs. He suggests that in many types of such constructions the 'possessor' NP (e.g. *John* in (36a)) is the argument expression and the other NP (e.g. *analysis of himself*) represents a function (from NPs to NPs, syntactically speaking). Consequently the principle (31) permits coreference in (36a) but blocks it in (36b), where the argument expression is a pronoun.

(36a) (*John's*) (analysis of *himself*)
   (b) *(*his*) (analysis of *John*)

Examples like *Every country's president attended the meeting* illustrate that the scope rule in (32) applies correctly to these structures assigning wider scope to *every* (rather than the reading in which there is a president such that he is the president of every country and he attended).

Given this analysis, it seems that independently motivated semantic considerations determine coreference options, and that the coreference rule may apply directly to logical representations (function-argument expressions) and need not refer to syntactic relations at all. Keenan himself does not make this claim. He argues only that coreference facts in natural languages would not violate the Functional Principle (30), though independent syntactic constraints are needed to yield the full range of coreference facts. However, the functional principle has been adopted and developed recently by Bach and Partee (1980) who argue that, in fact, the anaphora restrictions do apply directly to semantic representations. Of the several function-argument restrictions they propose, the one relevant for the cases of definite NP coreference that we have examined so far (in the previous chapters) is (37).

(37) A pronoun cannot be a stipulated coreferent to an NP that occurs in a constituent interpreted as a function with the pronoun as argument. (Bach and Partee, 1980, principle B'.)

Similar to the structural restriction we have been assuming, (37) determines only when coreference is impossible and in all the cases not blocked by it, coreference is free, regardless of the order of the pronoun and the antecedent. For example, coreference is, correctly, permitted in the cases of (38).

(38a) (The teacher *he* likes) (gave *Dan* an A).
  (b) (Jokes about *her*) (upset *Rosa*).
  (c) (*Her* parents) (are convinced that *Rosa* is a genius).

Although the pronoun in these sentences is part of the argument expression and the antecedent is in the function expression, the pronoun is not itself the argument, and (38) prohitibs coreference only if the pronoun is the direct argument.

Given the logical syntax (function-argument structures) assumed by this semantic approach, principle (37) yields, indeed, identical results to those of the c-command restriction, in all the cases we examined in the previous chapters. In fact, this is precisely what the theory I propose here predicts. Note that the function-argument representations proposed by Bach and Partee (e.g. 1980) and by Keenan and Faltz (1978) are not arbitrary. They assume a choice among many equivalent representations for the same sentences, and the one selected is that which is 'isomorphic' with the syntactic structure of the sentence. (Another way to put it is that their coreference restriction applies, in fact, to a level of logical syntax which reflects properties of the surface structure.)

These isomorphic representations are precisely the ones determined by c-command relations, and in Chapter 9 (Section 9.1) I state the rules mapping surface-structures onto function-argument representation in these terms. This mapping yields the result that a c-commanding NP is interpreted as an argument of a function consisting of the interpretations of all (and only) the nodes in its domain, so, obviously, a restriction stated in argument-function terms would be equivalent to a restriction stated directly in terms of c-command. The few cases where they are not equivalent are those which are, independently, problematic for both approaches – the cases where the semantic representations seem to be not isomorphic to the surface structure.[7]

Since the two approaches are equivalent (except for the cases I just mentioned), the choice between them cannot be based on empirical grounds, and it depends on the overall theoretical picture of natural language – an area which I shall not enter into here. I should mention only that there is no obvious advantage for the semantic approach in terms of providing an explanation for why coreference should be restricted the way it is. It may seem that the functional principle (30) provides such an explanation, since the requirement that the argument must be identifiable independently of the function may make sense, semantically. Note, however, that although the functional restrictions (37) yields the right coreference results, the results themselves do not conform to principle (30). Thus, (37) correctly permits coreference in the sentences of (38), e.g. (38a) (*the teacher* **he** *liked*) (*gave* **Dan** *an A*). However, the coreference interpretation of this sentence actually violates the requirement of principle (30), since the reference of the argument expression *the teacher he liked* cannot be determined independently of the reference of *Dan* in the function expression.[8] So it seems that principle (30), as stated, is simply not a correct generalisation, and, in any case, it is not what explains restriction (37) (whose results do not conform with it). If this is the case, (37) is as 'mechanical' a restriction as the syntactic restriction, and it has no 'explanatory' advantages over the latter.

Notes

1. The source of the confusion which underlies Hind's principle (1) is the lack of a distinction between the reference of pronouns and their functional role in the sentence. The referent of a pronoun is often assumed to be known to the hearer (or to be in a way one of the discourse topics). However, this does not mean that the pronoun itself functions in its sentence as the topic (or as the thematic element). If the distinction between NPs and their referents is ignored, the distinction between theme and rheme is completely empty when applied to coreferential NPs. On this point, see also Reinhart (1981b).

2. A famous test for this claim is possible question-answer sequences. Thus (iia) is a more appropriate answer to (i) (when asked with normal question intonation) than (iib).

   (i) A: Did Rosa meet Dan at the party?
  (iia) B: No, at the restaurant.
   (b) B: No, Bill./ No, she met Bill.

3. Note that there is no independent restriction preventing stressed focus-NPs from being pronouns, as illustrated in (i).

   (i) Rosa's brother suggested that we invite HER.

4. Bolinger (1977, 1979) has noted several counterexamples to the assumption that subjects can never be pronominalised intrasententially. (While some of them are of the type explained here syntactically in Section 3.2.2, many others are not.) However, these examples are independent of the topic-function of the subject (in all his relevant examples the subject *is* the topic). They include mainly cases of pragmatic 'separation' as in (i) or cases of enjoined sentences as in (ii).

(i) He was recognizable, I tell you, the moment John arrived. (Bolinger, 1979, p. 188)

(iia) He didn't do as he was told, so John had to take the consequences. (Bolinger, 1977, p. 123)

(b) He won't help you, unless you can convince John that you are sincere. (ibid., p. 115)

While (i) is indeed a pragmatic violation of the c-command restriction, we have already noted in Section 2.7 that there are no sentence level restrictions on conjoined sentences — i.e. the cases in (ii) do not violate the c-command restriction since the pronoun does not c-command the antecedent. In Section 7.4, I return to 'pragmatic violations' of the structural restriction, and the account I propose there will capture another type of Bolinger's counterexamples.

5. Johnson and Postal (1981) suggest briefly that it is plausible that 'pronominalisation constraints' could be captured within relational grammar by the 'outrank' relation. However, as they state (in Section 11.3), they do not attempt the specification of this restriction. (Their definition of outrank is not the one I offer below for 'outrank with respect to coreference'.) Throughout the discussion I assume the earlier and more familiar version of relational grammar introduced in Perlmutter and Postal (1974). It is possible that few (certainly not all) of the problems posed below for a relational constraint can be better handled by the more elaborate theory presented by Johnson and Postal.

6. It may seem that a relational restriction would fare better in stating the conditions for reflexivisation, which is believed to be a simplex S phenomenon. Note, however, that even here a relational restriction will fail to capture the subject-object asymmetry in the case of preposed constituents. In (i) both the subject and the indirect object can control reflexivisation of the oblique NP, which is consistent with the relational hierarchy. However, when the oblique NP is preposed, only the subject, as in (iia), but not the object, as in (iib), may control its reflexivisation.

(ia) *John* always talks to Rosa about *himself*.

(b) John always talks to *Rosa* about *herself*.

(iia) About *himself*, *John* always talks to Rosa.

(b) *About *herself*, John always talks to *Rosa*.

(The c-command restriction on reflexivisation will be discussed in the next chapter.)

7. This is primarily the case with certain types of PPs, some of which I shall return to in Chapter 8. As shown in Bach and Partee (1980), in such cases the semantic restriction yields correct results where the c-command rule fails, and it is indeed in this area that an attempt to evaluate the two approaches should concentrate. However (as was pointed out to me by Barbara Partee, personal communication), the semantic approach works here only at the cost of giving up the crucial requirement of isomorphism or compositionality. Consequently, it is not clear that it has an advantage over an attempt to solve these problems syntactically by reanalysis or some *ad hoc* rules.

8. A similar point was made by Dowty (1980).

5 BOUND ANAPHORA

So far we have examined the anaphora options of definite NPs only, and ignored in the examples cases with indefinite or quantified antecedents. This was necessary since while the latter observe the anaphora conditions we examined ((17) and (40) of Chapter 2) these conditions are not sufficient to handle all anaphora facts of quantified NPs, which seem to require a special, stronger condition. We have also considered in the previous discussion only anaphora involving non-R(eflexive or reciprocal) pronouns, since the latter, too, while observing the general anaphora conditions require a specific, stronger restriction.

What these two cases (anaphora with quantified antecedents and with R-pronouns) have in common is that the anaphora interpretation of the pronoun in both cases involves its translation as a bound variable, and in this chapter we will examine the structural conditions that restrict this type of interpretation. The discussion here is, again, limited to the structural aspects of bound anaphora. I will turn to the semantic interpretation of pronouns in Chapter 7, where I will argue also that the anaphora problems can be restated in a way that does not require separate conditions for general anaphora and for bound anaphora, and, in fact, the bound anaphora problem is the only sentence-level anaphora problem.

5.1 Quantified Antecedents

5.1.1 The problem

The general anaphora condition we discussed ((17) of Chapter 2) blocks coreference between any given NP and any non-pronouns in its domain, e.g. it blocks anaphora interpretation in both (1) and (2).

(1) *He* exploits the secretary that works for *Felix*.
(2) *He* exploits the secretary that works for *each of the managers*.

The point is, however, that when we consider quantified antecedents, there are many cases where the general anaphora condition allows, inappropriately, anaphora interpretation. Compare, for example, the sentences in (3) with those in (4).

(3a) The secretary who works for *him* despises *Siegfried*.
  (b) The fact that *she* has already climbed this mountain before encouraged *Rosa* to try again.
  (c) In *his* flat, I saw *Bill* washing the dishes.
(4a) *The secretary who worked for *him* despised each of the managers.
  (b) *The fact that *he* has already climbed this mountain before encouraged *someone* to try again.
  (c) *In *his* apartment, I saw *nobody* washing the dishes.

In all these sentences the pronoun is not contra-indexed or marked as non-coreferential with the potential antecedent by the general anaphora condition. Nevertheless, while free coreference is possible in (3) the pronoun cannot be interpreted as bound by the operator corresponding to the italicised NPs in (4). The puzzling problem about these facts, known as the 'weak crossover' cases (Wasow, 1972) is that they do not follow from semantic considerations: we can see this if we compare (4a) and (5).

(5) The secretary who worked for *each of the managers* despises *him*.
(6a) (Each x: x a manager) (the secretary who works for him despises x).
  (b) (Each x: x a manager) (the secretary who works for x despises x).

The unavailability of anaphora interpretation in (5) is easily explained on semantic grounds: since in the semantic interpretation of the sentence the pronoun is not in the scope of the operator corresponding to *each manager*, it obviously cannot be interpreted as a variable bound by this operator. This, however, is not the case with (4a). A rough logical formula which can reasonably correspond to this sentence is the one given in (6a), in which the pronoun is in the scope of the operator and its translation as a bound variable which would yield the formula in (6b) should be perfectly acceptable. For some reason, however, the logical formula (6b) is not expressible in English by means of sentences like (4a), which cannot be so interpreted. It is also not the case that quantified NPs cannot bind pronouns at all in natural language — they obviously can, e.g. in (7).

(7) Each of the managers exploits the secretary who works for him.

So the unavailability of the anaphora (bound-variable) interpretation in the sentences of (4), or the difference between (4a) and (7), must be attributed to structural properties of their surface structure which the anaphora or coindexing conditions should then specify.[1] Postal (1970, 1971), who was the first to discuss such cases in detail, suggested that indefinite NPs obey a special restriction blocking any kind of backward pronominalisation. Though I shall soon argue that this is not the correct generalisation, some syntactic account is needed.

A similar famous problem arises in sentences to which *wh*-movement has applied, as we see if we compare (3) and (8).

(8a) **Who does the secretary who works for *him* despise *t*?
   (b) **The guy *who* those who have met *him* say *t* was dangerous was arrested.
   (c) **Who did the fact that *he* had climbed this mountain before encourage *t* to try again?
(9a) **Who did *he* say *t* was brave?
   (b) **The guy *who* I told *him* that I like *t* was offended.
(10a) *Who* *t* insisted that those who like *him* are crazy?
   (b) *Who* did you accuse *t* of killing *his* mother?

These cases have received several analyses that will be mentioned below. Within trace theory (as e.g. in Wasow, 1972, and Chomsky, 1975), which I will assume here, the problem presented by (8) concerns anaphora options of traces. Thus, in (10), it would be assumed that the trace *t* (rather than the *wh*-word itself) is anaphorically related to the pronoun to its right. Within this framework, the general coreference restriction we have examined is sufficient to block the sentences in (9): the trace is not defined as a pronoun, hence in the sentences in (9), we find a non-pronoun (t) in the domain of a pronoun, which violates the requirements for anaphora. These sentences are, then, blocked in the same way as sentences like **He *said that* Bill *was brave* and **I told* him *that I like* Bill. This same coreference restriction, however, is not sufficient to block the sentences in (8): the traces in (8) are not in the domain of the pronouns (the pronouns do not c-command the traces). Hence, the coreference restriction as stated so far permits anaphora in these cases. As with quantified NPs, it is not the case that traces can never have anaphoric relations with pronouns. In (10), where the trace happens to precede the pronoun, anaphora is permitted, while in (8), where the pronoun precedes the trace, anaphora is blocked. It is clear, therefore, that a special restriction is needed to determine the conditions for anaphora of traces.

As observed in Chomsky (1976), what quantified NP anaphora and *wh*-trace anaphora have in common, is that in both cases an anaphoric pronoun is interpreted as a bound variable. Within Chomsky's framework the (a)-sentences below will be assigned roughly the informal logical formulae in (b).

(11a) Someone kissed Rosa.
   (b) There is a person x such that [x kissed Rosa].
(12a) Who t kissed Rosa.
   (b) For which person x, [x kissed Rosa].
(13a) The man who t kissed Rosa is my friend.
   (b) The man x such that [x kissed Rosa] is my friend.

When such sentences contain a pronoun anaphoric to the relevant NP, this pronoun is translated, then, as the same variable that corresponds to the original position of the NP in surface structure. In the case of *wh*-trace, this is so because the antecedent itself (the trace) is interpreted as a bound variable). I will use here the term *bound anaphora* for all and only the cases where the pronoun is interpreted as a bound variable. This should not be confused with the way this term is used in much of the current EST literature, where it is a syntactic notion which does not necessarily have a unique semantic interpretation.[2]

The problem we face is that within this framework pronouns in all other cases are not interpreted as bound variables. Therefore, whether the pronoun is interpreted as a bound variable depends upon the antecedent it is anaphorically linked to, i.e. on whether this antecedent is interpreted either as a variable binding operator, or as a bound variable itself (as with *wh*-traces). So it turns out that a semantically determined class of NPs (the antecedents in this case) obeys a syntactic restriction which does not follow independently from their semantic properties. In Reinhart (1976), I attempted to avoid this problem by defining this set syntactically, and I will mention other attempts along such lines in Chapter 7. There is very little hope for such attempts, since it is not true that all syntactically quantified or indefinite NPs obey the special bound-anaphora condition.[3] .

As is well known (e.g. Postal, 1971; Wasow, 1972; and Hawkins, 1978) generic and specific indefinite NPs are not subject to the bound anaphora restriction (although they are commonly believed to correspond to variable binding operators as well). Consider the following sentences from Wasow (1972, p. 53) (the first two are quoted from Postal):

(14a) If *he* has a boring wife, *a man* should find a mistress.
  (b) The fact that *he* is being sued should worry *any businessman*.
  (c) That *he* was not elected upset *a certain leading candidate*.
  (d) The woman *he* loved betrayed *a man I knew*.

In all these cases the antecedent is an indefinite NP, but 'backward anaphora' is possible. Attempting to define the class of NPs which obey the stricter restriction on anaphora, Wasow (ibid.) has distinguished between two classes of NPs: determinate NPs include definite NPs, generic indefinites as in (14a, b), and specific indefinites, as in (14c, d). Indeterminate NPs are nonspecific, nongeneric indefinite NPs. It is only the last class of NPs that requires a stricter anaphora restriction, or, in our terms, that obeys the bound anaphora restriction.

Wasow offers several convincing examples showing similarities between the types of NPs included in the determinate NP class. However, the precise logical analysis of determinate NPs, which distinguishes them from indeterminate NPs, is still an open question. In any case, even if this distinction can be made explicit, it remains a semantic distinction and we are left where we started. Furthermore, there are many other types of counterexamples to any possible bound anaphora restriction on quantified NPs. The most famous cases are the so called 'donkey sentences' and pronouns of laziness, e.g.

(15a) Every man who owns a donkey beats it. (Geach, 1962)
  (b) The man who gives his paycheck to his wife is wiser than the man who gives it to his mistress. (Karttunen, 1969)
  (c) John wants to catch a fish and Bill wants to eat it. (Partee, 1978)

In all these cases the pronoun is both outside the scope of the quantified antecedent, and does not meet the syntactic conditions allowing bound anaphora which we will examine directly. Nevertheless it can be anaphorically linked to the antecedent. Another type of problem is that there is always a difference between cases where the pronoun is singular or plural: universally quantified NPs can often control the reference of plural pronouns when they fail to bind a singular pronoun, as in (17b), and plural quantified NPs can always do so, as, e.g. in (16).

(16a) The secretary who works for *them* despises *all the managers*.

(b) Everybody who has any experience with *them* is convinced that *some politicians* are corrupt.

(17a) *The guy who read *every book in the library* says that *it* is absolutely boring.

(b) The guy who read *every book in the library* says that *they* are absolutely boring.

Obviously, such counterexamples to the potential bound anaphora condition cannot be handled syntactically to begin with, since in these cases the quantified NP can control coreference also outside the sentence. For example; *every boy* failed the exam. Should we give *them* another chance? What these cases seem to have in common is that in the interpretation of the sentence, some pragmatic reference is established for the quantified NP in the discourse. So these are not cases of bound anaphora, but of coreference, where the pronoun is not interpreted as a bound variable, which is also clear from the fact that in many of the problematic cases the pronoun cannot be in the scope of the quantifier under any semantic analysis (for some discussion of this extensively studied problem see Kasher and Gabbai, 1976; Partee, 1978; and Kamp, 1980). So once an analysis of the pragmatic interpretation of such quantified NPs is found, they are not, in and of themselves, counterexamples to the structural condition I will propose here. However, they clearly indicate that there is no hope of defining the set of NPs that obey this condition syntactically.

I will postpone the conclusions to be drawn from this problem until Chapter 7, and here we will concentrate only on the question under what structural conditions a pronoun can be interpreted as a bound variable (assuming that the semantic conditions can be handled separately). For the time being, I will continue to refer to the class of relevant antecedents as 'quantified' NPs, which will include here *wh*-traces. However, in evaluating the judgements in the following sections it would be crucial that the only interpretation considered for the sentences should be the bound-variable interpretation for the pronoun, and all potentially referential interpretations (which result, for example, from interpreting the antecedent as generic or specific) should be avoided.

5.1.2 The non-relevance of 'Precede'

The most common treatments of the bound anaphora condition are in terms of linear order. The condition (18) which had first been proposed (with a different formulation) by Postal (1970, 1971) is still assumed, e.g. in Chomsky (1976) and Higginbotham (1980b).

(18)   Quantified NPs and *wh*-traces can have anaphoric relations (or can be coindexed) only with pronouns to their right.

That this restriction is incorrect can be shown in two ways. First, there are many cases of impossible anaphoric relations not blocked by these restrictions; secondly, there are a few cases where the restriction incorrectly blocks possible anaphoric relations. Let us see this first in the case of quantified NPs.

We have seen already some cases where forward-anaphora of quantified NPs is impossible, e.g. (17a) or (5), repeated in (19a) and the same is true for (19b, c).

(19a) *The secretary who worked with *each of the managers* despises *him*.
   (b) *The fact that the nurse expected *one more patient* to get undressed embarrassed *him*.
   (c) *Since the nurse expected *one more patient* to get undressed, she shouted at *him*.

However, in these cases the unavailability of anaphora can be attributed to independent scope considerations: in standard analyses the pronoun is not in the scope of the operator corresponding to the antecedent. So, we should look at cases where no independent semantic account is possible, such as (20)–(23). (I am using the *each of* quantifiers in most of the examples since it seems to be harder to be interpreted referentially.)

(20a) *People from *each of the small western cities* hate *it*.
   (b) *Gossip about *every businessman* harmed *his* career.
   (c) *The neighbours of *each of the pianists* hate *him*.
(21a) *We changed the carpets in *each of the flats* to make *it* look more cheerful.
   (b) *I placed the scores in front of *each of the pianists* before *his* performance.
(22a) *So many patients called *a psychiatrist* that *he* couldn't handle them all.
   (b) *We fired *each of the workers* since *he* was corrupt.
(23a) In *Felix's* office, *he* is an absolute dictator.
   (b) *In *everyone's* office, *he* is an absolute dictator.
(24a) According to *Felix*, *he* is a real democrat.
   (b) *According to *every candidate*, *he* is a real democrat.

In all these examples standard logical analyses may include the pronoun in the scope of the quantified NPs. Still, despite the fact that the antecedent precedes the pronoun, the pronoun cannot be understood as bound by the operator corresponding to it. None of these cases is blocked also by the general anaphora conditions, since the pronoun does not c-command the antecedent. As we saw in Section 3.2 of Chapter 3, the sentences in (23) and (24) are examples for preposed sentential PPs, which are attached to a node higher than $\bar{S}$, and, as illustrated by the (a)-sentences, definite NP coreference is possible in such cases, though the bound anaphora in the (b)-sentences is impossible. What all these cases have in common is that the antecedent does not c-command the pronoun, and we shall see more examples of the failure of the linear restriction when we examine the alternative c-command restriction.

An alternative formulation of the restriction on anaphoric relations or indefinite NPs was suggested by Ross (1972 b). This restriction states that the antecedent must both precede and have primacy over the pronoun, which amounts to saying that the antecedent must both precede and command the pronoun. (A similar restriction in terms of precede-and-command was suggested briefly in Lasnik, 1976.) The problems for a restriction couched in terms of 'precede-and-command', rather than 'precede' alone, arise in environments similar to those which provide counterexamples to the 'precede-and-command' restriction on the co-reference of definite NPs. While the modified definition of command I mentioned in Chapter 1, which defines any cyclic node as relevant for the relation, can handle the sentences in (20), in all the other examles we considered in (21)–(24), the preceding antecedent commands the pronoun, so this stricter restriction fails as well. Furthermore, this restriction will fail just like (18) because the other type of counter-evidence for any linearly based account for bound anaphora holds here as well: backward-bound anaphora is possible.

(25a) In *his* own way, however, *each man* is petitioning for the same kind of administration. (NYT, 21 Jan. 1977, quoted in Carden, 1978)

  (b) As *its* major source of income, *each club* collects a playing fee from the players every half hour. (*SOCIAL PROBLEMS* 28.557, 77, quoted in, Carden, 1978)

(26a) Near *his* child's crib *nobody* would keep matches.

  (b) *Near *his* child's crib you should give *nobody* matches.

  (c) You should give *nobody* matches near *his* child's crib.

(27a) Thinking about *his* problems, *everyone* got depressed.

(b) *Thinking about *his* problems, I pitied *everyone*.
(c) I pitied *everyone*, thinking about *his* problems.

In (25), (26a) and (27a) the pronoun precedes (and also commands) the antecedent, but anaphoric relations are still possible. We have already seen in Chapter 2 (Section 2.2) that no ordering solution is possible for coreference problems. That such a solution would fail here as it did in the case of definite NPs is indicated by (26) and (27). We see that in the (b)-sentences, unlike the (a)-sentences, an anaphoric relation is impossible, although prior to the preposing of the PP, as in the (c)-sentences, the same sentence is acceptable on the anaphoric reading. The differences between the (b)- and (c)-sentences also indicate that, as was the case with definite NPs, a mere distinction between anaphora options of subjects and objects will not do, since in both the antecedent is an object and the pronoun is in a PP (i.e. 'lower in accessibility'), yet anaphora is permitted only in the (c)-sentences.

Turning now to *wh*-traces, it is more difficult to illustrate the irrelevance of linear order to such cases, since many of the sentence-structures we used as counterexamples for (18) have no parallel with traces. For example, the PP in (24) is higher than COMP, so, obviously, it is not an extractable position; in the sentences in (20) extraction from the subject is impossible as illustrated in (30). Still, we may consider those cases where extraction is possible, as in (28), and note also that in (29), where extraction is difficult regardless of anaphora, it is still much worse in the (b) than in (a) cases.

(28a) *Who did you place the scores in front of *t* before *his* performance?
   (b) ?Which worker did you fire *t* since *he* was corrupt?
(29a) ?Which businessman did the gossip about t cause a national scandal?
   (b) *Which businessman did the gossip about *t* ruin *his* partner's career?
(30) *The city all the people from t voted for Carter will suffer a financial disaster.

These cases have the general character of the weak crossover cases just like the sentences in (8) above, namely anaphora is very difficult to obtain, despite the fact that the trace antecedent precedes the pronoun, as required by (18). We may note here that, generally, 'cross-over' judgements in the case of *wh*-traces are less clear than in the case of (genuinely) quantified NPs. Possibly this is so because they can be more easily interpreted with a referential interpretation to the *wh*-antecedent. In any case, in judging such examples their 'echo' question interpretation should be carefully avoided, since echo questions are known to violate all sentence-level restrictions.

Examples of appropriate 'backward pronominalisation' with traces are even harder to find. The examples in the case of quantified NPs (in (26) and (27) above) were of sentences with preposed PPs. *Wh*-movement is usually impossible in such cases (e.g. **Who, in the box, put the book?*), so they cannot be used as counterexamples. However, we may look at the following cases cited by Wasow (1972), in which the pronoun does precede the trace.

(31a) On December 23rd, the postman brought a large envelope which, when I opened it at breakfast, *t* shed a lot of silvery tinsel into my plate. [from Graham Greene]
   (b) He was the kind of man who, when *he* loses *his* collar stud, *t* bellows the house down. [from Agatha Christie]

Two alternative solutions have been proposed for the problem of anaphora in sentences to which *wh*-movement has applied. Postal (1971, 1972) has faced the problem with a derivational constraint. His constraint, summarised roughly, blocks sentences in which a *wh*-word has been fronted over (crossed over) a coreferential pronoun. As was pointed out in Wasow (1972), trace theory provides a way to capture whatever information is captured by derivational constraints (at least in the case of movement rules which leave traces). The predictions made by Postal's crossover constraint are thus identical to those made by the restriction blocking anaphoric relations when the pronoun precedes the trace. Consequently, it would also fail in exactly the same environments.

The other solution is the one suggested briefly in Keenan and Comrie (1978) for relative clauses (which can, perhaps, be extended to *wh*-movement in general). Within the framework of trace theory, their 'preferred reference condition' can be stated to require that the trace must be higher on the accessibility hierarchy[4] than the pronoun, or that an anaphoric relation between a trace and a pronoun is impossible if the trace is not higher in the hierarchy. As Keenan and Comrie note, when dealing with simple sentences of SVO languages, like English, their 'preferred reference condition' yields very similar results to Postal's crossover constraint, since in such languages, if a constituent B is to the right of a constituent A, B is usually lower in the accessibility than A. Thus

their constraint, just like Postal's, blocks coreference in sentences like
The man that **he** *met* **t**, since the trace (or the NP relativised) is lower
in the hierarchy than the pronoun. However, as we saw in Section 5.1.1,
within trace theory, there is no need for a special constraint to block
such sentences, since they violate the general restriction on anaphora
prohibiting coreference in case a non-pronoun (here the trace) is in the
domain of a pronoun. When it comes to more complicated cases, like
the ones discussed in this section, the constraint of Keenan and Comrie
is not sufficient to block impossible coreference. For example, in (28b)
the object trace should be higher on the hierarchy than the pronoun in
the subordinate clause, and in (28a) both antecedent and pronoun are
oblique, so the restriction does not apply to block these cases.

5.1.3 The C-Command Restriction

We can now see that in fact the anaphora restriction on bound anaphora
operates on precisely the same syntactic domain as the restriction on
definite NPs coreference. The difference is only that NPs of the first
type are more limited in their anaphora options than definite NPs,
which means that they obey a stricter restriction: the one given in (32).
Here again I state it as a general output condition rather than an actual
coindexing procedure. (The coindexing mechanism will be discussed in
Chapters 6 and 7.)[5]

(32)   Quantified NPs and *wh*-traces can have anaphoric relations
        only with pronouns in their c-command syntactic domain (as
        defined in (17) and (12) of Chapter 1).

This means that unlike definite NPs, quantified NPs cannot have any
anaphoric relations outside their domain.[6]

As was the case with the alternative restrictions on coreference discussed in Chapter 2, the alternative formulations of the bound anaphora
restriction in (18) and (32) intersect in their predictions in a large number
of cases (though not as large as in the previous case).[7] The restriction
(18) blocks coreference in all the cases where a pronoun precedes a
quantified NP. In most structures of a right-branching language, when
NP_2 is to the right of NP_1, NP_2 does not c-command NP_1 (i.e. NP_1 is not
in the domain of NP_2). Hence, in such structures, when a pronoun, NP_1,
precedes a quantified NP, NP_2, the restriction (32) blocks anaphora,
since NP_1 is not in the domain of NP_2.

The way the two rules intersect in the case of 'backward pronominalisation can be illustrated with the sentences in (33)–(36), which have
the structure (37).

(33) *Those who know *him* are kissing *someone* in Rosa's film.

(34) *Those who know *him* are drinking champagne in *someone's* film.

(35) *Those who are lucky are kissing *him* in *someone's* film.

(36) *Who do those who know *him* kiss *t* in Rosa's film?

(37)

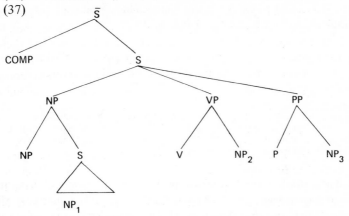

In (37), NP_1 precedes NP_2 and NP_3, and NP_2 precedes NP_3. Hence the restriction (18) seems to give the right predictions, blocking the sentences (33)–(36), in which the preceding NP is a pronoun. However, if we look at the domain relations of the NPs involved, rather than their linear order, we see that in (37) an NP to the left is not in the domain of an NP to the right: NP_1 is not in the domain of NP_2, since NP_2 is dominated by the VP which does not dominate NP_1. The restriction (32), then, blocks bound anaphora between NP_1 and NP_2 in (33) and (36), because the pronoun is not in the domain of the quantified NP or the trace and not because the pronoun precedes it. The same is true for NP_1 and NP_3. NP_3 in the PP in (37) does not c-command NP_1 (the domain of an NP in a PP is only the PP). Hence, anaphora is blocked, as in (34). For the same reason, NP_2 is not in the domain of NP_3 and the restriction (32) blocks anaphora in (35).

The fact that 'backward pronominalisation' is usually not permitted with quantified NPs is, thus, a consequence of the requirement that the pronoun be in the domain of the quantified NP for coreference to be possible. This consequence holds, however, only for the cases in which the NP to the left is not in the domain of the NP to the right. Although this is the common case in right-branching languages, there are several structures in which NP_1 is to the left of NP_2, but NP_1 is still in the domain of NP_2. In these constructions, the restrictions (18) and (32) will differ in their predictions. The other and more substantial difference in the predictions of the two restrictions shows up when the quantified NP precedes the pronoun. The 'precede' restriction (18) permits anaphora in all such cases, while the c-command restriction (32) permits it only when the pronoun is, furthermore, within the domain of the quantified NP. Thus, the two types of cases that should be examined in evaluating the alternative restrictions are I and III of (38):

(38)   anaphora is blocked by the   anaphora is blocked by the
       'c-command restriction (32)   'precede' restriction (18)

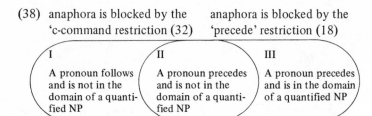

I	II	III
A pronoun follows and is not in the domain of a quantified NP	A pronoun precedes and is not in the domain of a quantified NP	A pronoun precedes and is in the domain of a quantified NP

The cases of type I, unlike type III, are very common in a right-branching language, and these are the cases we should consider primarily. In fact, the counterexamples for (18) we considered in (10)-(24) and (28)-(30), some of which are repeated in (39), are of this type.

(39a) *The neighbours of *each of the pianists* hate *him*.
   (b) *People from *each of the small western cities* hate *it*.
   (c) *We changed the carpets in *each of the apartments* to make *it* look more cheerful.
   (d) *In *everyone's* office *he* is an absolute dictator.
   (e) *Which businessman did the gossip about *t* ruin *his* partner's career?
   (f) *Who did you place the scores in front of *t* before *his* performance?

For the c-command restriction these are just the expected results. In the sentences of (39) the antecedent is dominated by a PP, hence it does not c-command the pronoun, so they cannot be coindexed. Although such cases are sufficient to argue for the c-command rule, we will examine a few further supporting cases.

One test for the linguistic relevance of the c-command domain (and the non-relevance of the precede-and-command domain) which has been mentioned in previous chapters, is the asymmetry between the relations of subjects and objects to constituents dominated by S (i.e. the S which dominates the subject). While subjects have the whole sentence in their domain, the domain of objects consists only of the VP. The same type of evidence supports the 'c-command' restriction (32): this restriction predicts that a quantified object NP cannot have anaphoric relations with pronouns outside the VP, while quantified subjects can. Let us check this first in cases with PPs:

(40a) *Each of the kids* kisses Rosa in *his* picture.

(b)

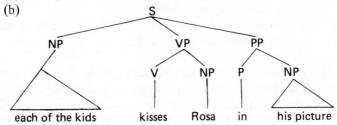

(41a) *Rosa kisses *each of the kids* in *his* picture.

(b)

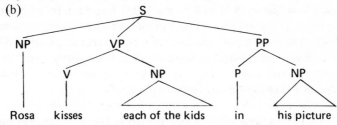

(42a) Rosa put *each of the books* in *its* box.

(b)

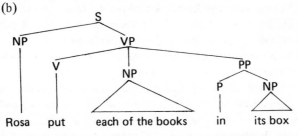

As we saw in Chapter 3, (section 3.1) the PP in (40) and (41) is sentential, which means that it is in the domain of the subject, but not in that of the object. Consequently, anaphora is permitted in (40), but in (41), where the quantified NP *each of the kids* is in the VP, it does not c-command the pronoun, or the pronoun is not in its domain, and anaphora is correctly blocked by restriction (32). In (42), the quantified NP is also an object, but in this case the PP is verb-phrasal, hence it is in the domain of the object and an anaphora is permitted by (32). The asymmetry of subjects and objects shows up as well in (43) and (44).

(43a) *Anybody over 60* had to resign in order to receive *his* insurance.
   (b) *We had to fire *anybody over 60* in order to pay *his* insurance.
   (c) We had to send *anybody over 60* home to live on *his* pension.
(44a) *Anybody remotely connected with the assassination* will be arrested in spite of *his* alibi.
   (b) *The police will arrest *anybody remotely connected with the assassination* in spite of *his* alibi.

As was mentioned in Section 3.2, *in order to*-clauses are always sentential. Hence, anaphoric relations are permitted only when the quantified NP is the subject as in (43a). In (43b), anaphora is blocked, since the pronoun in the *in order to*-clause is not in the domain of the object. The *to*-phrase in (43c), on the other hand, is verb-phrasal (arguments can be found in Williams, 1974, and Faraci, 1974), hence it is in the domain of the object and anaphora is permitted. Similarly, the *in spite of*-phrase in (44) is sentential, hence a pronoun in it can be coindexed with a quantified subject, as in (44a), but not with a quantified object, as in (44b).

The examples below illustrate the same domain asymmetry between subjects and objects in cases involving traces.[8]

(45a) The actress who *t* kissed Brando in *her* latest film will win the Oscar.
   (b) *The actress who Brando kissed *t* in *her* latest film will win the Oscar.
   (c) *What actress did Brando kiss *t* in *her* latest film?
(46a) Who *t* was arrested in spite of *his* alibi?
   (b) *Who did the police arrest *t* in spite of *his* alibi?
   (c) *The guy who the police arrested *t* in spite of *his* alibi has filed a complaint.

In the (b) and (c) cases, the trace precedes (and commands) the pronoun, but anaphora is nevertheless blocked, since the pronoun is not in its c-command domain.

Another test for the relevance of c-command domains is provided by sentences which have undergone extraposition. We saw in Chapter 2 (Section 2.5) that the coreference options of the matrix object in such sentences depend upon whether the extraposed S is attached to the VP or to the matrix S. In cases like (47a), the extraposed sentence is attached to the VP, while in the case of result-clause extraposition as in (47b) or extraposition from NP as in (47c), the extraposed sentence S_2 is attached to the matrix S.

(47a) *[S_1 It [$_{VP}$ amused *him* [S_2 that so many people wrote to *Brando*]]]

   (b) [S_1 So many reporters [$_{VP}$ *called him*] [S_2 that Brando couldn't answer them all]]

   (c) [S_2 Many people [$_{VP}$ hate *him*] [S_2 who had the chance to work with *Brando* on a film]]

Consequently, in the case of definite NPs, the general restriction on anaphora blocks coreference in (47a), where the NP in S_2 is in the domain of the object and, thus, must be a pronoun in order to be coreferential with the object. But it permits coreference in (47b) and (47c), since the extraposed S_2 is not in the domain of the object (being outside the VP), and thus, there are no restrictions on coreference options of the object and NPs in S_2.

In the case of quantified NPs, the situation is reversed — 'forward pronominalisation' is permitted only in the structure where 'backward pronominalisation' of definite NPs is blocked:

(48a) It surprised *each of the candidates* that *he* was not elected.

   (b) *So many people interviewed *each of the candidates* that *he* couldn't remember them all.

   (c) *Many people interviewed *each of the candidates* who knew nothing whatsoever about *his* background.

(49a) It surprised *nobody* that *he* wasn't elected.

   (b) *Many people interviewed *nobody* who had nothing to offer *him*.

(50a) Who did it bother *t* most that *he* wasn't elected?

   (b) *The actor whom so many reporters called *t* that *he* couldn't see them all is now in Paris.

   (c) *Which book do people recommend *t* most who know anything about *it*?

The domain relations of the objects and the NPs in the extraposed clauses are, of course, identical to those in (47). The restriction on bound anaphora applies, thus, to precisely the same domains. However, since this restriction permits an anaphoric relation only in case the pronoun is in the domain of the quantified NP, it blocks anaphora in the

(b)- and (c)-sentences, where the object does not c-command the pronoun. In the (a)-sentences, on the other hand, the pronoun is properly
in the domain of the NP, and anaphora is possible. ('Backward pronominalisation' parallel to that of (47b, c) is blocked in the case of
quantified NPs, since an NP in the extraposed clause does not c-command
anything outside this clause).

The asymmetry of subjects and objects shows up again in sentences
of this type. The c-command restrictions predicts that pronouns in
extraposed sentences of types (b) and (c) in the sentences above (i.e.
cases where the extraposed S is attached to the matrix S) can be anaphoric to quantified subjects of the matrix sentence, since the subject,
unlike the object, does c-command the extraposed S. That this is indeed
the case is illustrated in (51). And compare also (22a), repeated in (52a)
to (52b).

> (51a) *Each of the candidates* was interviewed by so many people
> that *he* couldn't remember them all.
> (b) *Nobody* was interviewed who didn't bring *his* c.v. and proofs
> of his loyalty.
> (c) The actor who *t* received so many phone calls that *he* couldn't
> answer them all is now in Paris.
> (52a) *So many patients called a *psychiatrist* that *he* couldn't handle
> them all.
> (b) A *psychiatrist* was called by so many patients that *he* couldn't
> handle them all.

We have seen that there is considerable evidence supporting the c-command restriction on bound anaphora in cases of type I of (38) — namely,
cases where the precede (or precede-and-command) restriction permits
anaphoric relations, while the c-command relation blocks them. We
should check now the other type of non-intersecting prediction of the
alternative restrictions, namely III of (38), where the c-command restriction permits 'backward anaphora', which is prohibited by the precede
(and command) restriction.

There are much fewer structures of this type (in a right-branching
language) and the major cases are sentences with preposed constituents.
In such structures a pronoun in the preposed constituent can be bound
by a quantified NP in the main clause, as we already saw in examples
(25)–(27) of the previous section, two of which are repeated in (53)
and (54).

(53a) Near *his* child's crib *nobody* would keep matches.

 (b) *Near *his* child's crib you should give *nobody* matches.

 (c) You should give *nobody* matches near *his* child's crib.

(54a) Thinking about *his* problems, *everyone* got depressed.

 (b) *Thinking about *his* problems, I pitied *everyone*.

 (c) I pitied *everyone*, thinking about *his* problems.

(55a) For *his* birthday, each of the employees received a Mercedes.

 (b) *For *his* birthday we bought *each of the employees* a Mercedes.

Given the full definition of c-command (see (17) of Chapter 1) the sub-ject c-commands nodes attached to $\bar{\mathrm{S}}$, hence it c-commands the pronoun in the PP in the (a)-sentences. As predicted by (32), bound anaphora is permitted, although the pronoun precedes the antecedent. The same subject-object asymmetry we observed before shows up here as well: in the (b)-sentences, the object does not c-command the pronoun and bound anaphora is impossible. Before the preposing of the PP in the (b)-sentences as in (53c) and (54c) the object c-commands the PP and anaphora is permitted. Other constructions of type III of (38) in a right-branching language are cases with double objects, or indirect objects which c-command the preceding direct object. (It would be recalled that in Section 2.6 of Chapter 2 indirect objects were analysed so as to c-command nodes in the VP.) It seems indeed that in such constructions bound anaphora is sometimes possible as, e.g., in (56).

(56a) 'We are . . . lawyers who go into court to . . . return to *her* class-room a *pregnant girl* illegally suspended from school'. (Adver-tisement, Children Defense Fund, Nov. 78, quoted in Carden, 1978.)

 (b) We are lawyers who go into court to return to *his* classroom *each of the students* who were suspended for political activities.

In the real-discourse example (56a), the antecedent is specific, so this example is not sufficient for our purposes. However, it seems that (56b) with a genuinely quantified antecedent is also possible. It may, never-theless, be argued that the NP shift which applied to these examples is a later stylistic rule, in which case the bound anaphora rule applies to the underlying structure where the pronoun follows the antecedent. While bound anaphora in examples where this could not be the case is harder, it seems, nevertheless, that the sentences (57)–(59) are not altogether impossible, but perhaps require some discourse justification, as is always the case with backward anaphora.[9]

(57) ?The secretaries reported the progress on *his* project to *each of the managers.*

(58) ?We will give *his* examination back to *every student* who shows up between 8 and 10 a.m.

(59) ?You may show *his* files to *each patient* who wants to see them.

We may conclude that the c-command restriction (32) comes much closer to handling the bound anaphora cases than the linear restriction (18). There are still several types of structures where the c-command restriction, as stated, fails systematically to capture the facts. Since these structures represent general problems for the c-command rules (and not just for the bound anaphora condition) I will discuss them all together in Chapter 8. Here, however, we may look at Higginbotham's (1980b) counterexamples to the c-command restriction on bound anaphora that I have proposed here and in Reinhart (1976).

Higginbotham offers two types of structures where the c-command restriction seems to be violated. The first are cases where the quantified NP is the determiner of a possessive NP as in (60)-(61).

(60) *Every boy's* mother thinks *he* is a genius.

(61) *Whose* mother loves him?

Anaphora in such cases is possible for many speakers, although the antecedent c-commands the pronoun. This, indeed, is one of the general problems for c-command, which I duscuss in Chapter 8, and I propose there an (*ad hoc*) modification of c-command to handle these problems in English. (As noted by Higginbotham the possibility of anaphora in such cases might be language-specific.) The other type of structure involves a quantified PP embedded in a quantified NP as in (62).

(62) Every daughter of every professor in *some small college town* wishes she could leave *it.*

While it is true that anaphora is possible in (62) although the antecedent does not c-command the pronoun, it is also the case that the antecedent in this example is specific. Hence, this may be simply a case of co-type of structure) is specific. Hence, this may be simply a case of co-reference rather than bound anaphora. Once we consider genuinely quantified antecedents, as in (63), anaphora is much harder to obtain.

(63a) *Every daughter of some professor in *each of the small university towns* hates *it.*

(b) *Some jokes about *everyone* upset *him.*

It would seem then, that such structures do not systematically violate the c-command restriction, but the counter examples they still provide require further study.[10,11]

5.2 Reflexive and Reciprocal Pronouns

R(eflexive or reciprocal) pronouns unlike regular pronouns, do not have a deictic or referential use. Their reference can be obtained only from an antecedent in the sentence. For example, a sentence like (64) where the R-pronoun has no intrasentential antecedent is uninterpretable, unlike the sentence in (65).

(64) *Zelda bores himself.
(65) Zelda bores him.

This means, then, that R-pronouns are interpretable only as bound variables. (This will become clearer in Chapter 7.) We should note, however, that R-pronouns and particularly the reflexive ones can also be used emphatically, or as marking point-of-view (see, e.g. Cantrall, 1974), and in that use they are known to violate sentence-level restrictions. We will not consider this pragmatic use of R-pronouns, but only their standard use, in which they are interpreted as bound variables.

If the bound anaphora condition we examined restricts the interpretation of pronouns as bound variables, we would expect it to apply also in the case of R-pronouns' interpretation, and this is indeed the case. While R-pronouns obey also further conditions not applying to quantified NP anaphora, they cannot be anaphoric to a non c-commanding NP, as illustrated in (66)–(67).

(66a) *Felix's* wife respects *himself*.
   (b) *The rumour about the *new neighbours* bothered *each other*.
(67a) *I spoke about *Rosa* with *herself*.
   (b) *I put near *the boys each other's* toys.

As with the other cases of bound anaphora, the linear order does not play a role in determining anaphora options of R-pronouns. In the (a)-sentences below, the pronoun precedes the antecedent, but since the antecedent c-commands the pronoun, anaphora is permitted.

(68a) Which fancy story about *himself* did *Felix* tell you this time?
   (b) *Which fancy story about *himself* did you tell *Felix* this time?

(69a) *To each other the women* introduced the smartest men.

(b) *To each other, the woman introduced *the smartest men*.

(c) The woman introduced *the smartest men* to *each other*.

(70a) In *each other*'s arms, *the lovers* found peace.

(b) *In *each other*'s arms, God gave *the lovers* peace.

(c) God gave *the lovers* peace in *each other*'s arms.

The subject-object asymmetry typical to c-command domains is also observed in these examples. In the (b)-sentences, where the potential antecedent is the object rather than the subject, anaphora is impossible. Before the preposing of the PP, on the other hand, the R-pronoun is in the domain of the object, and anaphora is, indeed, possible as in (69c) and (70c).

The same subject-object asymmetry can be observed also in cases which do not involve PP preposing:

(71a) *Felix and Zelda* are adored in *each other*'s family.

(b) *Everyone adores *Felix and Zelda* in *each other*'s family.

(72a) *Felix and Zelda* always come out perfect in *each other*'s stories.

(b) *People always adore *Felix and Zelda* in *each other*'s stories.

As we saw in Section 3.1, the PPs in (71) and (72) are sentential. Consequently, they are in the domain of the subject but not of the object. An R-pronoun in this PP can be anaphoric with the subject, as in the (a)-sentences, but not with the object, as in the (b)-sentences.

Just as in the case of quantified NP anaphora, there are several cases where the c-command bound anaphora restriction systematically fails. In Chapter 8 where we will consider these cases we shall see that the bound anaphora restriction fails in the same environments in both cases, which suggests that, regardless of the details of c-command, quantified NP anaphora and R-pronoun anaphora obey the same bound anaphora conditions.[12]

However, as is well known (see e.g. Chomsky, 1973), R-pronouns obey a further specific restriction which distinguishes them from regular pronouns. Roughly, they can be bound within their S or NP cycle, but not, for example, in (73).

(73a) *Zelda believes that Felix adores *herself*.

(b) *The managers like Zelda's presents *to each other*.

In Chomsky (1981) the syntactic environment which allows reflexivisation is defined as the minimal governing category, a notion which will be surveyed in the next chapter. The condition (74), then, combines the general bound anaphora requirement that the antecedent c-commands the pronoun, and the specific restriction on R-pronouns.

(74) An R-pronoun must be interpreted as anaphoric (or coindexed) with, and only with, a c-commanding NP within a specified syntactic environment, e.g. its minimal governing category.

(74) follows essentially the formulation of the R-pronouns rule in Chomsky (1981), and we shall see more of the details of this system in the next chapter.

Notes

1. It is interesting to note that Bach and Partee (1980), who provide the only systematic attempt I am aware of to define all the anaphora conditions on semantic rather than syntactic representations (or at least on a level of logical syntax), do not provide a condition capturing these 'crossover' cases but rather note that 'some constraint will have to be placed on the syntactic operations of our Theory' (p. 18 of the original ms.), i.e. they acknowledge that a syntactic condition might be needed for these cases.

2. Since 'bound' is an established and recognised semantic term it seems to me more reasonable to maintain its use for semantic phenomena and to invent a different name for the relevant syntactic phenomena, rather than conversely. In Section 7.3.2 I suggest that the appropriate syntactic term may be simply 'coindexed'.

3. A similar criticism of the syntactic attempt in Reinhart (1976) was made in Bosch (1980), who mentions several of the cases I bring below.

4. The Accessibility Hierarchy suggested by Keenan and Comrie is given in (i):

(i) Subj DO IO Object of Preposition Possessive NP Object of Comparatives

NPs higher in the hierarchy can more easily be relativised or extracted.

5. A similar condition, using *in constructing with*, has been proposed by Evans (1977, 1980). But Evans's condition assumes also linear order, requiring that the pronoun must be both to the right of and in construction with (i.e. c-commanded by) the antecedent.

6. As is well known, two occurrences of the same quantified NP can never be coindexed (i.e. they cannot be interpreted as operators binding the same variables). This is captured by (32) which allows quantified NPs to have anaphoric relations only with pronouns (in their domains). It would appear that this formulation of (32) does not allow coindexing of a trace by a c-commanding trace in COMP (in the case of iterative *wh*-movement, since traces can be coindexed only with c-commanded pronouns, and the c-commanded trace is not a pronoun). However, when we consider the actual coindexing procedure for such cases in Chapters 6 and 7, we will adopt Chomsky's (1981) output conditions on coindexing, where this problem does not arise, since they restrict only anaphora options of NPs in 'argument position' (i.e. not in COMP). An NP trace can still be coindexed with another NP since NP traces are defined as anaphors (like R-pronouns).

7. We saw in the previous section that if the restriction on bound anaphora has to mention precede, then a more adequate formulation seems to be that of Ross (1972b), which requires that the antecedent must both precede and command the pronoun, and which can be reformulated as in (i):

(i) A quantified NP can have anaphoric relations only with pronouns to its right which are commanded by it.

The restriction in (i) has a much larger intersection with the c-command restriction in (32) than does the restriction in (18). Nevertheless most of the examples we will consider count against (i) as well.

8. As is often the case with bad anaphora in *wh*-sentences, it is much improved if the sentences are interpreted as 'quiz-show' or 'echo' questions. Thus (45c) might be possible as a title in a Hollywood gossip column. However, the (b) and (c) cases of (45) and (46) are unacceptable as a genuine request for information.

9. I should mention that, possibly, there is another structure of type III of (38) (namely an NP to the left is c-commanded by an NP to the right) in which the c-command restriction does not fare so well: in coordinate NPs as in (i), anaphoric relations are impossible in the (b) cases, where the pronoun precedes.

(ia) *Each of the employees* and *his* wife will be invited to the party.
 (b) **His* wife and *each of the employees* will be invited to the party.
 (c) ?*His* wife and *Ben* will be invited to the party.

There may be some special discourse constraint on coordinate constructions, which is indicated by the fact that coreference with definite NPs in (ic) is also hard to get. However, (ib) is much worse. If conjoined NPs are analysed as sister nodes, this is a counterexample to the c-command restriction which requires an *ad hoc* constraint. However, it is possible that, as proposed in Ross (1967), the second conjunct forms a constituent with the *and*, in which case the antecedent in (ib) does not c-command the pronoun. See also footnote 7 of Chapter 2.

10. Particularly, it seems that the cases with wh-antecedents of this structure, which are mentioned by Higginbotham, are generally acceptable, as illustrated in (i).

(i) Which books about *which politician* annoyed *him* (this year)?
(ii) Which books about which politician were published this year?

Possibly, cases like (i) have a restricted use which is not truly quantificational: It seems that a multi-value answer (e.g. a book about Carter and a book about Nixon) would not be as natural here as it is with a regular question of this type, as in (ii) (See also note 8). However, in the absence of an analysis along such lines, they still are a problem for the c-command rule.

As pointed out in Reinhart (1976), sentences of this quantificational type pose a problem for the c-command restriction on the interpretation of scope, which we shall examine here in Chapter 9. However, it does not follow automatically that they should present a systematic problem for the bound anaphora condition as well. If, as I argue in Chapter 7, bound anaphora is determined by surface-structure coindexing, independently of the assignment of quantifier scope, we may get, in principle, cases where a given quantified NP has a pronoun in its scope, but it cannot, nevertheless, bind it.

11. Bach and Partee (1980) also argue against the c-command restriction proposed here and in Reinhart (1976). In the only counterexample they cite, given in (i), we seem to disagree on the judgment.

(i) Every student claimed that *one of his professors* was a genius in order to influence *her*. (Bach and Partee, 1980, p. 65)

(ii) Some student claimed that *none of his professors* is a genius in order to upset *her*.

However, even if anaphora is possible in (i), Dowty (1980) has pointed out that the pronoun in this sentence can be analysed in the intended reading as (Cooper's) contextual pronoun, rather than as a bound variable. In a sentence like (ii), where a contextual interpretation is inapplicable, anaphora is impossible. So it seems that this example falls under the more general problem of the interpretation of apparently referential quantified NPs.

12. Since R-pronouns can occur only in a restricted set of syntactic environments (which we shall specify directly), most of the supporting tests for the c-command restrictions are not available here. The counterexamples here seem, therefore, more striking. Because of these counterexamples, the c-command restriction on R-pronouns which was proposed in Reinhart (1975b) was not included in Reinhart (1976). However, in view of the fact that quantified NP anaphora poses precisely the same problems for c-command, there is no reason to assume that a different restriction is needed for R-pronouns.

6 THE INDEXING SYSTEM OF INTERPRETATIVE SEMANTICS

6.1 A Summary of the Anaphora Conditions

In our discussion of anaphora we have assumed general conditions that restrict anaphora interpretation, regardless of the semantic nature of the antecedent, and one stricter condition determining the interpretation of pronouns as bound variables, which, as I presented it so far, applies when the antecedent is a quantified NP or a *wh*-trace. The interpretation of R-pronouns shares properties with that of bound anaphora, (both since they are interpretable as bound variables and since they obey the bound anaphora condition), but, on the other hand, it applies to all cases involving R-pronouns, regardless of the semantics of the antecedent, so in this sense it may be viewed as part of the general conditions on anaphora. The general conditions are then stated in sum in (1), where (1a) is the anaphora condition proposed originally in Reinhart (1976) and (1b–c) are recent adoptations of the reciprocal rule and the disjoint reference rule proposed in Chomsky (1973):

(1a) A non-pronominal NP must be interpreted as non-coreferential with any NP that c-commands it. (This entails that a pronoun must be interpreted as non-coreferential with any full NP it c-commands.)

  (b) A reflexive or reciprocal pronoun (an R-pronoun) must be interpreted as coreferential with (and only with) a c-commanding NP within a specified syntactic domain (e.g. its minimal governing category).

  (c) A non-R-pronoun must be interpreted as non-coreferential with any c-commanding NP in the syntactic domain which is specified for (1b).

Given the theoretical assumptions I surveyed in Chapter 2 (Section 2.1), (1b) specifies the conditions for obligatory, or stipulated, anaphora, (1a) and (1c) determine the conditions for obligatory non-coreference interpretation, and when neither of these conditions apply, the sentence allows free, or optional coreference. (1a) captures Lasnik's (1976) observation, that coreference is blocked both when a pronoun c-commands its potential antecedent and when a full NP c-commands another full NP. (1b) captures the fact that R-pronouns must be anaphoric and they are not otherwise interpretable (as, e.g. in *Max bores herself*), the fact that an R-pronoun can be anaphoric only to NPs that c-command it, and the fact that R-pronouns can be controlled only within a restricted domain (roughly the same clause of NP cycle, but not, e.g. in *The new neighbours expected that Zelda will respect each other*), which is defined in Chomsky's (1981) model as the minimal governing category (see below). In environments which allow an NP to be coreferential with an R-pronoun, no other NP can be coreferential with the given NP. Condition (1a) already blocks anaphora in sentences like *Zelda bores Zelda*, since a full NP must be interpreted as non-coreferential with any c-commanding NP. But it does not block coreference in sentences like: *Zelda bores her*. In such sentences condition (1c) applies and marks the pronoun as non-anaphoric. The bound anaphora condition we assumed in Chapter 5 is repeated in (2).

(2)　Quantified NPs and *wh*-traces can have anaphoric relations only with pronouns in their c-command domain.

Pronouns may have anaphoric relations with quantified NPs and *wh*-traces only in the syntactic environments specified by (2), which would mean, once the translation procedure for such cases is defined in the next chapter, that the conditions on the translation of pronouns as bound variables are stricter than the conditions on their coreference interpretation.

The conditions in (1)-(2) are stated as informal output conditions specifying the appropriate output of the various interpretative procedures, rather than the procedures themselves. The way they are incorporated into the grammar is dependent upon the syntactic framework assumed. In fact, the conditions in (1) are largely assumed in the recent interpretative framework and there are several proposals as to the way they are incorporated, which I will now survey. The condition (2) is believed, within this framework, to apply independently of the general anaphora condition, possibly at a different level of linguistic analysis, and I will postpone the details of how it is formulated until the next chapter.

6.2 The Indexing System

Within current interpretative semantics (e.g. Chomsky, 1980, 1981) it is believed that anaphora interpretation and movement rules both obey the same general conditions, which are stated as conditions on appropriate coindexing. A moved constituent leaves behind a trace (an empty node) which carries the index of the moved constituent. If we assume, further, that anaphora interpretation is governed by appropriate syntactic coindexing, we may observe the similarity between the conditions governing the relations between anaphorically coindexed NPs and those governing the relations between a trace and the constituent which have left the trace, i.e. conditions on the appropriate coindexing of a given node with an empty node. Chomsky has recently proposed two ways to formulate the coindexing mechanism, the first of which I will review only briefly, omitting the details relevant to movement rules.

In Chomsky (1980) it is assumed that all NPs are base-generated with indices called 'referential' indices, and then three further indexing procedures guarantee the outputs consistent with (1): (a) All R-pronouns are obligatorily coindexed with any c-commanding NP, which means that their base-generated referential index is replaced with that of the c-commanding NP. (b) All other NPs (including non R-pronouns) are negatively coindexed, or contra indexed with all c-commanding NPs. Formally, this is achieved by adding to the referential index (rather than replacing it by) the referential index of the c-commanding NP, which is called 'anaphoric index' (meaning 'contra-anaphoric' index). (c) An index-cancelling procedure then applies to all pronouns (R or non-R) equally cancelling coindexing and contra-indexing in the appropriate syntactic environment — say, if a pronoun is coindexed or contra-indexed outside its minimal governing category (whose definition I shall survey directly). This system, thus, establishes explicitly a three-valued coindexing system: two NPs may end up coindexed, contra-indexed or free (i.e. neither of the first two).

In Chomsky (1981) an attempt is made to reduce the indexing system to just two relations: coindexed (or 'bound') and 'free'. Formally, the contra-indexing procedure is abandoned and, unlike the previous framework, also non-R-pronouns can be coindexed with a c-commanding NP. In this analysis, coindexing is obtained either by movement leaving a coindexed trace or by arbitrary coindexing. The same output conditions govern both, filtering out derivations with inappropriate coindexing. Obviously, I will give here neither a full nor a precise survey of the proposal but I will focus only on the aspects relevant to our previous discussion.

Some of the terminology assumed is the following. *The governor* of a given node α is, intuitively, the node which assigns case to α, and it can be e.g. N, V, INFL or P (this is a broader notion but its definition is not crucial now). The governing category of α (GC) is any S or NP node containing both α and the governor of α. *The minimal governing category of* α (MGC) is the GC of α which contains no other GC of α (i.e. the S or NP node most immediately dominating α which dominates also its governor). NPs are grouped into three classes: *pronominal NPs* are non-R-pronouns and PROs; *anaphors* are R-pronouns, NP-traces and PROs; 'lexical' NPs are case-marked NPs not belonging to the previous classes, including *wh*-traces. *Argument position* will be, for our purpose only, any position not immediately dominated by COMP or $\bar{S}$. A rough approximation of the output binding conditions is, then, stated in (3)–(4), where (4) ignores several of the entailments of the more precise formulation. A derivation not meeting these conditions (i.e. where an NP is either inappropriately coindexed or fails to be coindexed) will be filtered out.

(3)   *Definitions*:
  (a) An NP is *bound* if it is coindexed with a c-commanding NP in argument position.
  (b) An NP is free if it is not bound.
(4)   *Output conditions*:
  (a) Lexical NPs must be free in each of their governing categories.
  (b) Anaphors must be bound in their minimal governing category.
  (c) Pronominals must be free in their minimal governing category.

With respect to the anaphora problems we have been discussing, the conditions in (4) are similar to the conditions in (1a, b, c) respectively (with 'free' replacing 'non-coreferential'). However, they have much broader applications: (4a) filters out both the coindexing in (5) and inappropriate *wh*-movement into a non-COMP position as in (6b, c), since in both cases a lexical NP (*Felix* or *t*) is bound by definition (3), while it is required to be free by condition (4a).

(5)   *Rosa told him$_i$ that she loves Felix$_i$.
(6a)   Rosa told e that she loves whom$_i$.
 (b)   *Rosa told whom$_i$ that she loves t$_i$.
 (c)   *Whom$_i$ did Rosa tell t$_i$ that she loves t$_i$.

Similarly, (4b) handles both reflexivisation and NP-movement, blocking the derivations in (7) and (8), where the anaphor is inappropriately free in its MGC and allowing the derivations in (9) and (10) where it is appropriately bound in its MGC.

(7)   *Felix expects that [himself will be elected].
                        MGC

(8a)   e is expected that Felix will be elected.
(b)   *Felix$_i$ is expected that [t$_i$ will be elected].
                        MGC

(9)   [Felix$_i$ promised himself$_i$ that he will be elected].
(10)   [Felix$_i$ was promised t$_i$ that he will be elected].
       MGC

(4c) both prevents coindexing in, e.g. *Felix$_i$ appointed him$_i$* and controls the interpretation of PROs (given some further mechanism not discussed here).

In this system, it is possible for an NP to be coindexed but not bound, e.g. if it is coindexed with a c-commanding NP in COMP-position which is not an argument position. Although the trace in (11) is coindexed in its (higher) GC, the derivation is, correctly, not filtered out by (4a), since its not 'bound' by definition (3) and condition (4a) only filters out 'bound' derivations.

(11)   Tell me [$_\bar{S}$ who$_i$ [$_S$ Felix met t$_i$]].

This summary captures the essential details of the coindexing system and some remaining issues not covered here will be mentioned in Section 7.3.2 of the next chapter.

7 THE INTERPRETATION OF PRONOUNS: A RE-STATEMENT OF THE ANAPHORA PROBLEMS†

So far, I have concentrated only on the structural conditions governing anaphora. A major question still to be answered is what is actually meant by anaphora or coreference. While much attention has been paid in recent studies of anaphora to the structural conditions governing anaphora, the basic conception of which problems should to begin with be captured by sentence-level anaphora conditions has, essentially, remained the same since the earliest studies of anaphora in generative linguistics. Anaphora studies still concentrate primarily on the conditions for definite NP anaphora and avoid, in most cases, the problem of the interpretation of pronouns (e.g. whether they are interpreted as bound variables or as referential expressions) by postulating notions like co-reference, or non-coreference, governed by a coindexing mechanism. However, the coindexing mechanism is a syntactic device which needs to be interpreted semantically, and, similarly, notions like 'coreference' are useful only if there is a clear semantic analysis for them.

We will see first, in Section 7.1, that this point of departure, which results in an anaphora model of the type I presented in the previous chapters and in Reinhart (1976), leads to enormous problems and complications. I will argue, further, that although some of the problems seem to be specific to analyses assuming non-coreference rules, as in Chomsky (1973, 1980), Lasnik (1976) and Reinhart (1976), there is no way to avoid them as long as the anaphora questions are put the way they are.

All these problems are avoided once we pay more attention to the distinction, observed by many semantians, between the bound-variable interpretation of pronouns, and their referential interpretation, a distinction which, as we shall see in Section 7.2, is empirically testable. While the structural conditions governing anaphora will remain the same (i.e. they are restricted by c-command domains), I will argue that the problems for the model I presented result from attempting to capture within the grammar the conditions on the referential interpretation of pronouns, which is essentially a pragmatic, rather than a sentence-level problem. In the analysis I will propose, the only sentence-level mechanism needed to handle anaphora is the one governing the translation of pronouns as bound variables, i.e. the bound-anaphora mechanism as restated in Section 7.3. However, the range of application of this condition is much wider than we assumed so far. The answers to the traditional problems of definite-NP coreference, or non-coreference, follows from this mechanism pragmatically (i.e. outside the grammar) in a way specified in Section 7.4. Once this is established, we would be able to see how the anaphora interpretation of pronouns is fully consistent with the general hypotheses concerning the restrictions on semantic interpretation rules I proposed in Chapter 1.

7.1 The Problems with the Current Anaphora Picture

7.1.1 Problems with Non-coreference Rules

7.1.1.1. As we saw in Section 2.1 of Chapter 2, the anaphora model we have been considering assumes, crucially, a 'three-valued' system of coindexing: NPs can be positively coindexed, negatively coindexed or neutrally indexed (i.e. neither positively nor negatively coindexed). This corresponds to the three types of anaphora relations we illustrated in (6) of Chapter 2, repeated in (1).

> (1a) *Obligatory (stipulated) coreference*, e.g.:
>   Zelda bores herself.
>   (b) *Obligatory (stipulated) non-coreference*, e.g.:
>   Zelda bores her.
>   She adores Zelda's teachers.
>   (c) *Optional (free) coreference*, e.g.:
>   Zelda adores her teachers.
>   Those who know her adore Zelda.

The non-coreference relation, captured by contra-indexing, is needed to distinguish the (b) cases of (1) from the (c) cases. If all the rules of the grammar did was to prohibit coindexing in the (b) cases, nothing could prevent the pronouns in these sentences from nevertheless being assigned the reference Zelda, from a source outside the sentence (e.g. from a previous discourse). This is so, because non-R-pronouns can be used deictically or referentially, in which case, they select their reference from outside the sentence, and such a selection cannot be governed by a sentence-level rule.

In accordance with this observation, two of the general conditions on anaphora we assumed (which are summarised in (1) of Chapter 6) have been stated as conditions assigning non-coreference. In fact, the three-valued system these conditions are based on is assumed, at least implicitly, in all current analyses of anaphora within interpretative semantics.[1] We already saw in Chapter 6 that in Chomsky's (1980) framework these 'three values' were explicitly formalised. We also saw there that in Chomsky (1981) an attempt was made to reduce the indexing system to just two relations: 'bound' and 'free'. However, we may note now that if the system is supposed to capture the cases we examined so far, the reduction to just two indexing relations is only apparently successful. Given the definition of 'bound', and the conditions on appropriate binding, all the pronouns in (2)–(3) are equally defined as free. (It would be recalled that in (3) of Chapter 6, an NP was defined as bound, if it is coindexed with a c-commanding NP in argument position.)

    (2)   The flowers that we bought for Zelda cost her trouble.
    (3a) Zelda entertains her.
    (b)   She doesn't like the flowers that we bought for Zelda.

In (2) *Zelda* does not c-command the pronoun, hence by the definition of 'bound' the pronoun cannot be bound, i.e. it is free. In (3a) and (3b) the pronoun must be free, i.e. not coindexed with *Zelda*, otherwise the derivation will be filtered out by the output conditions on binding ((4c) and (4a) of Chapter 6 respectively).

However, our point of departure has been to distinguish (2), where coreference is possible, from (3), where it is not. If the model still intends to capture these facts, 'free' cannot be defined as 'not bound' but, rather as contra-indexed.[2]

There are further theoretical consequences of the assumptions of this framework, which are stated in Lasnik (1976). It follows that sentence-level grammar has nothing to say about the interpretation of optionally coreferring pronouns as in (1c). This problem is reduced to the general problem of deciding what a given expression (e.g. a definite description) refers to and it is believed that there is nothing special about the assignment of reference to a (non-reflexive) pronoun. Thus, in the famous debate concerning whether pronouns are interpreted as bound variables or as referential expressions,[3] this analysis takes unequivocally the latter stand. An apparent support for this stand comes from Lasnik's observation which we discussed in Section 2.1.2 of Chapter 2, that when the non-coreference rule applies to a pair of a pronoun and a full NP, it also applies to two full NPs, as in (4), but when this rule does not apply, as in (5), full NPs coreference is possible.

(4a)   **She* liked the flowers that we bought for *Zelda*.
  (b)   **Zelda* liked the flowers that we bought for *Zelda*.
(5a)   The flowers that we bought for *her* pleased *Zelda*.
  (b)   The flowers that we bought for *Zelda* pleased *Zelda*.

Such examples seem to suggest, then, that the coreference interpretation of the pronoun in (5a) is not substantially different from the coreference interpretation of the full NPs in (5b) and that the non-coreference rule, applying to (4), determines non-coreference equally for pronouns and non-pronouns, so there is no reason to distinguish between pronouns and referential NPs or to establish some specific semantic interpretation procedures for pronouns. A final consequence of this picture is that a sentence containing an optionally coreferring pronoun is never ambiguous, but only vague, since there is nothing in the sentence-level syntax or semantics that distinguishes its coreferential interpretation from its non-coreferential interpretation.

7.1.1.2. The major problem for the anaphora model outlined above is that there is no explicit semantics for its complex indexing system. Indexing devices, however formal and intricate they may get, are just syntactic devices, and whether they make sense or not depends (at least in part) on whether they are interpretable semantically. While a syntax that has a two-valued indexing system allowing NPs to be either co-indexed or not, is easily interpretable semantically (say — coindexed NPs unlike the non-coindexed ones, are interpreted as variables bound by the same operator), it is very difficult to see how a three-valued indexing system can be interpreted. It turns out in this system that a pronoun can be interpreted as non-coreferential in two cases: either if it is contra-indexed or if it is neutral or 'free'. Similarly, it can be interpreted as co-referential either if it is coindexed or if it is 'free'. (Recall that in Chomsky's, 1981, model non-R-pronouns can also be coindexed.) How, then, is a neutral pronoun to be distinguished semantically from either a coindexed or from a contra-indexed pronoun? Or, to put the question differently, suppose that coindexed pronouns are indeed interpreted as bound variables, how then should the contra-indexed pronouns be interpreted? If they are interpreted either as referential expressions or as free variables, they are indistinguishable from the neutral or free pronouns, which are also so interpreted. To maintain the distinction it seems that some negative semantic operator should be introduced, whose formal properties are not easy to define.

Note that this problem must be solved for the system to work in the case of anaphora. For other cases it might be argued that the indexing system is just a syntactic device to filter out bad derivations and it need not be semantically interpretable. This is true, for example, for ruling out inappropriate *wh*-movement. However, in the case of anaphora, if we interpret the binding conditions as just ruling out coindexed derivations like *Felix$_i$ adores him$_i$*, we have not solved the problem we posed. Obviously, the same sentence with no coindexing will not be filtered out and the problem raised by Lasnik still holds, i.e. we have to explain why the pronoun *him* cannot choose the reference of *Felix*, from outside the sentence.

The source of the difficulties in interpreting the coindexing system is, then, the contra-indexing relation. Even if some arbitrary semantic device can be postulated to interpret this type of indexing, there are further problems with it, which are pointed out in detail in Evans (1980), and which I shall mention only briefly: assuming non-coreference rules or contra-indexing, there is no explanation for identity statements like *He is Zelda's husband* (uttered e.g. as an answer to the question *Who is the man with the flowers over there?*). Contra-indexing must explicitly mark *He* as disjoint in reference from *Zelda's husband* so any interpretation in which they overlap in reference would be plainly ungrammatical, or filtered out by the binding conditions. Some unnatural mechanism will be needed, therefore, to handle such cases. Furthermore, it seems that the definition of non-coreference (disjoint-reference), which is, presumably, a semantic, or at least a sentence-level notion, should be relativised to speaker's intentions to handle cases like the following: Suppose that in a visit to a desolate Greek island I see from a distance a woman with a purple hat who reminds me of Zelda and I say *She looks just like Zelda*, if, when she approaches, I find out that this is, in fact, Zelda, it turns out that my sentence was mistaken (since *look like* sentences implicate non-identity of the arguments), but given the non-coreferential rule it would furthermore turn out to be ungrammatical, since the NPs are not disjoint in reference as required by the rules. Although both these problems are acknowledged by Lasnik (1976), their solution is not obvious. Evans points out several cases where intended violations of the contra-indexing requirement are also possible in appropriate context, and we shall return to such cases in Section 7.4. Even if one believes that the problems pointed out by Evans are not, in and of themselves, a sufficient reason to reject non-coreference rules, combined with the general interpretability problem of a three-valued indexing system they do provide sufficient grounds for questioning the whole enterprise. In Section 7.2, I will return to the other theoretical consequences of this framework which I mentioned above, and argue that they are, in any case, empirically inadequate.

We should note, in conclusion, that the problems posed in this section are not inherent to the framework outlined above. They stem from the way the anaphora question has been put to begin with, namely the assumption that the question is when a pronoun can (or cannot) corefer with a definite NP. This question necessarily leads to Lasnik's problem of how to prevent 'accidental' coreference, and, in fact, I believe that this and the resulting problems are unsolvable within any model that shares this point of departure including, as we shall see directly, that of Evans. As we saw, Chomsky's (1981) model, as explicitly stated, fails in any case to answer this question. Our next step, in Section 7.4, will be to argue that it need not do that. But first we should look at the second set of problems for the current anaphora framework, which will provide the clue for posing the anaphora question differently.

7.1.2 Bound Anaphora Problems

Further problems for the model I assumed in the previous chapters arise in the case of the bound anaphora condition (which is summarised in (2) of Chapter 6). A serious question concerning the bound anaphora condition is at which level of linguistic analysis it could apply. As we saw in Section 5.1.1, the peculiar property of bound anaphora is that on the one hand, it obeys a syntactic restriction, but on the other, the class of NPs that this restriction applies to is determined semantically, and does not constitute a syntactic set. (Even the quantified NPs mentioned in the bound anaphora condition are not a syntactic set – they may include indefinite NPs as well as NPs introduced by a quantifier phrase.) Therefore, presenting the condition as a surface-structure syntactic condition as in Reinhart (1976) is just an attempt to avoid the problem.

To capture this, it has been proposed that the bound anaphora condition applies, in fact, to logical forms (LFs) and not to surface structures, and determines when a pronoun can be coindexed with, or translated as, a bound variable (e.g. Chomsky, 1976, and Higginbotham, 1980a,b). (Freidin and Lasnik, 1981, propose that even other coindexing procedures apply at this level.) We should note first that proposals along such lines have two interpretations, one of which is fairly dangerous: if the bound anaphora condition applies to actual logical formulae, i.e. to the output of the mapping of surface structures into semantic interpretations, there is no reason to expect that the structural relations of surface structure to which the condition is sensitive, will be preserved.

Or, in most cases, for any logical formula which is an appropriate translation for a given natural language sentence and which preserves some structural properties of the sentence, we can find an equivalent logical formula which does not do that and whose interpretation should be, nevertheless, an appropriate semantic interpretation for the sentence.[4] To maintain the proposal that the bound anaphora condition applies to LFs literally, we have to assume that LF is an intermediate level of logical syntax which contains both semantic information, such as semantic operators and bound variables, and a specific syntactic structure corresponding to surface structure. However, the initial hypothesis of interpretative semantics (quite similarly to that of Montague semantics) has been that it should be possible to define the procedures mapping syntactic structures directly into some familiar semantic language. The idea that an intermediate logical syntax, specific to natural language (or some specific natural language semantics) might be needed is as alien to interpretative semantics as it is to the original Montague framework.

However, in the extremely careful development of this analysis in Higginbotham (1980b), such problems are avoided. The procedure governed by the bound anaphora condition applies not directly to LFs but to the operations mapping surface structures into LFs, so in fact this is a syntactic procedure. To capture this, Higginbotham assumes, crucially, the rule of Quantifier Raising (QR) of May (1977), which adjoins a quantified (or indefinite) NP to S, leaving a trace in its original syntactic position. Once this is assumed, the missing syntactic link between quantified NPs and *wh*-traces is obtained, e.g. the sentences in (6) have, after QR has applied to (6a), the similar structures in (7).

(6a) His neighbours hate everyone.
  (b) Who do his neighbours hate?
(7a) Everyone$_1$ [$_S$ his neighbours hate e$_1$].
  (b) Who$_1$ [$_S$ do his neighbours hate e$_1$].

Higginbotham then introduces a coindexing procedure, which applies only to pairs of an empty node and a pronoun. Ignoring the details of his original procedure which, as we mentioned in Chapter 5, was stated in terms of linear order, the coindexing rule which is consistent with the bound anaphora condition we have been assuming, is stated in (8).

(8) Coindex a pronoun with an e-node that c-commands it
    (OPTional).

A pronoun which is coindexed with an e-node will be translated by later rules as the same variable which translates the e-node. The rule (8) cannot apply to the structures in (7), since the pronoun in these structures is not c-commanded by the e-node. But in cases where the e-node c-commands the pronoun, coindexing can apply and bound anaphora interpretation is obtained.

For many cases this analysis is straightforwardly equivalent to applying the bound anaphora condition to pre-QR surface structures. For the cases where it is not, Higginbotham proposes a special auxiliary constraint, which I shall not discuss here, and which renders the two analyses equivalent with respect to their empirical results, while Higginbotham's analysis has, furthermore, the advantage of mentioning only strictly-syntactic categories in his coindexing rule.

The only problem with this elegant solution (or, more precisely, with the anaphora facts that seem to necessitate it) is that it adds substantial complication to the grammar. We need to introduce a new coindexing procedure, which, it would seem, should be ordered after the general anaphora output conditions.[5] This procedure itself is fairly complex, requiring, apart from the rule in (8), a condition on cross-indexing and a condition for index transferring. But, in addition, if this solution is incorporated into a grammar that allows free indexing subject to output conditions, as the one surveyed in Section 6.2, a further mechanism will be needed to cancel arbitrary (accidental) coindexing, e.g. in cases like *The woman who invited him$_i$ praised every guest$_i$*, which are not filtered out by the general anaphora conditions. Such complications are, of course, tolerable, if that is how things must be, but a solution that can avoid them would be preferable.

Despite the fact that the bound anaphora problem is, as we saw, technically solvable, a puzzling question which remains is why should there be such a restriction in the first place. The assumption of QR as a syntactic transformation (which is otherwise not the only conceivable way to interpret quantifier-scope), provides a way around the problem of defining the class of NPs that obey this condition. But it still is the case that this is a semantic class. Why, then, should the semantic class of quantified NPs obey different anaphora conditions than definite NPs? Of course, if the difference could follow from their semantic differences (i.e. if this, to begin with, was a semantic question outside the level of syntax) there would be no puzzlement here. But, as we saw, in Section 5.1, the bound anaphora condition has no semantic explanation.

We should note that this question holds for all existing analyses of anaphora, including those which are semantically oriented like Bach and Partee (1980) (see footnote 1 of Chapter 5). Evans' (1980, p. 338) point of departure is that the analysis of anaphora should capture the 'common principle' that underlies the use of pronouns as bound variables (i.e. our bound anaphora) and as anaphoric pronouns (i.e. pronouns anaphoric to definite NPs). Nevertheless, he concludes by assuming the two distinct anaphora conditons in (9) for these two types of anaphora, more or less along the lines we have assumed here (ignoring the difference in the structural conditions, which we shall not pursue).

(9a) A pronoun can be interpreted as bound by a quantifier phrase iff it precedes and c-commands the pronoun. (Evans, 1980, p. 341)

(b) A pronoun can be referentially dependent upon an NP iff it does not precede and c-commands that NP. (Evans, 1980, p. 358)

The problem posed for Evans by the existence of these two distinct conditions is more severe than the problem posed by it to the framework we examined above (i.e. it is not just a matter of complications). To free the grammar from non-coreference rules, Evans distinguishes between coreference and referential dependency (as in (9b)). A pronoun is described as referentially dependent upon a given NP if it 'picks up its reference from that NP' (p. 358). The cases marked as non-coreferential by the contra-indexing procedures we have been assuming will be only cases where referential dependency is impossible, but coreference is still possible if the relevant reference for the pronoun is supplied from an independent source. Although I believe that the general spirit of Evans's analysis is correct, the problem with this specific solution is that no actual definition is offered for referential dependency. This is not an accident: a straightforward solution could be to define a pronoun as referentially dependent if it is interpreted as a bound variable, just as in the case of quantified NPs. If this is so, however, we cannot explain why referentially dependent pronouns do not obey the bound-anaphora condition (9a) like the other bound-variable pronouns. So this solution is not available in this analysis, and as long as there exists this difference between bound anaphora and definite-NP anaphora, referential dependency must be kept distinguished from bound anaphora, and there is no other obvious semantic property that could distinguish it, then, from coreference. In the absence of such a definition, this distinction is just arbitrary, particularly since there is no independent way to know when a pronoun is referentially dependent and when it is just coreferential.

For example, Evans points out, correctly, that coreference in a sentence like (10b), which violates the referential-dependency requirement (9b), is nevertheless possible in this peculiar context.

(10a) Everyone hates Siegfried. Even those who never met him hate Siegfried.
  (b) Everyone hates Siegfried. Even he (himself) hates Siegfried.

His analysis entails, however, that only in (10a) which meets condition (9b), can this pronoun be understood as referentially dependent, while in (10b) its reference can be determined only outside the sentence. And it is appropriate to ask how we could ever tell whether this is so or not.

7.2 Coreference and Bound Anaphora

Our starting point in restating the anaphora question will be to observe that the assumption that the bound anaphora condition holds only for the semantically-determined set of quantified NPs (and *wh*-traces) is simply incorrect, empirically. In fact, all pronouns can be interpreted as bound variables, regardless of whether the antecedent is a quantified NP or not, subject to the bound anaphora condition. Our next step will be to argue that the syntax, or sentence-level considerations, determine only when a pronoun can be so interpreted and not when it can corefer.

7.2.1. Sloppy Identity

That pronouns linked to a definite NP (or a proper name) can be ambiguous between a referential interpretation and a bound-variable interpretation is, in fact, well known (e.g. Keenan, 1971; Sag, 1976; Williams, 1977;Partee,1978).This ambiguity shows up, for example, in VP-deletion contexts such as (11).

(11) Felix hates his neighbours and so does Max.
(12) Max hates Felix's neighbours.
(13) Max hates Max's neighbours.
(14) (λx (x hates x's neighbours)) (Felix) and (λx (x hates x's neighbours)) (Max).

The second conjunct of (11) is ambiguous between the reading in (12) and the one in (13). This ambiguity is strictly within the coreference interpretation of (11). In addition, the sentence has, of course, a third reading in which both Max and Felix hate the neighbour of a third person, identifiable from the context. The reading (12) is obtained by fixing a referent for the pronoun in the second conjunct, in this case Felix, and then hating Felix's neighbours, which is predicated of Felix in the first conjunct, is predicated of Max in the second. The second reading (13) of (11) cannot be so explained. To obtain it, we need to assume that the first conjunct of (11) contains some open formula *x hates x's neighbours* which is satisfied by Felix in the first conjunct and by Max in the second, i.e. that some variable binding operator is involved, which is captured by the lambda representation in (14). So, in this reading of (11), which is labelled *sloppy identity*, following Ross (1967), the pronoun is interpreted as a bound variable.

What has gone unnoticed in the studies of sloppy identity is that, in fact, it obeys precisely the same conditions as quantified NP anaphora, i.e. the bound anaphora condition that we discussed in Chapter 5: the antecedent must c-command the pronoun for the sloppy identity interpretation to be obtained. The only cases of sloppy identity which have been studied extensively are those occuring with VP-deletion (as in (11)). Sag (1976) and Williams (1977) argue that these facts can be captured by a mechanism which they believe is needed anyway to handle the VP-deletion facts. Following Partee (1973), they assume as one of the obligatory operations mapping surface structures onto logical forms the derived VP-rule (DVPR), which creates a new predicate by lambda abstraction on the subject and is restricted to operate only on the (full) subject. This rule, then, applies to all sentences, regardless of anaphora. Once this is assumed, whenever a pronoun occurs in the scope of a lambda operator it can be translated as a variable bound by it, by a rule which Williams calls the *pronoun rule*. The way this works is illustrated in (15)–(17).

I will follow here and in the following discussion the informal lambda-notation introduced by Sag and by Williams, where the argument of the lambda predicate precedes the predicate as in (15b). This notation is convenient for its similarity to the surface-structure.

(15a) Los Angeles is adored by its residents and so is New York.
                                                             SLOPPY
   (b) *DVPR applied to the first conjunct*:
      Los Angeles (λx (x is adored by its residents)). (15b) is equivalent to (λx (x is adored by its residents)) (Los Angeles).)
   (c) *The pronoun rule*:
      Los Angeles (λx (x is adored by x's residents)).

(16a) The people who were born in LA adore its beaches but the people who were born in NY do not.   NON-SLOPPY

  (b) *DVPR*:

    The people who were born in LA (λx (x adore its beaches)).

  (c) *The pronoun rule*: inapplicable.

(17a) People from LA adore it and so do people from NY.   NON-SLOPPY

  (b) *DVPR*:

    People from LA (λx (x adore it)).

  (c) *The pronoun rule*: inapplicable.

In (16) and (17), where the pronoun rule is inapplicable, the sloppy-identity reading is correctly not obtained. In these examples, a restriction based on the bound anaphora condition and an analysis based on the DVPR yield identical results since in (16) and (17) the antecedent both does not c-command the pronoun and is not the subject and, conversely, whenever the antecedent is the subject, it also c-commands the pronoun.

The point is, however, that sloppy identity shows up also in cases where the antecedent is not the subject (and where the relevant 'deletion' is not VP-deletion) as in (18).

(18a) We paid the professor his expenses, but not the assistant.

  (b) The nurse referred Siegfried to his doctor, and Felix too. (meaning: she referred Felix . . . too.)

  (c) You can keep Rosa in her room for the whole afternoon, but not Zelda.

(19) *DVPR applied to (18b)*:

  The nurse (λx (x referred Siegfried to his doctor)).

In all these cases sloppy-identity interpretation is possible (e.g. (18a) can mean that we didn't pay the assistant the assistant's expenses, and (18b) that the nurse referred Felix to Felix's doctor.) But the DVPR-analysis obviously does not allow the coindexing of the pronoun, or its translation as a bound variable, since in its output, illustrated in (19), there is no operator binding the antecedent. However, in all these cases the antecedent c-commands the pronoun so in an analysis based on the bound-anaphora condition they can be coindexed which (given the appropriate mechanism we shall turn to in the next section) will guarantee the bound-variable interpretation of the pronoun. Let us see a few more examples for the claim that sloppy identity interpretation is possible whenever the antecedent c-commands the pronoun. In some of the following examples there are several ways to construe the deleted part, and attention should be carefully restricted to the one we intend to examine, which is indicated in the *i.e.* brackets.

(20a) Zelda bought *Siegfried* a present on *his* wedding day and Felix too. (i.e. and she bought Felix . . . too).   SLOPPY

  (b) Zelda thought about *Siegfried* on *his* wedding day and about Felix too.   NON-SLOPPY

(21a) *Siegfried* went to the party in order to please *his* wife, and Felix too / and so did Felix.   SLOPPY

  (b) We invited *Siegfried* to the party in order to please *his* wife and Felix too. (i.e. and we invited Felix . . . too).   NON-SLOPPY

  (c) We sent *Siegfried* home to be with *his* wife and Felix too. (i.e. and we sent Felix . . . too).   SLOPPY

(22a) (=18c) You can keep *Rosa* in her room for the whole afternoon, but not Zelda.   SLOPPY

  (b) Felix is kissing *Rosa* in *her* wedding picture but not Zelda. (i.e. he is not kissing Zelda . . .).   NON-SLOPPY

  (c) *Rosa* is wearing a pink dress in *her* wedding picture, but Zelda is not / but not Zelda.   SLOPPY

(23a) For *her* seventieth birthday *Rosa* requested a Stravinsky record and Zelda (did) too.   SLOPPY

  (b) For *her* seventieth birthday I bought *Rosa* a Stravinsky record and Zelda too. (i.e. For her seventieth birthday, I bought Zelda . . . too).   NON-SLOPPY

  (c) I bought *Rosa* a Stravinsky record for *her* seventieth birthday, and Zelda too. (i.e. and I bought Zelda . . . too).   SLOPPY

(24a) Upon entering *his* office, *Siegfried* found a suspicious object under the desk and Felix too.   SLOPPY

  (b) Upon entering *his* office Zelda found *Siegried* under the desk, and Felix too. (i.e. and she found Felix . . . too).   NON-SLOPPY

  (c) Zelda found *Siegfried* under the desk, upon entering *his* office, and Felix too. (i.e. and she found Felix . . . too).   SLOPPY

(25a) Thinking about *his* problems, *Siegfried* got depressed, and Felix (did) too.   SLOPPY

  (b) Thinking about *his* problems, I pitied *Siegfried*, and Felix too. (i.e. and I pitied Felix . . . too).   NON-SLOPPY

 (26) (Compare to (23a), (24a), and (25a):

(a) According to *him*, *Siegfried* is an unrecognised genius, and Felix (is) too.   NON-SLOPPY

(b) In *her* wedding picture, *Rosa* is wearing a pink dress, and Zelda (is) too.   NON-SLOPPY

(27a) According to *Siegfried*, *he* is an unrecognised genius, and according to Felix too.   NON-SLOPPY

(b) In *Rosa*'s wedding picture, *she* is wearing a pink dress, and in Zelda's wedding picture too.   NON-SLOPPY

The direct object of (20a), as in the examples of (18), c-commands the pronoun, and sloppy-identity interpretation is possible. In (20b), where the antecedent is in the PP, it does not c-command the pronoun and no sloppy-identity interpretation is obtained (i.e. that Zelda thought about Felix on Felix's wedding day). (This, however, is not true for all types of PPs, and we shall return to them in Chapter 8.) Sentences (21a) and (21b) illustrate the subject-object asymmetries with respect to a sentential PP-clause which disappear when the PP clause is verb-phrasal, as in (21c). (The structural differences between these sentences were mentioned in Chapters 3 and 5.) The relations of the object to sentential and verb-phrasal PPs is further illustrated in (22).

As we saw in Chapter 3, the PP in (22b) is sentential, unlike that of (22a). Hence, the object does not c-command the pronoun in the PP and sloppy identity, which is possible in (22a), is impossible here. (The sentence does not mean that Felix is not kissing Zelda in Zelda's wedding picture.) The subject in such a structure does c-command the PP, hence in (22c) sloppy identity (i.e. the interpretation in which Zelda wears a pink dress in Zelda's wedding picture) is possible. (23)–(25) illustrate subject-object asymmetries in cases of preposed constituents. The pronoun in the (a)-sentences is c-commanded by the subject antecedent, and sloppy-identity interpretation is obtained in all these cases. In the (b)-sentences where the potential antecedent is the object, no such reading is possible. For example, (23b) does not mean that I bought Zelda a Stravinsky record for Zelda's seventieth birthday (and since the non-sloppy-identity interpretation of the sentence is contextually unavailable here, this particular sentence seems meaningless). The sentential PPs in the sentences of (26), unlike those in (23)–(25) are, attached, when preposed, to a higher position than $\bar{\text{S}}$. (The syntactic evidence for this too was provided in Chapter 3, Section 3.2.) Hence, the subject does not c-command the pronoun in the PP, and sloppy-identity interpretation is indeed impossible. Finally, (27) illustrates cases where the antecedent is in the PP and hence does not c-command the pronoun.

The fact that sloppy identity is possible not only in VP-deletion contexts, and that it obeys the bound-anaphora restriction, indicates that
regardless of the question of whether the DVPR is needed at all as part
of the translation into LF in general, or for the analysis of VP-deletion
specifically, it is not this which accounts for sloppy identity. The independent coindexing procedure which is needed to capture the full
range of this phenomena will capture its occurrence in VP-deletion
contexts as well.

There are still problems with the claim that sloppy identity is possible
precisely when the antecedent c-commands the pronoun in surface
structure. However, these problems, to which we shall return in Chapter 8,
are general problems for the c-command condition. The crucial point
here is that sloppy-identity interpretation is possible precisely in the
same contexts where bound anaphora with quantified NP antecedents is
possible. The reader is invited to check this claim by substituting a
quantified NP for the antecedent in examples (15)–(27) and observing
that whenever sloppy-identity reading is impossible, the pronoun (which
can, nevertheless, corefer with the antecedent in the case of the definite
NP) cannot be anaphoric to the quantified NP. Here I shall illustrate
this comparison with only some of the examples:

(28a) (=15a) *Los Angeles* is adored by *its* residents and so is New
      York.   SLOPPY

  (b) *Each of the western cities* is adored by *its* residents.

(29a) (=17a) People from *LA* adore *it* and so do people from NY.
                                     NON-SLOPPY

  (b) *People from *each of the western cities* adore *it*.

(30a) (=25a) Thinking about *his* problems *Siegfried* got depressed
      and Felix (did) too.   SLOPPY

  (b) Thinking about *his* problems, *everyone* got depressed.

(31a) (=25b) Thinking about *his* problems, I pitied *Siegfried*, and
      Felix too.   NON-SLOPPY

  (b) *Thinking about *his* problems, I pitied *everyone*.

(32a) (=27a) According to *Siegfried, he* is an unrecognised genius.
      And according to Felix too.   NON-SLOPPY

  (b) *According to *everyone, he* is an unappreciated genius.

What is important in evaluating these examples is the correspondence
between the sloppy-identity judgment and the quantified-NP anaphora
judgment. Even if some readers disagree with my judgments here, I am
claiming that for each pair a reader who disagrees with my judgment on

the one, will, consistently, disagree also on the other. The point I am making here is thus independent of my structural analysis of bound anaphora; even if the c-command restriction is not the correct generalisation, it is still the case that these two phenomena obey precisely the same restrictions.

7.2.2 Implications

Given the facts we have just observed, the bound-anaphora puzzlement we observed in Section 7.1.2 (and in Chapter 5) disappears. We wondered why a syntactic condition should apply to a semantically-determined class. The answer is now clear: this condition is not, in fact, sensitive at all to the semantic properties of the NPs it applies to. Rather, it applies to all NPs determining when a pronoun can be interpreted as a variable bound by an operator which would correspond in the logical form to the given NP. It is still true that if a pronoun is prevented by the bound anaphora condition from being coindexed with a definite NP, as witnessed by the unavailability of the sloppy-identity interpretation, it can nevertheless happen to corefer with this NP (though it would not be interpreted as a bound variable), while such 'accidental' coreference is impossible if the antecedent is a quantified NP. This, however, follows strictly from semantic considerations and is not a syntactic issue, as we shall see in Section 7.4.

The examination of the sloppy-identity cases indicates, furthermore, that we have to abandon two of the assumptions underlying the non-coreference analysis of anaphora which we mentioned in Section 7.1.1. First, it is not true that there is nothing special about the coreference interpretation of pronouns, which distinguishes them from the coreference interpretation of two full NPs: a pronoun coreferring with another NP can, under the appropriate syntactic conditions, be interpreted as a bound variable, while a full NP that happens to corefer with another full NP cannot be so interpreted. Next, it is not true that sentences containing pronouns are always vague, rather than ambiguous: as we saw, in environments which allow for sloppy identity the sentences are always ambiguous between the bound-variable interpretation and the referential interpretation of the pronoun.

Both of the last conclusions have been in fact, widely acknowledged by semanticians (see, e.g. Partee, 1978, and the references cited there) and they entail a distinction between cases of bound anaphora, which are possible only if one of two NPs is a pronoun, translated as a bound variable, and cases of coreference, where two NPs (regardless of whether any of them is a pronoun or not) are assigned the same reference. The later is what Partee (1978) calls 'pragmatic coreference', what Evans (1980) calls 'coreference with no dependency', and, essentially, what Lasnik (1976) calls 'accidental coreference'. I will assume here that co-referring (but unbound) pronouns are interpreted as referential expressions (e.g. proper names) rather than as free variables, but this is not crucial to my analysis.

The problem for the theories of anaphora (including those which distinguish bound anaphora from coreference) result from attempting to define within the grammar the conditions for coreference, rather than for bound anaphora only. Whatever way we may specify conditions on the referential interpretation of unbound pronouns within the sentence, there is always the problem that such pronouns can corefer freely (i.e. subject to pragmatic conditions only) across sentences. So, unless we introduce the problematic non-coreference rules there is no way to prevent a pronoun from selecting the 'wrong reference' from outside the sentence. We shall see now that once the procedures determining bound-anaphora interpretations are specified, there is, in fact, no need to establish sentence-level coreference rules.

7.3 The Coindexing Procedure and the Interpretation of Coindexing

7.3.1 The Procedure

To capture the bound-anaphora facts we have been discussing, we shall assume that the syntax contains some mechanism allowing coindexing of pronouns with NPs in the appropriate syntactic conditions, and that this syntactic procedure has a unique semantic interpretation: coindexed pronouns, and only they, are translated as bound variables.

It may be recalled now that at least in one case the general anaphora conditions we assumed (which were summarised in Chapter 6) already required coindexing a pronoun with an antecedent (regardless of the properties of the antecedent): R(eflexive or reciprocal) pronouns obey condition (73) of Chapter 5, repeated with minor variations in (33).

(33) An R-pronoun must be coindexed with an only with a c-commanding NP within a specified syntactic domain (say, its minimal governing category).

If coindexing means that the pronoun is translated as a bound variable, it is not an accident that R-pronouns need be coindexed for the sentence to be interpretable: we saw in Chapter 5 (Section 5.2) that such pronouns are only interpretable as bound variables, which is why a sentence like *Zelda likes himself*, which contains no possible binder for the R-pronoun, is uninterpretable, unlike a sentence like *Zelda likes him*. We noted there further that condition (33) in fact collapses two distinct conditions. The one requires that the antecedent c-command the pronoun, and the other that the antecedent be dominated by the minimal governing category dominating the pronoun. The first of these is the bound anaphora condition we have been assuming, which is just what we should expect: since R-pronoun interpretation is a case of bound anaphora, we would not expect it to be possible when bound anaphora interpretation in general is impossible. However, R-pronouns also have the peculiar linguistic property specified in the second condition in (33), which cannot be reduced to the bound-anaphora rule and which has to be captured separately. Assuming a general coindexing mechanism governed by the bound-anaphora condition and special conditions on the distribution of R and non R-pronouns is thus just an extension of the mechanism we had to assume anyway in the previous model to capture the interpretation of R-pronouns. But I am claiming, further, that this mechanism is all that we need in the grammar to capture the anaphora facts, i.e. that it replaces all five conditions which were assumed so far (the four conditions summarised in (1) and (2) of Chapter 6 and the sloppy-identity rule exemplified in (15) above).

The coindexing procedure is stated in (34), ignoring the details of gender and number agreement. We assume that, apart from coindexing by movement, or cases of obligatory control, no other coindexing is permitted in the grammar; so only a pair containing (at least) one pronoun or empty node may end up coindexed. For convenience, (34) is stated as an actual coindexing mechanism. However, as we will see directly, it can be stated equally well as an output condition on free coindexing, along the lines of Chomsky (1981). In all syntactic details I assume here the analysis of the distribution of R- and non-R-pronouns as stated in Chomsky (1981) (see Chapter 6). However, nothing in my analysis hinges on this particular choice. A problem not captured by this analysis is that there exist exceptional contexts in which both R- and non-R-pronouns can occur anaphorically, i.e. either one can be coindexed with a c-commanding NP.

(34) Coindex a pronoun P with a c-commanding NP α (α not immediately dominated by COMP or $\bar{S}$).[6]
conditions: (a) If P is an R-pronoun α must be in its minimal governing category.

(b) If P is non-R-pronoun, α must be outside its minimal governing categories.

The procedure (34) is optional: no special obligatory requirement on R-pronouns is needed. Since R-pronouns are interpretable only as bound variables, and since only coindexed pronouns can be so interpreted, if an R-pronoun ends up uncoindexed, this particular derivation of the sentence will not be interpretable. A semantic interpretation rule with this effect is needed anyway to account for cases where (34) is inapplicable, such as (36c). The operation of the coindexing procedure is exemplified in (35)–(36).

(35a) Everyone$_i$ respects himself$_i$.
   (b) Felix$_i$ thinks that he$_i$ is a genius.
   (c) In his$_i$ drawer each of the managers$_i$ keeps a gun.
(36a) Zelda bores her.
   (b) He thinks that Felix is a genius.
   (c) Felix thinks that himself is a genius.
   (d) Those who know her respect Zelda.
   (e) Those who know her respect no presidents' wife.

While the pronoun can be coindexed in the sentences of (35), none of the pronouns in (36) meets the coindexing conditions. In (36a) it is because the condition (b) of (34) does not allow non-R-pronouns to be coindexed within their MGC, in (36b, d, and e) because the pronouns are not c-commanded by the potential antecedent, and in (36c), because R-pronouns cannot be coindexed with NPs outside their MGC. All these sentences, thus, leave the syntactic component with equal status. (36c), then, is filtered out as uninterpretable, and to the question what distinguishes the other sentences from each other, we shall return in the next section.

We need now a mechanism determining the interpretation of the co-indexing device. This mechanism should guarantee that all and only occurrences of coindexed NPs will correspond to variables bound by the same operator.[7] But the procedure I actually define here handles only the translation of pronouns and the binding of *wh*-traces requires a separate procedure.[8] We will say that for any string Φ and any NP β in non-COMP or $\bar{S}$ position in Φ, Φ^β/x is the result of replacing β and all pronouns coindexed with and c-commanded by β by x. The translation procedure for bound anaphora, then, is stated in (37). (For the λ notation used here, see the discussion of (15b) above.)

$$(37) \ [_{\bar{S}} \ \Phi] \Rightarrow [_{\bar{S}} \ \beta \ (\lambda x \ (\Phi^{\beta}/x))]$$

This rule thus operates in the $\bar{S}$ domain and λ-abstracts on the antecedent, i.e. that NP in a set of coindexed NPs which c-commands the others (which can only be pronouns, given the coindexing procedure (34)), and converts all other pronouns in this set to variables bound by the λ operator. The antecedent (β in (37)) can be any NP (definite, quantified or a pronoun) as long as it c-commands the pronoun it is coindexed with. The operation of (37) is illustrated in (38b)-(40b). The (a)-sentences represent coindexed surface structures — the output of the coindexing procedure (34).

(38a) Zelda$_i$ upset her$_i$ neighbours.
  (b) Zelda (λx (x upsets x's neighbours)).
(39a) Everyone$_i$ upsets his$_i$ neighbours.
  (b) Everyone (λx (x upsets x's neighbours)).
(40a) She$_i$ adores herself$_i$.
  (b) She (λx (x adores x)).

(39b) is either directly interpreted as, e.g. in Montague (1974), and Keenan and Faltz (1978), or it can be further translated into standard first-order logic notation. (QR can be used, if desired.) The pronoun *she* in (40b) is deictic (or pragmatic). As I mentioned, I assume here that deictic pronouns are interpreted more or less like proper names, so no further operations are needed for such cases.[9]

Obviously, nothing in my analysis hinges on the existence of a separate coindexing device. The translation procedure for pronouns can be stated directly on non-coindexed surface structures, λ abstracting on a given NP and translating all pronouns c-commanded by this NP (under the appropriate auxiliary conditions specified in (34), as variables bound by the λ operator. The reason I used coindexing here is that such procedures are currently assumed in the interpretive framework, where, as we saw in Chapter 6, coindexing is needed, independently, for syntactic movement rules, and where it is assumed that the same coindexing conditions govern both anaphora and movement. The crucial point in my analysis is that what is needed in the grammar to account for anaphora is a mechanism determining when a pronoun can be translated as a bound variable, while how this mechanism is formulated is theory-dependent.[10]

7.3.2 Output Conditions

The coindexing mechanism I proposed for anaphora is stated as an actual coindexing procedure, and is, thus, independent of details of the syntactic theory assumed. However, we shall see now that, with a certain modification, Chomsky's (1981) output conditions on indexing captures everything that (34) captures, so in fact, in this framework, there is no need to assume a separate coindexing procedure for pronouns.

As stated, Chomsky's output conditions which were summarised in Chapter 6 (Section 6.2) are not consistent with (34). We saw that this system distinguishes between binding and coindexing: the trace of (11) in Chapter 6, repeated in (41), is not bound, although it is coindexed with a c-commanding NP, since the definition of 'bound' holds only when the c-commanding NP is in 'argument position'.

(41)   Tell me $[_{\bar{S}}$ who$_i$ $[_S$ Felix met t$_i]$ $]$

In this way, the output conditions prevent movement of *wh*-constituents into an argument position, but allow them to move into COMP. Other structures allowing unbound coindexing are those where neither of the coindexed NPs c-command each other.

It is precisely this property of allowing 'unbound' coindexing which distinguishes this system from the coindexing mechanism I proposed in (34). The latter allows only pronouns and anaphors to be coindexed, and only with c-commanding NPs. Chomsky's mechanism allows binding in precisely the same conditions, but it still allows (unbound) coindexing of pronouns with non-c-commanding NPs as well as coindexing of two full NPs if neither c-command the other, since the conditions only filter out inappropriate binding but say nothing about other coindexing. So the generalisations on anaphora analysed in this chapter cannot be captured within the system as stated in (3) and (4) of Chapter 6.

We should note, however, that the only reason, in this framework, for permitting unbound coindexing of nodes when neither c-commands the other, is the need to allow for definite NP coreference in such cases. In no other case can we find coindexing of this type. Even though the binding conditions do not prevent coindexing of a *wh*-trace with a non-c-commanding constituent, such coindexing must be blocked, and at the present it is blocked independently by other conditions. For example, the binding conditions allow equally the unbound coindexing in (42) and (43b) below, since in both cases the coindexed lexical NP or the trace is defined as free. However, (43b) is ungrammatical, and it is filtered out independently by the θ criterion. Similarly, the inappropriate movement of a *wh*-constituent into a non-c-commanding COMP in (44b) is not, at the present, prevented by the binding conditions, but by an independent condition on logical forms.[11]

(42) Which people from the capital$_i$ adore the capital$_i$?
(43a) People from e adore which city$_i$?
   (b) *People from [which city]$_i$ adore t$_i$?
(44a) Felix realised [he is a failure] after whose remark.
        $\bar{S}$
   (b) *Felix realised [[after whose remark]$_i$ he is a failure] t$_i$.
        $\bar{S}$

The generalisation that the conditions on movements should (and have been intended to) capture is that ⎡movement⎤ is only possible into a position c-commanding the original position. It seems that the difficulties in capturing this generalisation directly by the binding conditions stem from the fact that coreference, unlike movement, is possible also when one NP does not c-command the other (hence it seems that coindexing might be allowed in such cases). However, my point in this chapter was to argue that coreference, to begin with, is not a sentence-level phenomenon, and bound anaphora is indeed possible only when the antecedent c-commands the pronoun, just as in the case of movement. If this is so, then there is no reason ever to allow coindexing when neither NP c-commands the other.

The only case which still requires unbound coindexing, then, is the case of *wh*-traces coindexed with a constituent in COMP. The same empirical results can, however, be obtained without assuming a distinction between binding and coindexing. A rough approximation towards capturing this is to replace the definition of 'bound' by a general condition on coindexing, as in (45a). The coindexing conditions can be then stated as in (45).

(45) *Output conditions on coindexing*
   (a) Two NPs may be coindexed only if (at least) one of them c-commands the other.
   (b) Lexical NPs cannot be coindexed with a c-commanding NP in argument position.
   (c) Anaphors must be coindexed with a c-commanding NP in their MGC.
   (d) Pronominals cannot be coindexed with a c-commanding NP in their MGC.

(45) is stated so as to maintain as much similarity to the conditions in (4) of Chapter 6 as possible. However, more concise formulations of (45) are possible.[12] The 'argument-position' requirement that was captured by the definition of 'bound' is incorporated into condition (45b) which, combined with (45a), has the effect of allowing *wh*-traces to be coindexed only with constituents in (a c-commanding) COMP-position.

Since in the theory assumed here an NP may end up in non-argument position (COMP) only via movement, lexical NPs other than traces may never end up coindexed with the COMP-NP, since in this case they are also coindexed with its trace and the derivation is filtered out by (45b) (see footnote 11). For this reason, also, the argument-position requirement need not be mentioned in conditions (45b, c). (The derivations mentioned in footnote 6 will be filtered out because of the coindexing of the pronoun and the trace.)

The conditions in (45) capture everything that the system in (3) and (4) of Chapter 6 intends to capture while preventing also *wh*-movement into a non c-commanding position. But, in addition, they have the effect of allowing anaphora-coindexing in precisely the same environments as the coindexing procedure I proposed in (34): coindexing is possible only when one NP c-commands the other, and only if the c-commanded NP is a pronoun (including anaphors) or an empty node – otherwise the derivation is filtered out by (45b). Assuming the modifications in (45), then, there is no reason to postulate a special coindexing procedure for pronouns as in (34) and the same mechanism does, indeed, guarantee the correct coindexing both for movement and for anaphora. Furthermore, in this system, there is no reason to assume two distinct coindexing relations ('coindexed' and 'bound'). The only syntactic device assumed is coindexing and there is no reason (at least in principle – see footnote 7) why it should not have a unique semantic interpretation where the pronoun or e node is translated as a bound variable along the lines of the translation procedure in (37).

7.4 Coreference

It remains to be shown that the conditions on bound anaphora are the only anaphora conditions which have to be captured within the grammar. The coindexing mechanism of the previous section determines that in all the sentences of (36), repeated in (46)–(49), bound anaphora is impossible.

(46) Those who know her respect Zelda.
(47) Those who know her respect no president's wife.
(48) Zelda bores her.
(49) He thinks that Felix is a genius.

This leaves unanswered the original question that motivated the anaphora study: why is coreference not possible in (47)–(49), although it is possible in (46)? The availability of coreference in (46) follows directly from the distinction we observed in Section 7.3.2 between bound anaphora and coreference. When two given NPs are referential it is possible, in principle, to select the same referent for them. Since non-R-pronouns can be used in natural language deictically, or referentially, they are not different from any other referential NPs in this respect. Thus, while the pronoun in (46) cannot be interpreted as a bound variable (as witnessed by the sloppy-identity test) the pronoun may choose its reference from a pragmatically-determined set, where one of the possible references is Zelda, whose choice then results in coreference.

This also automatically yields an answer to the question of what distinguishes (46) from (47). In (47), the NP *no president's wife* is not referential. Rather than fixing an individual, it is interpreted as an operator binding a variable. The only way a pronoun could be assigned the same interpretation as this NP is if it is bound by the same operator, which cannot be the case here, since the pronoun cannot be coindexed. In other words, in the case of genuinely quantified NPs the only type of anaphora possible is bound anaphora. Since they involve no reference, they also cannot involve coreference. (As we saw in Section 5.1.1, when a quantified NP can be interpreted pragmatically as fixing a reference, it can also corefer with pronouns not coindexed with it.) Thus, the apparent difference in the anaphora options of quantified NPs and definite NPs which all current anaphora theories have attempted to resolve within the syntax is nothing but a straightforward consequence of the difference in their semantics, within the analysis of anaphora that I have proposed here.

The crucial problem we are left with, however, is what distinguishes (46) from (48) and (49). Since I have just argued that pragmatic or accidental coreference is always possible between two referential NPs, why should this option not apply equally well to the sentences (48)–(49)? More generally, our problem is that bound anaphora and coreference have different distributions. It is neither the case that whenever bound anaphora is impossible coreference is impossible, nor that coreference is always free where bound anaphora is impossible. If both coreference and bound anaphora need to be captured with the grammar, we are back somewhere close to where we started: although we have reduced the number of conditions on anaphora, we will still have to reintroduce the problematic contra-indexing procedures. However, I will argue now that the distribution of coreference we observed in Chapters 2 and 3, and specifically ruling out coreference in (48)–(49) is not in fact governed by an independent condition of the grammar, but follows pragmatically from the bound anaphora conditions.

To see this, we will observe first that the non-coreference rules (1a) and (1c) of Chapter 6 are precise mirror-images of the bound-anaphora coindexing procedure in (34). This has always been recognised in the case of the R-pronouns condition (1b), repeated in (50a) and the non-coreference rule for the same syntactic environments (1c) repeated in (50b) ((50a) was, later, captured in our analysis by condition (34a)).

> (50a) An R-pronoun must be interpreted as coreferential with (and only with) a c-commanding NP within a specified syntactic domain (e.g. MGC).
> (b) A non-R-pronoun must be interpreted as non-coreferential with any c-commanding NP in the syntactic domain specified for (50a).

Since the earliest formulation of these conditions (in Chomsky, 1973) they were designed to apply in precisely the same environments, in order to capture the fact that where an R-pronoun can be coindexed with a given NP, no other pronoun (or NP) can be coreferential with this NP. Thus, assuming non-coreference as part of the grammar, two distinct rules were needed to capture this property of the distribution of R-pronouns. Now, precisely the same relation holds between the condition on bound anaphora, incorporated into the coindexing procedure (34), and the general condition on non-coreference in (1a) of Chapter 6. To make this easier to observe, I restate their respective effects informally, in (51) (which ignores, for simplicity, the MGC requirement for (51a)).

> (51a) Bound anaphora is possible if a given NP c-commands a pronoun (see (34)).
> (b) Coreference is impossible if a given NP c-commands a non-pronoun (see (1a) of Chapter 6).

So, both non-coreference conditions (51b) and (50b) have the effect of guaranteeing that whenever it is possible to express a bound-anaphora relation between two NPs, we will get non-coreference if we do not use this option which the grammar provides. In environments that allow R-pronouns to be coindexed this is the only option for bound anaphora. If we choose instead an option that does not allow coindexing as in (48) (*Zelda bores her*) we get non-coreference. Similarly, in environments that allow non-R-pronouns to be coindexed, if we avoid this option by using a non-pronoun in a position where a pronoun could be coindexed, we get non-coreference, as in (49),*He thinks that Felix is a genius.* (Had we used a pronoun instead of *Felix* here, i.e. had we reversed the order of the full NP and the pronoun, we could obtain bound anaphora.)

There is no reason, however, to assume that these mirror-image non-coreference results require special rules of the grammar to be captured, since they follow from Grician requirements on rational use of the language, for communication, as developed in Kasher (1976): in a rational linguistic exchange we would expect that if a speaker has the means to express a certain idea clearly and directly, he would not arbitrarily choose a less clear way to express it.

That non-coreference effects can be obtained via pragmatic considerations of this type rather than by rules of the grammar, has been argued by Dowty (1980) and Engdahl (1980). The principle that Dowty states (Dowty, 1980, p. 2), as well as Engdahl's informal description of the procedure, is based indirectly on the 'avoid ambiguity' principle. This principle captures successfully the mirror-image effect in the case of R- and non-R-pronouns, shown in (50): R-pronouns must be interpreted as anaphoric, while non-R-pronouns are referentially ambiguous. If the grammar allows the use of an unambiguous R-pronoun and the speaker avoids this option, as, for example, in *Zelda bores her*, he would assume that he is not violating the 'avoid ambiguity' norm but rather, that he does not intend coreference. However, the same principle cannot explain the other mirror-image effect, stated in (51), since there is no unambiguous way in English to express coreference with non-R-pronouns. Given, for example, the sentence *She bores Zelda's neighbours*, the alternative option *Zelda bores her neighbours*, which allows coreference, is nevertheless ambiguous between the anaphoric and non-anaphoric interpretation, so the 'avoid ambiguity' norm cannot tell us which of these sentences the speaker should have used if he wants to express coreference.

To capture both cases of non-coreference, then, the pragmatic inference here must be explained independently of ambiguity, and it needs, crucially, to consider the availability of the bound-anaphora interpretation for non-R-pronouns under the conditions proposed here. The relevant principle is the broader aspect of the 'manner' maxim (as I described it above): be as explicit as the conditions permit. When syntactically permitted, bound anaphora, whether of R-pronouns or of non-R-pronouns, is the most explicit way available in the language to express coreference, as it involves referential dependency. So, when coreference is desired, this should be the preferred way to express it. Even though in the case of non-R-pronouns the sentence is ambiguous, it is still the best option that the conditions permit (emphatic devices excluded).[13] Given these considerations, some approximation of the pragmatic strategy governing decisions about intended coreference can be stated as in (52).

(52a) *Speaker's strategy*: Where a syntactic structure you are using allows bound-anaphora interpretation, then use it if you intend your expressions to corefer, unless you have some reasons to avoid bound anaphora.

(b) *Hearer's stragegy*: If the speaker avoids the bound-anaphora options provided by the structure he is using, then, unless he has reasons to avoid bound anaphora, he did not intend his expressions to corefer.

The difference between (46) and (47), repeated in (53a) and (54a), is that in (53) the syntactic structure does not allow bound anaphora, regardless of the order or the positions of the NP and the pronoun (i.e. coindexing is impossible in (53b) as well), since neither of the NP positions c-commands the other.

(53a) Those who know her respect Zelda.

(b) Those who know Zelda respect her.

(54a) He thinks that Felix is a genius.

(b) $Felix_i$ thinks that he_i is a genius.

Since this structure does not allow bound anaphora, the hearer can infer nothing from it about the referential intentions of the speaker, and whether the NPs are intended as coreferential or not can be determined on the basis of discourse information only. In (54a), on the other hand, the structure allows coindexing. Had the speaker intended coreference he could use (54b) where coindexing is possible. A choice of (54a), instead, suggests therefore (by (52b)) that no coreference is intended. (The same is true for the choice of non-R-pronoun in (48) *Zelda bores her*, where the speaker could have used instead of the coindexed version *Zelda bores herself*.)

In its empirical results this analysis is largely equivalent to the non-coreference rules (50b) and (51b), which we assumed in the previous chapters (e.g. coreference is still blocked whenever a given NP c-commands a non-pronoun). In this sense, the c-command restriction on definite NP anaphora still holds, empirically, though it is not part of the grammar. However, there is a crucial difference between a pragmatic account for non-coreference, based on strategies like (52), and the syntactic account by means of non-coreference rules. While the latter marks each occurrence of a pronoun c-commanding a full NP as ungrammatical if the two are intended as coreferential, the first approach predicts that coreference should be possible in such cases if there are good pragmatic reasons to avoid bound anaphora (i.e. where the coreference and bound anaphora interpretations are distinguishable). These are precisely the counterexamples to the non-coreference rules which were pointed out in Evans (1980), some of which we have already mentioned in Section 7.1.1. (Similar examples were noted, from a different perspective, in Bolinger, 1977.) In the case of identity statements, e.g. *He is Zelda's husband*, the bound-anaphora interpretation expressible in *Zelda's husband$_i$ is himself* – (Zelda's husband (λ x (x is x))) – is clearly not what is intended: the speaker did not intend to express a tautology but rather to claim that being Zelda's husband holds of a certain pragmatically determined individual. Since there are good reasons to avoid bound anaphora here, identity statements do not violate the strategy (52).

Evans points out various other counterexamples to the non-coreference rule.

(55a) I know what John and Bill have in common. John thinks that Bill is terrific and Bill thinks that Bill is terrific. (Evans, 1980, p. 49)

   (b) Look, fathead. If everyone loves Oscar's mother, then certainly Oscar must love Oscar's mother. (Evans, 1980, p. 47)

(56) Everyone has finally realised that Oscar is incompetent. Even he has finally realised that Oscar is incompetent. (Evans, 1980, p. 52)

While all these sentences will be marked as ungrammatical on the coreference interpretation by the non-corefernce condition (51b), coreference is obviously possible in these contexts, and we can observe now that this too is consistent with the pragmatic strategy (52). Although the structures permit bound anaphora, it is not precisely the reading which is intended; e.g. in (55a) it is the property of finding Bill terrific which is taken to be common to John and Bill (while it is possible that x's finding x terrific is true of Bill but not of John). Therefore, avoiding the choice of bound anaphora interpretation is pragmatically motivated and coreference is not excluded.

The sentences in (57) and (58) illustrate the same point with reflexivisation environments, i.e. where coreference would be blocked by the syntactic condition (50b). The strategy (52) allows coreference here, since the bound-anaphora interpretation which will be obtained if the c-commanded NP is a reflexive pronoun is not the one intended here.

(57a) I know what Bill and Mary have in common. Mary adores Bill and Bill adores Bill / and Bill adores him too.
   (b) Everybody is expecting Begin to resign soon. Even he himself looks sometimes like he is expecting Begin to resign soon.
(58a) Only Churchill remembers Churchill giving the speech about blood, sweat, toil and tears. (Fodor, 1975, p. 134)
   (b) Only Felix voted for Felix.
   (c) Despite the big fuss about Felix's candidacy, when we counted the votes we found out that in fact only Felix himself voted for him.

The cases of (58) are particularly interesting since here the bound anaphora and the coreference interpretation are, clearly, semantically distinguishable because of the operator *only*. (58b), for example, has different truth conditions than *Only Felix voted for himself*. If, say, each participant voted for one candidate only, and each participant voted for himself, then the latter sentence is false, while (58b) is true. In such cases, then, no particular context is required for justifying the choice to avoid bound-anaphora configuration:[14] since the two readings are clearly distinct, the hearer will simply conclude that the speaker intended the coreference, rather than the bound-anaphora reading.

If the non-coreference understanding of a sentence is determined by pragmatic strategies rather than by syntactic non-coreference rules, there is also nothing problematic about the need to relativise it to speakers' intentions (which we mentioned in Section 7.1.1). Pragmatic questions are, to begin with, questions about speakers' intentions and their use of sentences rather than about properties of sentences, and (52) is stated accordingly as a strategy governing the expression of referential intentions rather than actual coreference. Furthermore, if non-coreference is determined pragmatically, we may expect that many discourse considerations not captured by (52) may also interfere. In fact, several studies point out less systematic empirical counterexamples to sentence-level restrictions on coreference such as proposed in Reinhart (1976) (e.g. McCray, 1980; Gueron, 1979; Koster, 1979). Such counter-examples need no longer bother the sentence-level linguist, though they should be taken into account when attempting a more precise pragmatic analysis of speakers' strategies in identifying coreference.[15]

Another problem that can be resolved if non-coreference is prag-matically determined is that, in general, violations of the previous non-coreference rules which involve two full NPs are much easier to process than violations involving a pronoun and a full NP. (I mentioned already, in Section 2.1 of Chapter 2, that Lasnik's ,1976, observation about the similarity between the two cases, which was incorporated into the non-coreference rules, has been often challenged. See also Evans, 1980; Bach and Partee, 1980.) For example, it is much easier to find a context allowing the 'violations' in (55) than (56) or in (58b) compared to (58c). The strategy in (52) also does not explicitly distinguish these two cases since, in both, bound anaphora is equally impossible. However, since what is involved here is the ease of identifying coreference when the bound-anaphora option needs to be avoided, it is generally so that the reference of a full NP is more easily recoverable than the reference of a pronoun. So, independently of (52) it should be easier to identify intended coreference of two identical full NPs than of a pair of a pro-noun and full NP which does not allow bound-anaphora interpretation.

We may conclude, then, that while it greatly simplifies the anaphora mechanism of the grammar, the exclusion of all (unbound) coreference conditions from the domain of the grammar is not just throwing the problems into the 'pragmatic waste-basket'. In fact, the pragmatic analysis of coreference is much closer to yielding empirically correct results than its syntactic analysis.

7.5 Summary

Anaphora studies have been attempting to resolve within the grammar the questions of coreference, rather than of bound anaphora. This has dictated the grouping of the anaphora facts in a particular way, illustrated in (59)–(61), where the first group are the cases allowing definite NP coreference, the second are cases where coreference is impossible, and the third are cases of quantified NP anaphora, which required special treatment.

(59a) Felix thinks he is a genius.
   (b) Felix adores himself.
   (c) Those who know him despise Felix.
(60a) He thinks Felix is a genius.
   (b) Felix adores him.
   (61) Those who know him despise every manager.

It is primarily this grouping of the facts which led to the enormous complications in the theory of anaphora that we observed in Section 7.1. Once we shift the question from coreference to bound anaphora it turns out that the groups in (59)–(61) do not constitute grammatical or sentence-level classes. Rather, the crucial distinction is between the (a)- and (b)-sentences of (59), where bound anaphora is possible, i.e. where the pronoun can be translated as a bound variable, and all the other sentences where it cannot. The coreference differences among the sentences that do not allow bound anaphora follow from semantic and pragmatic considerations outside the syntax. This classification, or more generally, the distinction between bound anaphora and coreference in the case of definite NPs, is not arbitrary (as was the case with notions like 'referential dependency'), and it is directly testable in each case by the sloppy-identity test.

Clarifying this confusion between bound anaphora and coreference enables us to observe that the three previously unrelated phenomena of reflexivisation, quantified NP anaphora and sloppy identity (which each required a separate mechanism in previous treatments) are all instances of the same phenomenon and they observe the same bound-anaphora conditions. All we need in the grammar to capture anaphora is the rather simple mechanism governing the translation of pronouns as bound variables stated here in (34) and (37), or any of its possible equivalents.

We may return now to the two hypotheses I proposed in (19) and (21) of Chapter 1 concerning the restrictions on semantic interpretation rules. They require that such rules can operate on two given nodes only if one of them is in the domain of the other, and if they involve 'primacy' or dependency relations, primacy is given to the head. Once the anaphora rule is appropriately stated, we see that it obeys strictly these requirements. The anaphora rule determines when a pronoun can depend on a given NP for its reference. This dependency is defined formally: the pronoun is translated as a variable bound by the operator corresponding to this NP. Such dependency is possible only when the pronoun is c-commanded by the given NP, in accordance with the first hypothesis. This means that the dependent node (the pronoun) is in the domain of

which the independent node (the antecedent) is a head, in accordance
with the second hypothesis.

Notes

† Several sections of this chapter were published in Reinhart (1983) and are reprinted with permission of D. Reidel publishing company.

1. I am arguing here only that such a three-valued system is, in fact, assumed.
This, however, is not the only logical option of capturing the facts in (1). It is
possible, in principle, to reduce the system to the two relations: positively and
negatively coindexed. This would imply that the sentences in (1c) are ambiguous:
the pronouns can be either positively or negatively coindexed with the NPs, which,
as we shall see directly, is inconsistent with Lasnik's (1976) analysis. In any case,
an analysis along such lines will not fare any better in handling the problems for
negative coindexing that we shall mention below.

2. It might be argued that the difference between (2) and (3a,b) within this
system is that in (2) the pronoun may still end up coindexed with the full NP,
though not 'bound', but in the latter it cannot, since it is required to be free.
However, Lasnik's question of why 'accidental' coreference is impossible in (2b,c)
still holds.

3. For a survey on the extensive literature debating this point see Evans (1980)
and Partee (1978).

4. To take a trivial example, suppose that (ib) is some informal approximation
of a logical formula corresponding to (ia).

(ia) His neighbours hate everyone.
(b) ($\forall$x: x a person) (his neighbours hate x).

In this logical formula, translation of the pronoun as x is correctly blocked since
the variable antecedent does not c-command (and follows) the pronoun. However,
(ii) is an equivalent formula in which the same variable does c-command the
pronoun. We should be able, then, incorrectly, to coindex them in this formula,
getting a bound variable reading for the pronoun in (ia).

(ii) ($\forall$x: x a person) (hate (his neighbours, x)).

5. Although it has never been stated explicitly, this seems to be the case, since,
unlike Higginbotham's coindexing procedure, the general anaphora restrictions are
currently stated as output conditions. If they are permitted to apply to the output of QR, they would filter out as ungrammatica, e.g. the sentence (ia) whose
structure after QR is (ib).

(ia) I told every boy some stories about himself.
(b) [Every boy]$_1$ [some stories about himself]$_2$ [$_S$ I told e$_1$ e$_2$].

In (ib) the R-pronoun will be defined as 'free' or uncoindexed in Chomsky's
(1981) framework, since there is no c-commanding NP in argument position that
it could be coindexed with. Consequently, since reflexives must be coindexed, the
sentence will be filtered out. This, incidentally, counts against some recent moves
within EST to state all anaphora conditions as output conditions on LF (e.g. Freidin and Lasnik, 1981).

6. The requirement that α be in a non-COMP or $\bar{S}$ position is the equivalent of the requirement that it be in 'argument position', which, as we saw in Chapter 6, was introduced in Chomsky (1981). In the particular case of the coindexing procedure for pronoun, this requirement is a convenient way to prevent a situation where the pronoun, which cannot be coindexed with a given trace nevertheless ends up coindexed with the NP that left the trace, as in (i).

(ia) *Felix$_i$, himself$_j$ likes t$_i$.
(b) *Who$_j$ do you think that he$_i$ likes t$_i$?
(ii) Himself$_i$, Felix$_i$ likes t$_i$.

Since *Felix* and *who* of (i) are in COMP or $\bar{S}$ position, the given requirement does not allow the pronouns to be coindexed with them, and since the coindexing procedure does not allow these pronouns to be coindexed with the traces which do not c-command them, such derivations cannot be obtained. In (ii), on the other hand, (54) allows correctly coindexing of the R-pronoun with *Felix*, since the pronoun is not required to be in non-COMP-position. (Note that if indexing is governed by output conditions, rather than by conditions on the procedure as I state it here, this problem does not arise, since the derivations in (i) are blocked because of the inappropriate coindexing with the trace.)

7. In the current interpretative forework it is not assumed that there is a unique semantic interpretation for the coindexing devices: while *wh*-traces are translated as variables bound by the operator corresponding to the *wh*-source, NP traces are not interpreted as bound variables. So my all-and-only claim here may seem too strong in this framework. Note, however, that in principle there is no reason why in a theory assuming the existence of NP traces they cannot be interpreted as bound variables. They can be viewed as distinguished syntactically from *wh*-traces, but not semantically, just as *wh*-traces are distinguished syntactically from pronouns, although they are interpreted in the same way.

8. This is so because the *wh*-antecedent must be interpreted itself as a variable binding operator, roughly as in (ib), and applying λ abstraction to (ia) as in (ic) does not yield an obviously interpretable output.

(ia) Who$_i$ t$_i$ came?.
(b) (wh x: x a person) (x came).
(c) Who (λx (x, x came).

The requirement that the antecedent be in non-COMP position, in the procedure I state directly, excludes *wh*-antecedents (in COMP position), even if they happen to be coindexed with a pronoun. Further study is needed on the interaction of the procedures of bound-anaphora translation and trace translation.

9. Note that R-pronouns can never be translated as the argument of the λ predicate: even though there exist cases where an R-pronoun c-commands a coindexed pronoun, since they never meet the conditions we specified in our notation for the β of (37). E.g. in a sentence like *even herself$_i$ she$_i$ can't stand,* she is the only possible β because, although *she* is a pronoun c-commanded by *herself*, the latter is not in a non-COMP or $\bar{S}$ position as required by the definition of β.

10. This point is also independent of whether one assumes that this mechanism is governed by surface-structure considerations, as I do here, or by considerations of the logical syntax (function-argument structures) as in Bach and Partee's (1980) analysis which we examined in Section 4.3. The analysis proposed here is directly translatable into their framework.

11. A potential problem for the conditions as stated is that they allow coindexing an arbitrary full NP with a *wh*-trace. In (i) such coindexing is prevented because the trace is inappropriately 'bound' by *Max*.

(i) *Who$_j$ did Max$_i$ kiss t$_i$?
(iia) *Who did the people who know Max$_i$ kiss t$_i$?
(b) The people who know Max$_i$ kissed Max$_i$.

In (iia), however, the trace is not bound by *Max*, since *Max* does not c-command it and (unbound) coindexing is permitted here, as in (iib). *Max* is also not bound by *who*, since the latter is not in argument position, so in fact nothing prevents this derivation. (It would be recalled that in this model coindexing is free so such a derivation can be obtained.)

12. For example, the four conditions in (45) can be collapsed with equivalent results to the three conditions in (i) (ignorning, as we have done in Chapter 6, the problem of the government of PRO).

(ia) If two NPs are coindexed then (at least) one of them c-commands the other.
(b) If an NP is coindexed with a c-commanding NP in argument position outside its MGC then it is pronominal.
(c) If an NP is coindexed with a c-commanding NP inside its MGC then it is an anaphor.

13. Fiengo and Higginbotham (1981) argue that pronouns like *his own* in (ia) are R-pronouns. If this is true, it is a problem for the pragmatic analysis of non-coreference, since the availability of explicit bound anaphora here would predict that avoiding it as in (ib) would result in non-coreference, which is not the case.

(ia) Max read his own book.
(b) Max read his book.

However, Dowty (1980) argues convincingly (replying to an independent comment by Bach and Partee) that such pronouns cannot be R-pronouns, since they have also a deictic use as in (iia), while R-pronouns cannot be used in this way, as illustrated in (iib). Such pronouns seem to function emphatically, similarly to the emphatic use of the apparent R-pronouns in (iii).

(iia) That's his own book.
(b) *That's about himself.
(iii) Max wrote it himself.

14. Nevertheless, the use of a pronoun in such cases is harder than the use of a full NP and it may depend more crucially on the context. It is sufficient for our purpose that such contexts can be found, as in (58c), and we shall return to the difference between pronouns and full NPs in this respect directly.

15. We should keep in mind that the counterexamples to the c-command syntactic rule are still counterexamples to the strategy (52), since, as I said, the two are empirically equivalent, except for when there are reasons to avoid bound anaphora. But since coreference is governed now by a pragmatic rule, there is more room to attempt an explanation for the counterexamples.

8 UNSOLVED PROBLEMS OF ANAPHORA

I shall conclude the discussion of anaphora with a brief survey of the cases where my analysis either fails to capture the facts or can do so only with some *ad hoc* modifications. The problems pertain primarily to the syntactic aspects of the analysis, i.e. to the c-command requirement. We will see that there are three types of constructions where the c-command condition on bound anaphora is violated. Violations may show up in other cases as well, but often they vary more with speakers and with a particular choice of examples and are not fully decisive. In the cases I survey, on the other hand, the condition fails systematically. So these are real problems that should be solved, but at the moment I do not have any impressive solution. We may note, first, that although the problems appear to be specific to the c-command requirement, they have no obvious solution in any other framework. For example, they would pose a difficulty for a semantically based theory as well. Next, it is interesting to note that each of these problems shows up equally in all the three types of bound anaphora we observed in Chapters 5 and 7. This means that although the precise conditions on bound anaphora may not be fully understood yet, the theoretical claim of Chapter 7 is not affected by such problems: reflexivisation, quantified NP anaphora and sloppy-identity interpretation still obey precisely the same conditions.

8.1 PP Problems

NPs in certain types of PPs behave as if they c-command NPs outside them. We have observed this first in Section 2.7 of Chapter 2 with respect to (definite NP) coreference: indirect objects have identical coreference options to those of direct objects. For example, while coreference is permitted in (2), where the PP is locative, in (1b) anaphora is blocked just as in (1a). And the same is illustrated in (3a,b).

(1a) *It should have bothered *her* that *Rosa*'s driving is dangerous.
   (b) *It should have occured to *her* that *Rosa*'s driving is dangerous.
   (2) Someone was shouting behind *her* that *Rosa*'s driving was insane.
(3a) *I met *him* in *Ben*'s office.

(b)   *I spoke to *him* in *Ben*'s office.
(c)   *I talked with *him* in *Ben*'s office.
(d)   ?I was thinking about *him* in *Ben*'s office.

While the problem of indirect objects can be easily solved, if we assume that in fact they are not analysed as PPs but as case-marked dative NPs (as I proposed in Section 2.7), a more serious difficulty arises when we observe that certain oblique NPs behave the same way. Thus, coreference is blocked in (3c) where the pronoun is in a *with* phrase (while (3d) is acceptable for many speakers, as predicted by the c-command restriction).

Given the reanalysis of the anaphora restricting I proposed in Chapter 7, the problem here is not directly with the non-coreference rule, since we no longer assume it to operate independently. Rather, the non-coreference in (1) and (3) reflects the fact that bound anaphora is permitted in such cases, with the reverse order of pronoun and antecedent.

This is illustrated for the *with* case in (4). Although the antecedent does not c-command the pronoun, all three types of bound anaphora are permitted.

(4a)   I talked with the neighbours$_i$ about each other$_i$.
 (b)   I talked with every student$_i$ about his$_i$ problems.
 (c)   I talked with Max$_i$ about his$_i$ problems, but not with Bill.
                                                    SLOPPY
 (5)   *I talked with *him* about *Max*'s problems.

An NP in this position can control reflexivisation, as in (4a), or can be interpreted as an operator binding the pronoun as in (4b) and in the sloppy-identity interpretation of (4c) (i.e., *I did not talk with Bill about Bill's problems*). The non-coreference in (5) (as well as in (1) and (3) above) follows, then, from the pragmatic conventions stated in (52) of Chapter 7 according to which if a speaker avoids an available option to express bound anaphora he does not intend his expressions to corefer.

The problem for our analysis, then, is the availability of bound anaphora interpretation in sentences like (4), where a pronoun is coindexed with an NP that does not c-command it.

A syntactic solution to this problem seems to lie along the lines of reanalysis proposals as, for example, in Williams (1980) and Hornstein and Weinberg (1981) — the preposition of the PP is reanalysed to form a constituent with the verb, allowing, thus, the NP to c-command nodes in the VP. However, at least in the second of these studies, reanalysis applies to all verb-phrasal PPs, which would yield the wrong results for the application of the anaphora restrictions: verb-phrasal locative PPs, as well as instrumental PPs always function as PPs with respect to anaphora. (We saw several examples of this in Chapters 5 and 7.) The other PPs behave less systematically, as can be illustrated, for example, with the pair in (6).

(6a) I spoke with Rosa$_i$ about herself$_i$.
  (b) *I spoke about Rosa$_i$ with herself$_i$.

Bach (1979) and Bach and Partee (1980) have noted that this type of problem arises when there are also other reasons to believe that the appropriate interpretation for the sentence is that in which the oblique NPS is interpreted as the argument of the whole VP function. So a semantically-oriented analysis of anaphora seems promising here. However, as I have mentioned already in Section 4.3 this solution is not without cost within this semantic approach, since the semantic representations have to be non-isomorphic to the surface structures. (See footnote 7 of Chapter 4.)

In any case, a syntactic solution for this problem requires more study into the interaction of anaphora and the problems of movement which have motivated reanalysis proposals, and I leave it here as an open problem.

8.2 Possessive NPs

For many speakers, bound anaphora is permitted when the antecedent is the determiner of a possessive NP. We noted this in Section 5.1.3 of Chapter 5, in the case of quantified NP anaphora, illustrated again in (7).

(7a) Everyone$_i$'s mother thinks he$_i$'s a genius.
  (b) Nobody$_i$'s students should respect him$_i$.
  (c) We'll discuss each of the boys$_i$' problems with his$_i$ parents.

The antecedent does not c-command the pronoun here, so the bound-anaphora restriction we observed in Chapters 5 and 7 cannot allow their coindexing. Although it is not the case that such sentences (particularly (7b and c)) are perfect for all speakers, many speakers systematically accept them.[1] Furthermore, for such speakers the problem shows up also in the other type of bound anaphora exemplified in (8).

(8a) Felix$_i$'s mother thinks he$_i$'s a genius and so does Siegfried's
     mother.   SLOPPY

(b) We'll discuss Rosa$_i$'s problems with her$_i$ parents and Sonya's
     problems too.   SLOPPY

Although sloppy-identity interpretation is supposed to be impossible in
such cases (see, e.g. Sag, 1976), the speakers who get the anaphora interpretation in (7) can get the sloppy-identity reading in (8) (e.g. for
(8a) that Siegfried's mother thinks Siegfried is a genius). This, as we saw
in Chapter 7, means that the pronoun here is translated as bound variable, i.e. that it is coindexed with the full NP, although the latter does
not c-command the pronoun.

This problem is specific to the determiner of possessive NPs and does
not characterise NP structures in general (e.g., bound anaphora is not
possible in (9)).

(9a) *The mother of each of the students$_i$ kissed him$_i$.

(b) The friends of Felix respect him, but the friends of Siegfried
     do not.   NON-SLOPPY

(c) Some friends of Felix respect him and so do some friends of
     Siegfried.   NON-SLOPPY

Although some speakers may disagree with my judgments of (9), such
disagreements are not systematic and vary with the examples. At the
moment, I can only face the possessive NP problem with an *ad hoc*
modification of c-command which allows the determiner (and only the
determiner) of possessive NPs to c-command whatever the NP c-commands. An *ad hoc* solution would seem less disastrous if we consider
the fact that the problem at issue might be language specific (see Higginbotham, 1980a), as well as 'dialectal' — in the sense that not all speakers
of English allow this type of anaphora, so possibly, not all of them apply
the proposed *ad hoc* condition.

An apparent problem for this modification is that it seems that it
should, incorrectly, allow also reflexivisation in such cases, as in (10),
since the determiner *Siegfried* is now defined as c-commanding the
R-pronoun.

(10) *Siegfried$_i$'s mother adores himself$_i$.

However, we observed already that R-pronouns require a stricter restriction anyway on their distribution than the general bound-anaphora

condition, i.e. they are subject also to requirements in terms of minimal governing categories (MGC). The coindexing in (10) can be prevented by a minor modification of the condition on R-pronouns' coindexing in (34b) of Chapter 7 which would require that the R-pronoun and its antecedent must be dominated by the *same* MGC (i.e. the same minimal S or NP). This is just a matter of formulation which has no other effect on the grammar.

Another problem is that the same proposed modification should determine, via the pragmatic strategy governing coreference ((52) of Chapter 7), that coreference is impossible, e.g. in (11).

(11a) *His* mother thinks thàt *Felix* is a genius.
   (b) We'll discuss *his* problems with *Siegfried*'s parents.

Since the proposed modification defines the determiner pronouns here as c-commanding the full NP's, for speakers who have this modification in their grammar the reverse positions of pronoun and antecedent would yield a possible bound-anaphora interpretation (as in (7)). So avoiding it should indicate a non-coreference intention. In Reinhart (1976, Chapter 4) I argued on the basis of an informal survey I conducted on several (linguist) speakers, that this is indeed the case, and speakers who accept bound anaphora in, for example, (7) do not accept coreference in (11), while those who allow for coreference in (11) do not allow bound anaphora in (7). However, I have not found decisive support for this claim in my latter informal surveys, and it might be incorrect.

8.3 'Experiencing' Verbs

The object of an experiencing verb can in many cases control a pronoun in the subject, although it does not c-command it, e.g.:

(12a) Jokes about his$_i$ wife upset Max$_i$, but not Felix.   SLOPPY
   (b) The jokes about her$_i$ boss pleased each of the secretaries$_i$.
   (c) The jokes about each other$_i$ amused the neighbours$_i$.

Higginbotham (1980b) has suggested a syntactic solution for a subset of these cases. However, it seems that the problem arises also when no syntactic solution is possible as, for example, in (13).[2] So this is an unsolved problem.

(13a) That people hate him$_i$ disturbs Felix$_i$ but not Max.   SLOPPY

(b) That people hate him$_i$ disturbs every president$_i$.

Another puzzle about these cases is that here there is, clearly, no correlation between the distribution of bound anaphora and coreference. Since bound anaphora is permitted in the sentences of (12) and (13), our pragmatic convention governing coreference ((52) of Chapter 7) predicts that if this option is avoided, e.g. by reversing the positions of the pronoun and the full NP, as in (14), we will get non-coreference. Nevertheless, coreference is perfectly acceptable in (14).

(14a) Jokes about *Max* upset *his* wife.

(b) That people hate *Felix* (should) disturb *him*.

Notes

1. Bach and Partee (1980) argue that cases like (7) are not, in fact, instances of bound anaphora, but of the 'pronoun of laziness' phenomenon. However, in standard examples of the latter type we will not obtain bound anaphora by the sloppy-identity test. The fact that here we do, as we will see directly, indicates that for the speakers who allow the sentences of (7) this is genuine bound anaphora.

2. These facts were pointed out to me by Haj Ross, personal communication.

Within the interpretative-semantics framework, it is necessary to define the procedures mapping surface structures onto semantic representations — a level at which the interpretation of the sentences is determined. We have defined formally only one such procedure — the rule translating coindexed pronouns as bound variables ((37) of Section 7.3.1). However, throughout the discussion we have noted several correlations between anaphora interpretation and other aspects of the interpretation of sentences which the theory of semantic interpretation should explain. For a semantically-oriented approach of the type we considered in Section 4.3 such correlations suggest that the anaphora rule operates on semantic representations rather than on syntactic representations. But within the interpretative approach, the same correlations would be explained if it turns out that the different procedures mapping surface structures onto semantic representatives, which apply independently of each other, each obey the same syntactic conditions.

It would be recalled, now, that in Chapter 1, I proposed the hypothesis that the anaphora restrictions are just a particular case of more general conditions restricting the operation of semantic-interpretation rules. These conditions ((19) and (21) of Chapter 1) are repeated in (1) and (2).

(1) Sentence-level semantic interpretation rules may operate on two given nodes A and B only if one of these nodes is in the domain of the other (i.e. A is in the domain of B, or B is in the domain of A, or both).

(2) If a rule assigns node A some kind of prominence over node B, A must be a D-head of the domain which contains B.

If this hypothesis is true, it would follow that we should find correlations between different interpretative properties of the sentence, although none of these properties is derived from the other.

In this chapter I will examine this hypothesis with respect to the two interpretative procedures that came up most frequently in the discussion of previous chapters — the assignment of function-argument representations and of relative quantifier scope. Since the introduction of the relation c-command in Reinhart (1976), several other interpretative procedures have been stated in these terms, i.e. in accordance with (1) and (2), but I will not survey such proposals here. (See, particularly, Williams, 1980.)

Another correlation we observed throughout the discussion was between anaphora options and functional (theme-rheme) relations in the sentence. Although these relations are pragmatic rather than semantic, I will argue briefly in Section 9.3 that to the extent that they are governed at all by sentence-level considerations, these considerations are consistent with condition (2).

9.1 Function-argument Representations

One of the advantages of the c-command relations for interpretative rules is that it makes use of the full range of constituents in the sentence (unlike the relation *command* which considers only cyclic nodes). This means that the compositional requirement (i.e. that the interpretation of a constituent is determined by the interpretations of its subconstituents) can be stated in terms of c-command. Although it would not have been necessary to introduce this relation just for this purpose, the compositional interpretation of sentences is consistent with the general c-command condition (1) on interpretative rules. This condition determines that if neither of two given nodes c-command the other, as, for example, is the case with nodes d and c of tree (3), they cannot be directly related by an interpretative rule, which in this case means that it is impossible to translate either of these nodes as a function taking the interpretation of the other as an argument. Thus, the PP *with the binoculars* in (4), which has this constituent structure, cannot be interpreted as a function taking the interpretation of the verb *kissed* as argument (which would yield the interpretation we get for a sentence like *The lady kissed Max with the binoculars*).

(3)

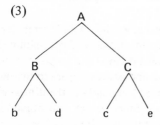

(4)   The lady with the binoculars kissed Max.

Such interpretation would, of course, violate the compositionality requirement.

However, compositionality puts stricter requirements on the interpretation of surface structures than (1). For example, in both the structures (6) and (7), the verb c-commands the PP, so condition (1), in and of itself, does not prevent an interpretative rule from operating directly on these two nodes in either tree.

(5)   Max saw the lady with the binoculars.

(6)

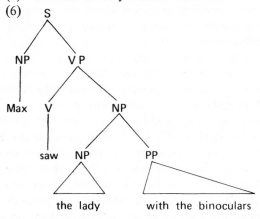

(7)

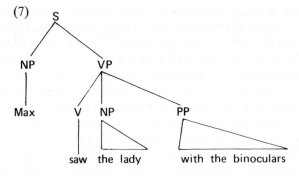

So, if the assignment of function-argument relations is governed only by (1), nothing prevents interpreting the PP of (6) as a function taking the verb as argument, which will yield, incorrectly, an interpretation identical to that of (7). This means that although this assignment never violates condition (1), a further restriction on its operation is needed. A first approximation of this restriction is stated in (8), which does not specify the translation procedure itself but rather a condition on its

output. As we shall see directly, (8) restricts the set of possible translations in a particular way which is not assumed by all semanticians.

(8)   A function-argument formula $F(a_1, a_2, \ldots, a_n)$ is an appropriate
      logical translation of a phrase α only if there is a node F' in α
      which corresponds to F, and, for each argument expression a_i
      there is a corresponding node a_i' in α, and F' and a_i' c-command
      each other.

Since (8) requires the expressions corresponding to the function and
the argument to c-command each other in surface structure, it excludes
the inappropriate interpretation of (6) we have just observed: the PP
cannot be interpreted as a function ranging over the interpretation of
the verb since it does not c-command the verb. However, condition (8)
is stated as a necessary but not as a sufficient condition. Further conditions are needed to determine function-argument representations
when more than two nodes c-command each other. This, for example,
is the situation inside the VP in tree (7). Although the structure in (7) is
simplified (ignoring one VP) the c-command relations of the nodes in
the VP of the full tree are identical to those in (7). (We shall return to
this point directly.) Therefore, condition (8), as stated, cannot prevent
the PP from being translated as a function taking the interpretation of
the NP as an argument, which would yield the wrong result. Note, further,
that (8) does not determine which nodes in the tree would be translated
as function and which as arguments. For example, (8) permits a logical
representation in which the subject corresponds to the function and the
VP to the argument. This choice of interpretation is determined by
independent considerations of the semantic theory.

To illustrate further the operation of (8), let us consider an example
of the correlation between syntactic and logical structures which was
discussed in detail in Sectin 3.1.2. We saw that sentential adverbs or
PPs, as in (9), are interpreted as functions from formulae to formulae,
while V-phrasal adverbs or PPs, as in (10), are interpreted as restricting
functions from functions to functions. This guarantees that entailments
such as (11) hold for sentences with V-phrasal PPs and V-phrasal adverbs
but not for sentences with sentential PPs or sentential adverbs.

(9a)   See diagram on next page.

(b)   Rosa is riding a horse $\left\{ \begin{array}{l} \text{in Ben's film} \\ \text{probably} \end{array} \right\}$

(c)   Ben is an absolute dictator in his office.

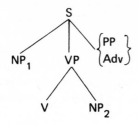

(d) Ben is a genius according to him.
(10a)

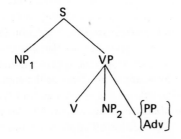

(b) Rosa rode a horse $\begin{Bmatrix} \text{in Ben's pasture} \\ \text{gracefully} \end{Bmatrix}$

(c) Ben found a brass bed in his office.

(d) Ben holds a candle in front of him.

(11) (10b) → Rosa rode a horse.

    (10c) → Ben found a brass bed.

    (10d) → Ben holds a candle.

The correspondence rule from syntactic structures to function-argument representations must guarantee, therefore, that the PP or Adv in (10a) will not be interpreted as a function over the whole sentence (namely a function whose arguments are the translations of the subject NP_1 and the VP). This is precisely the type of restriction that is captured by (8): since the PP does not c-command the subject, NP_1, the latter cannot be interpreted as its argument. The PP or Adv of (9), on the other hand, is permitted by (8) to take the interpretations of the NP and the VP as arguments since it reciprocally c-commands these nodes.

It is easy to see that in many cases condition (8) puts stronger restrictions on the interpretation of sentences than required by purely logical considerations. Thus, a sentence like (12) permits (among several others) the two interpretations in (13), which are logically equivalent.

(12a) Rosa kissed Dan.

(b)

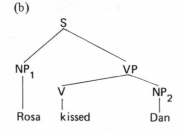

(13a) (kiss) ⟨Rosa, Dan⟩
(b) (kiss ⟨Dan⟩) ⟨Rosa⟩

But of these two representations only (13b) is permitted by (8). In the corresponding tree (12b) the node V corresponding to the function *kissed* has only the object NP_2 in its domain, hence the function *kissed* can take only the translation of NP_2 as an argument (but not the translation of NP_1, as in (13a)). The node VP, on the other hand, which corresponds to the function (*kissed* ⟨*Dan*⟩) has the subject NP_1 in its domain, hence given the condition (8), (13b) is an appropriate representation for (12b).

In effect, then, a condition like (8), which takes into account the full range of the constituent structure of surface structures, assigns to these structures semantic representations of the type proposed in Keenan (1974) and developed, for example, in Keenan and Faltz (1978) (which we discussed in Section 4.3). This is not surprising, since the point of departure of such studies has been to preserve as much as possible the correspondence between surface structure and the logical syntax. In any case, this particular result of (8) explains the correlation we observed in Section 4.3 between the c-command restriction on anaphora and the semantics-oriented approach which assumes this type of logical syntax. The node corresponding to the argument is required by (8) to c-command the node corresponding to the function, so, as long as this correspondence is preserved, the 'functional' restriction is equivalent to the c-command restriction.

We may conclude with a note on the role of the relation c-command in condition (8). It may appear that the use of this relation is superfluous, in the sense that it can be replaced with the independently defined relation of sisterhood. (The nodes corresponding to the function and the argument must be sisters.) Note, however, that the relation of reciprocal c-command (A and B c-command each other) is not equivalent to the relation of sisterhood. In the previous examples of VP structure (7 and 10), I have used for ease of presentation a simplified tree. In fact, the VP structure of, for example, sentence (7) is (14).

(14)

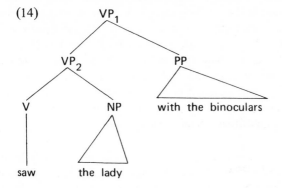

(15a) Max saw the lady with the binoculars and Rosa did so with her lorgnette.
   (b) Max hit the lady with his binoculars and Rosa did so with her lorgnette.
   (c) *Max hit the lady with his binoculars and Rosa did so the gentleman.

Apart from considerations of phrase-structure rules, the structure (14) is required by independent syntactic considerations since certain rules can operate on VP_2 alone, as illustrated with the *do-so* cases in (15a) and (15b). (Since *so* substitution works better the more 'active' the verb is, the point may be clearer in (15b).) Assuming that syntactic rules can operate only on constituents, VP_2 must be a constituent. (Note that the do-so rule, in particular, cannot operate only on 'part' of the VP as in (15c).)

In tree (14), therefore, the verb and the PP are not sisters. However, given the full definition of c-command ((17) of Chapter 1), the verb still c-commands the PP, so reciprocal c-command holds here, but not sisterhood. If the translation condition required that the nodes corresponding to the function and the argument be sisters, the only semantic representation that could be assigned to (14) is that where the PP corresponds to a function which takes the interpretation of the whole VP_2 as argument. Condition (8), on the other hand, allows it also to take the interpretation of the V alone as argument (forming, thus, a complex transitive verb), subject to lexical considerations. That such an interpretation may be required in many cases has been proposed, e.g. in Bach (1979).

In other words, the distinction between VP_2 and VP_1 in (14) does not correspond to a domain distinction, and the domain relevant for the operation of semantic rules is only VP_1 (see the definition of domain in (12) of Chapter 1). The structural details of VP_1 are, therefore, irrelevant for condition (8), and the decision which nodes take which as an argument is restricted only by lexical and semantic considerations. It would be recalled that the special provision in the formulation of c-command (for the cases of S over S or VP over VP) was required precisely since there are certain properties of constituent structures which are required for the proper operation of syntactic rules, but which do not affect semantic interpretation. The internal semantic analysis of the VP may turn out to be a further instance of such cases.

9.2 Relative Scope of Quantifiers

9.2.1 The analysis

In Chapter 3 we observed a striking correlation between c-command domain relations and relative scope of quantifiers. I will suggest now that this correlation is due to the fact that the rules which assign relative scope to quantified expressions in surface structure operate within the same domain hypothesis (1) and (2) above, which restrict the interpretation of anaphora. The output condition on these rules which I propose is stated in (16).

> (16) A logical structure in which a quantifier binding a variable x has wide scope over a quantifier binding a (distinct) variable y is a possible interpretation for a given sentence S only if in the surface structure of S the quantified expression (QE) corresponding to y is in the domain of the QE corresponding to x.[1]

Condition (16) mentions 'quantified expressions' rather than 'quantified NPs' to allow it to apply to quantified PPs. This formulation attempts to avoid a problem which arises here: given a quantified PP like *in all the rooms*, if we consider strictly the node Q which dominates the quantifying word (*all*), its c-command domain under any syntactic analysis cannot extend beyond the PP (and under some syntactic analyses it consists only of the NP *all the rooms*). Counting the whole PP as the QE means that the relevant domains in determining the relative scope of such quantifiers are those of the PP. Similarly, in a quantified possessive NP like *everyone's father* the quantifier may have wide scope over quantifiers outside the possessive NP. So the whole possessive NP counts as QE. (Though in this case this is not crucial, since the *ad hoc* modification of c-command we introduced in Section 8.2 assigns the determiner of such NPs the domain c-commanded by the NP.)[2]

Condition (16) can be tested by checking the following claims which it implies:

(a) The linear order of QEs in surface structure plays no role in determining their relative-scope interpretation.

(b) A QE in head position will be assigned wide scope over a QE in its domain, in accordance with hypothesis (2).

(c) If neither QE is in the domain of the other, neither of the corresponding quantifiers in the logical representation is in the scope of the other, i.e. they are not scope-related, in accordance with hypothesis (1), and

(d) scope ambiguity is possible if each of the QEs is in the domain of the other, since in this case, both expressions meet the condition stated in (16). Let us consider, first, examples supporting these claims.

Although it is often the case (in a right-branching language) that a preceding QE is interpreted as having wider scope over a QE to its right, the sentences of (17) and (18) show that this is not always the case. In these sentences QE_1 precedes (and commands) QE_2, but QE_1 cannot, nevertheless, be interpreted as having wider scope over QE_2. (The trees, particularly (17a), are again simplified.)

(17a)

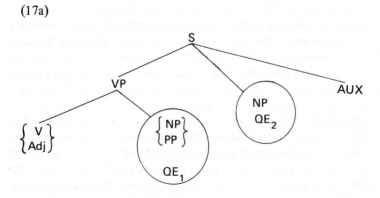

(b) Fond of some boy every girl is.
(c) (. . . and) break all the plates someone finally did.
(d) Opposed to all laws though some revolutionaries are, they all support the right of abortion.

(18a)

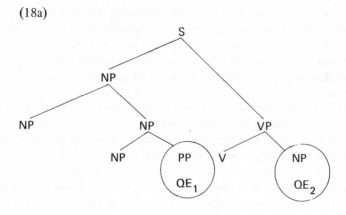

(b) Ben's letters to all the girls annoyed some boys.
(c) Ben's letters to some girls annoyed all the boys.

An intuitive way to verify that, in (17b), the quantifier corresponding to QE_1 (*some boy*) does not have wide scope over the quantifier corresponding to QE_2 (every girl) is to observe that if it did, the sentence would logically imply that all the girls are fond of the same boy, which it does not. In the sentences (17c,d) and (18b), where QE_1 is universally quantified, it is easier to see that the choice of reference for the existentially quantified QE_2 is independent of the choice of reference for QE_1. For example, in (17d) it must be the case that there is at least one revolutionary who is opposed to all laws, and it is not sufficient that for each law there is a revolutionary who opposes it (possibly a different one for different laws).

If we look now at the trees underlying these sentences, we see that in both (17a) and (18a), QE_2 is not in the domain of QE_1 (since QE_1 is dominated by the VP node which does not dominate QE_2). (16), correctly, does not allow QE_1 to be assigned wide scope over QE_2. It is clear, therefore that, in these examples, it is not the linear order of the QEs that determines their relative-scope options.[3]

A further examination of the structure (17a) reveals that while QE_2 is not in the domain of QE_1, QE_1 is in the domain of QE_2. (16) predicts, therefore, that in (17b-d) QE_1 is interpreted as being in the scope of QE_2. This is the correct interpretation. The choice of a boy in (17b) may depend on the choice of a girl, i.e. it is sufficient that for each girl we pick out, there would be at least one boy whom she likes, possibly a different boy for different girls. The same can be seen to be true for the other sentences of (17) if we reverse the order of quantifiers, e.g. in the sentence *Opposed to some law though all revolutionaries are . . .* the choice of a law may vary with the choice of a revolutionary. These facts, thus, exemplify the second claim implied by restriction (16), namely, that a QE in head position (QE_2 in this case) is assigned wide scope over QEs in its domain (and, again, regardless of the linear order of the QEs).

The third claim implied by (16) is that when neither QE is in the domain of the other, neither is interpreted as being in the scope of the other. Such a situation is exemplified in (18). We have seen already that in (18), as in (17), QE_2 is not in the domain of QE_1 and is also not interpreted as being in its scope. But (17) and (18) differ with respect to the domain of QE_2. In (18), QE_2 does not have QE_1 in its domain. The sentence (18c) *Ben's letters to some girls annoyed all the boys*, shows that, in accordance with (16), the choice of reference for the variable corresponding to QE_1 (*some girls*) is independent of the choice of QE_1 (*all the boys*). The resulting picture is that neither of the quantifiers corresponding to QE_1 and QE_2 is in the scope of the other, or that they are scope-independent. This may mean that such sentences require analysis in terms of branching quantifiers, but I will not elaborate on this point here.

Let us return now to the scope-cases we observed in Chapter 3; their analysis also provides examples for the fourth implication of (16) regarding scope ambiguities. The correlation between relative scope and anaphora was illustrated in Chapter 3 by paradigms like (19)-(22), which consist of four syntactic structures, two of which (in 20) and (21)) have identical domain relations and differ only in the linear order of their constituents. (Here too, the structures are simplified.)

Verb-phrasal PPs in final position;

(19a)

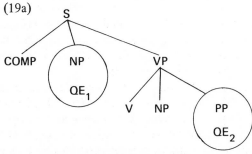

(b) Some reporters put tape recorders in every room. (— not ambiguous: $(\exists x)(\forall y) . . .$ is the only interpretation)

Sentential PPs in final position:

(20a)

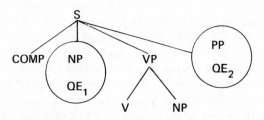

(b) Some reporters worship Kissinger in every town he visits. (—ambiguous.)

(c) Somebody ends up stripping in all of Ben's films. (—ambiguous.)

Preposed V-Phrasal PPs:

(21a)

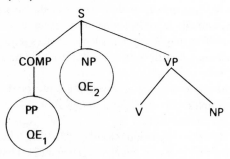

(b) In every room, some reporters have put tape recorders. (—ambiguous.)

Preposed sentential PPs:

(22a)

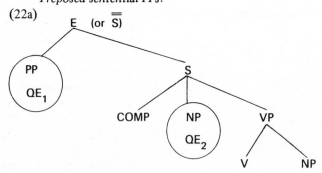

(b) In every town he visits, some reporters worship Kissinger. (—not ambiguous. $(\forall x)\,(\exists y)$ . . . is the only interpretation.)

(c) In all of Ben's films, somebody ends up stripping. (—not ambiguous.)

(The arguments for the structural analysis of these sentences are given in detail in Chapter 3.) In the structure (20) and (21), the quantified subject and the quantified PP c-command each other. This is precisely the environment in which (16) predicts scope ambiguity, regardless of the order of the QEs, and indeed the sentences of both structures are ambiguous. (An intuitive, though not exact illustration of this is the fact that in both (20b) and (21b) it could be either the same reporters or different reporters that the quantified subject refers to.) In tree (19), the quantified PP is in the domain of the quantified subject but not conversely, and consequently, with normal intonation, the sentence is not ambiguous, and the quantified subject has wider scope. In tree (22) the situation is reversed — the subject is in the domain of the PP, but not conversely. Here again there is no ambiguity — the quantified PP has wider scope than the quantified subject. Condition (16), then, captures correctly the relative-scope interpretation of all these different structures.

An obvious consequence of (16) is that the famous sentence (23), below, has only one logical interpretation, namely the one with wider scope to *everybody*, since in the syntactic tree (24) of this sentence the quantified expression NP_2 (*two languages*) is in the domain of the quantified expression NP_1 (*everybody*), but not conversely. (The disagreement among judgments here will be noted directly.)

(23) Everybody speaks two languages.
(24)

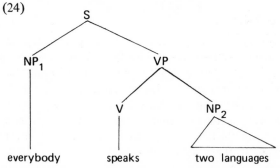

Given a sentence like (25a), on the other hand, (16) allows, correctly, two scope-interpretations, since in the syntactic tree (25b) of this sentence the quantified expressions are in each other's domains.

(25a) Two languages, everybody speaks.

(b)

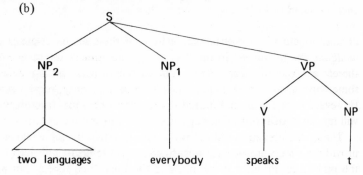

It can be observed, now, that, if correct, the restriction put by (16) is very similar to the 'functional' restriction on scope proposed in Keenan (1974) which was surveyed in Section 4.3. We saw in the previous section that the 'functional' analysis crucially assumes function-argument representation in which the argument expression c-commands the function expression in surface structure. Hence, the condition that quantified expressions in the function can be in the scope of quantified expression of its argument, but not conversely, corresponds to the c-command requirement (16). We see, then, that in order to capture the correlation between scope and anaphora there is no need to apply these rules to semantic representations and it follows from the fact that their interpretation is independently restricted by the same general domain conditions on interpretative rules. However, since the predictions made by (16) are not accepted by all linguists we should attempt a further evaluation of this condition.

9.2.2 Some Problems

Condition (16) only restricts the set of possible logical interpretations for a given sentence. It does not require that all the possible logical interpretations it defines be acceptable in any given sentence. It has, for example, been observed (Ioup, 1975) that lexical quantifiers differ inherently in their tendency to take wide scope. Consequently there will be cases where (16) permits in principle two scope arrangements, but in fact, only one of them would be acceptable. Thus, while (25a) is indeed ambiguous (perhaps with intonational differences), a sentence like *some teachers, everybody likes*, which has the same structure as that of (25a), will give a strong (if not exclusive) preference to the interpretation of *some* as having wider scope since, as Ioup argues, it is both the case that *some* tends to have wider scope than *every* (when possible), and that quantified expressions in topic position have stronger preference for a wide scope interpretation than subjects. In other cases, an interpretation which is permitted by (16) may be excluded on semantic grounds. Thus, in a sentence like *the policeman found a bomb in every mailbox*, the quantified expressions are in each other's domains and, therefore, (16) permits two interpretations, one of which is that there is some bomb such that the policeman found this same bomb in every box. However, since this interpretation is semantically bizarre, the sentence will not, in practice, be judged ambiguous.

The crucial question concerning (16) is, therefore, not whether it provides a sufficiently strong restriction on the set of possible interpretations of a given sentence, but whether the restriction it provides is not too strong. Many linguists have argued, for example, that sentences like (23), *Everybody speaks two languages*, are, in fact, ambiguous, contrary to the claim I have made here. However, this is, I feel, a relatively minor problem.

In the first place, most putative examples of such ambiguities which are discussed in the literature are ones where one interpretation entails the other (e.g. the interpretation ($\exists$ two languages x) ($\forall$y) . . .) entails the interpretation ($\forall$y) ($\exists$ two languages x) . . . So our intuitions distinguishing ambiguity and vagueness in these cases are less clear than in cases where the two interpretations are logically independent.

In the second place, although there may be cases where speakers' disagreement cannot be reduced to the claim that the sentence in question is vague rather than ambiguous, and we will have to assume then that these speakers permit a violation of (16), it appears that the violation is highly restricted with respect to the NP pairs which tolerate it. Thus, Ioup (1975) has observed that 'scope ambiguity' may be possible between quantified subjects and quantified objects, but judgments of such ambiguity are much harder to obtain between quantified subjects and other NPs within the VP. This may be illustrated in (26): (26b) and (26c) are unlikely to be interpreted as ambiguous even by speakers who consider (26a) and (23) ambiguous.

(26a) Some tourists visited all the museums.
   (b) Some tourists spent an afternoon in all the museums.
   (c) Some tourists were disgusted with all the museums.

A more substantial problem for (16) arises in the case of PPs within complex NPs, on which there is no disagreement in judgments. It has been observed (e.g. in Gabbai and Moravcsik, 1974) that in complex NPs like those occurring in (27) and (28) the quantified PP must have wider scope than the quantified NP.

(27a) Santa Claus brought some gifts to every girl.
(b)

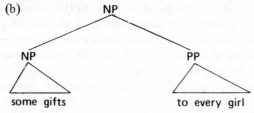

(28a) All the gifts to some girl were wrapped in red paper.

Such examples do not yet pose a serious problem for (16). The quantified expressions in the underlying tree (roughly presented in (27b)) are in each other's domains. (16) therefore permits scope ambiguity. But as we have seen, this does not mean that other semantic considerations may not impose further restrictions on the set of interpretations permitted by (16). However, the more serious problem here is that the same order of quantifier scope holds when further PPs are embedded, e.g.:

(29a) Santa Claus brought some gift to every girl in some country.
(b)

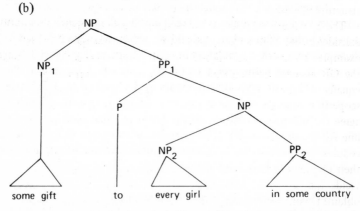

(29a) has only one correct scope interpretation — the one which assigns wide scope to *some country* (i.e. there is some country such that for every girl in that country, there is a gift such that . . .). But in the corresponding tree (29b), the quantified NP_1 (*some gift*), is not in the domain of the quantified expression PP_2 (*in some country*) so (16) does not allow this scope arrangement.

In Reinhart (1976, 1978) I proposed an *ad hoc* solution to this problem. However, this is the strongest case against the c-command-based restriction, and it was used to argue against it in May (1977). May proposes as an alternative that the scope of QEs is not determined in their domain. Rather, he assumes a syntactic operation of Quantifier Raising (QR), which I have mentioned already in Chapter 7. This operation adjoins the QE to S, subject to island conditions similar to those restricting *wh*-movement. The scope of a QE can, then, consist of the whole S it is attached to. In (29), for example, PP_2 can be raised, since it is not in an island, so it can have wider scope over QEs that c-command it in its original position.

Note that this interpretation of QEs does not directly violate the domain hypotheses (1) and (2): the operation QR, itself, is consistent with these conditions. The position into which the QE is raised c-commands its original position, so condition (1) does not prevent linguistic rules from operating on these two positions.[4] Once QR has applied, the QE is in D-head position and it is allowed by condition (2) to have primacy over nodes in its domain. If more than one QE is raised, they c-command each other, so condition (2) allows both to have 'primacy' over the other, i.e. it predicts scope ambiguity. Nevertheless, the analysis based on QR differs substantially from the analysis proposed in (16) since it results in QEs not being interpreted directly in their surface-structure position.

The evaluation of the two analyses crucially depends on empirical considerations. Most of the judgments concerning scope relations in the examples I surveyed in this section still seem to me solid facts, while the QR analysis predicts that all the examples we considered here are equally ambiguous. On the other hand, it also seems to be the case that scope interpretation is one of the areas where speakers' judgments disagree the most, so a restriction like (16) may be too severe. A possible line for a solution would be to assume that there are, in fact, two procedures for interpreting quantifier scope: the first interprets QEs in their original (surface-structure) position, subject to condition (16) and yields the unmarked interpretation − or the one which is easiest to obtain. On the other hand, QR can also optionally apply, thus changing the scope interpretation of QEs. However, interpretations obtained via QR are marked, harder to get and depend more on the appropriate context. A similar solution stated in semantic terms is proposed in Keenan and Faltz (1978).[5]

Except for the PP cases illustrated in (29) (which still require an *ad hoc* account), it is generally acknowledged (even, e.g. by May, 1977) that the interpretation predicted by rule (16) is the easiest to obtain even for those who can get both interpretations. So if the alternative interpretation requires a special operation not required by the first, this may explain why it is more marked or 'costly'.

9.3 Theme-rheme Relations

The 'theme', or the 'topic' of the sentence is a pragmatic relation which is identifiable only with respect to the context of its utterance. As such, we should not expect the process of identifying the topic to be subject to the domain conditions which restrict only the application of sentence-level operations. Nevertheless, we observed in Chapter 3 (primarily Section 3.2.3) certain systematic correlations between thematic (topic) relations and domain relations, and in Section 4.1 we saw that to a certain extent the domain restrictions on anaphora overlap with functional, topic-oriented accounts. So this partial correlation needs to be explained.

Despite the pragmatic nature of the topic relation, it is generally believed that sentence-level properties may affect the choice of a topic for a given sentence, in a given discourse (though they are clearly not the only parameters). For example, as is well known, there is a strong preference in discourse to interpret the grammatical subject as the topic, or to place the topic in subject position. Thus, in 'normal' intonation (30) seems more appropriate than (31) or (32) in a context in which we have been discussing Felix or we intend to assert something about him.

(30) Felix goes out with Rosa.
(31) Rosa goes out with Felix.
(32) Rosa was kissed by Felix.

This preference is only a matter of tendency. The intonation, the context, and other considerations may always dictate the choice of non-subjects as topics. However, the subject is the unmarked, or easiest, candidate for being used as topic.[6]

Assuming that such correlations exist between sentence-level considerations and preferred selections of topic, we can ask what are the relevant sentence-level considerations. The strongest preference for subjects is consistent with our syntactic domain analysis. In most cases the subject is the D-head of the S domain, so it seems easiest to place the topic of the sentence in its D-head position. We may view topichood as a sort of weak 'pragmatic' primacy relation, since the reference of the topic, i.e. what the sentence is about, should be known independently of what is said about it. In this case selecting the D-head as topic is consistent with the domain hypothesis (2). The other examples of thematic relations we examined provide further support for this analysis:

We examined in Chapter 3 examples for structures where the subject is not the D-head of the whole sentence: cases involving 'left dislocation' and preposed sentential PPs. In such structures the subject does not c-command the preposed constituent. So only the latter is the D-head of the whole sentence (E or $\bar{\bar{S}}$). Indeed, as we saw in detail in Section 3.2.3, in such cases the strongest and perhaps only possible preference for a topic is the preposed constituent. (On the thematic role of 'left-dislocated' constituents see also Gundel, 1974.)

In the cases of topicalisation and preposed verb-phrasal PPs, on the other hand, the subject and the preposed constituent c-command each other, and they are both D-heads of the same S domain. The hypothesis (2) marks them both, then, as candidates for being assigned 'primacy' and, as we saw in the same section, in such cases both tend to be topics (so this is a case of 'double' topic construction).

When we examined the relations between anaphora and the functional analysis of sentences in Section 4.1 we observed that a gradient analysis of thematic material might be helpful here (i.e. an analysis which determines the degree of the information of an expression relative to others). Gradient analyses such as Firbas's (1975) also assume that one of the parameters determining the degree of 'communicative dynamism' is structural, and they consider the relevant structural property to be linear order: material in final sentence-position tends to be most 'rhematic'. So if expression A precedes expression B, A tends to be more thematic than B. However, we have observed at least one clear case in English where this is not true: the sentential PPs in final position which we examined in Section 3.1.2 tend, as we saw, to be thematic (in the unmarked case) despite their final position. This, again, would be consistent with the condition (2), since such PPs are D-head of the S domain. This distinguishes them from verb-phrasal PPs in final position which, indeed, usually represent the rhematic information.

The situation here is similar to the other cases where we compared the c-command restriction to conditions based on linear order. In a right-branching language the c-commanded node is often to the right of the c-commanding node. So, in these cases the linear restrictions may seem to work. However, in structures where this is not so, the linear order fails, where c-command works. We should note also that in subject-final languages such as Malagasy the attempt to determine functional relations by linear order would lead to particularly wrong results: subjects would be described as the most rhematic information of the sentence. Nevertheless, I do not wish to claim that linear order plays no role whatsoever in determining the hierarchy of the information in the sentence. Since this is a discourse procedure, such considerations may interfere. The point is, however, that generally, if expression A c-commands B, it would be easier to interpret A as more thematic than B, than conversely.

We may conclude, then, that the easiest selection of topic or thematic material is the one consistent with the domain condition (2). (Although, again, this is only the sentence-level parameter and pragmatic parameters may outweigh it.) What we still need is an explanation for why it should be so. Since identifying the topic is not a semantic, or sentence-level procedure, why should it conform even partially to this condition? The answer seems to lie in considerations of the processing of sentences which I will develop in the next chapter.

Notes

† Sections 9.1 and 9.2 of this chapter are extensively revised versions of Sections 4 and 5 in Reinhart (1978) and the overlapping parts are reprinted with permission of D. Reidel Publishing Company.

1. Note that (16) only restricts the relative scope of two given quantifiers, i.e. their *relative* position in a logical structure. It does not state where they will go, nor does it restrict the position of a quantifier relative to anything which is not a quantified expression.

2. A full analysis of the interpretation of relative scope would, of course, require a more rigorous specification of what counts as a QE.

3. Lakoff (1971) has argued on the basis of examples like (17b) that preposing rules do not affect the scope interpretation of sentences, which, if true, would mean that the relative scope of this sentence could be determined by the linear order of the QEs in deep structure (or before preposing). Note, however that this is not true for all types of preposing. In (i), where only the NP *some boy* is preposed, the relative scope does change (and the sentence is ambiguous).

(i) Some boy, every girl is fond of.

The same will be exemplified below with other sentences. Condition (16) captures the difference between (17b) and (i): since in (i), unlike (17b) the second QE is in the domain of the first, the first may be interpreted as having wide scope over the second.

4. Since QR is a syntactic operation, it is not subject directly at all to condition (1) as stated. However, in the next chapter I argue that condition (1) applies in fact to all sentence-level rules, including syntactic rules and it allows such rules to operate on two positions in the tree only in case one c-commands the other.

5. Keenan and Faltz propose that QEs are interpreted in their original position in the logical syntax, subject to the functional principle. However, λ-abstraction can freely apply to such expression yielding the second type of interpretation which they also consider marked. It is easy to see that their λ-abstraction is empirically equivalent to the syntactic QR.

6. Other sentence-level considerations effecting the choice of topics are discussed in Reinhart (1981b).

10 THE PSYCHOLOGICAL REALITY OF THE C-COMMAND CONDITIONS

The last question I shall deal with here is what could explain the domain conditions we observed, i.e. why should different semantic interpretation rules obey these particular syntactic conditions. Obviously, by posing this question we go beyond the relatively defendable grounds of testing the correspondence of a linguistic theory to linguistic facts into a 'much deeper, and hence much more rarely attainable level – that of explanatory adequacy . . .' (Chomsky, 1965, p. 27). Nevertheless, we may attempt to see what an answer might look like within the framework I have been assuming here, and more generally, within the picture of natural language proposed by Chomsky (e.g., 1965, 1975).

Our first step will be to observe, in Section 10.1, that the domain conditions are not specific to semantic interpretation rules. In fact, they restrict the operation of all sentence-level rules, including syntactic rules. If the same conditions restrict the operation of unrelated rules at various levels, this suggests that they may reflect general properties of the processing ability of the mind. In Section 10.2 we will consider the possibility that these properties are reflected also in the actual processing of sentences.

It would be recalled that the domain conditions (DC) we are considering are the two repeated in (1) and (2) of the previous chapter. The first restricts all rules, requiring that they operate on two given nodes only if one is in the domain of the other, and I will refer to it as the *general DC*. The second – hereafter *primacy DC* – assigns primacy, in the relevant cases to D-heads.

10.1 Syntactic Rules

That syntactic rules conform to the general DC is now widely recognised. It follows directly from the fact that in the Extended Standard Theory movement restrictions are just a particular case of the binding conditions, and that the current formulations of these conditions, which we surveyed in Chapter 6, are stated in terms of c-command. Nevertheless, let us look briefly at some of the empirical motivation for this claim, which was presented in Reinhart (1976, Section 5.2). The discussion here is

restricted to showing that syntactic rules conform empirically to the
DC. This does not mean that each syntactic rule must be restricted
directly by the DC. How this conformity is captured within the linguistic
theory, e.g. whether the conditions on syntactic movement are stated as
output binding conditions, is an independent issue.[1]

The predictions of the general DC may be illustrated first with structures like (1).

(1a)

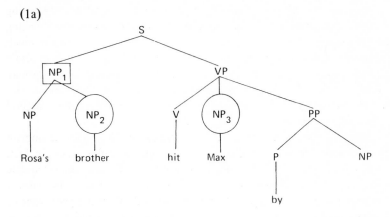

(b) Max was hit by Rosa's brother.
(c) *Rosa's Max was hit by brother.

Neither of the circled nodes in (1a) c-commands the other. The general
DC, then, prevents linguistic rules from operating on them. And as (1c)
illustrates, the rule of passive cannot indeed operate on these two nodes.
On the other hand, the general DC permits the rule to operate on the
node NP_3 and (the boxed) node NP_1 to yield (1b), since NP_1 does
c-command NP_3.

Next consider the tree in (2a).

(2a) See diagram on next page.
(b) COMP the fact that Rosa said COMP she is in love shocked who.
(c) Who did the fact that Rosa said she is in love shock$_t$.
(d) *The fact that Rosa said who she is in love shocked$_t$.

Here again, neither of the circled nodes is in the domain of the other
and the general DC predicts that rules cannot operate on these two
nodes. If we look at tree (2a) linearly (that is, at the sequence in (2b)),

(2a)

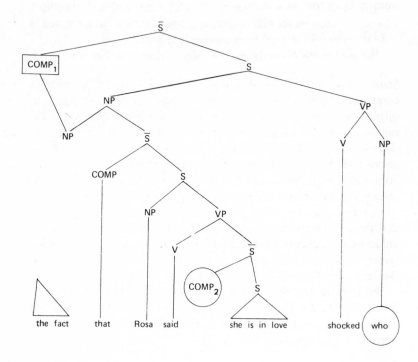

the first *COMP* available for the *wh* to move into is *COMP₂*. Nevertheless the *wh* cannot be moved into this position to yield (2d). The boxed comp (COMP₁), on the other hand, does c-command the *wh*, which means that an operation involving these two nodes is permitted, as in (2c).

These types of facts do not, in and of themselves, provide direct evidence for the DC. The proper application of the rules exemplified above is assured by conditions like the A-over-A condition and the subjacency condition (the latter of which prohibits rules from operating on two nodes if there is more than one cyclic node which dominates the one, but not the other, as is the case with the circled nodes in (2a)).

These conditions are needed independently and cannot be reduced to the DC. Thus, in the case of passive, the DC does not block the rule from applying to *John* and *Rosa* in (3a) since *John* c-commands *Rosa*.

(3a) John hit Rosa and Max.

(b) *Rosa was hit and Max by John.

Some version of the A-over-A principle is needed to block (3b), and this constraint, clearly, cannot be reduced to the general DC. The same considerations hold for the subjacency condition, since the general DC cannot block, for example, extraction from complex NP into a c-commanding COMP. It is still the case that the operations exemplified above apply in conformity with the general DC (in the sense that they do not violate it), but to test the DC more directly we should look at cases which are not reducible to these independent constraints.

One example is provided by extraposition. We saw in Section 2.5 that there is substantial syntactic evidence that *extraposition-from-NP*, unlike extraposition of sentential subjects, cannot attach the extraposed clause to the VP, but must attach it to S. There is no obvious reason for this fact, except that that is how things are.

But now we may note that if the extraposed relative clause were to be attached to the VP, as in tree (3), the DC would be violated, since neither of the nodes (or positions) affected in (3) c-commands the other.

(3)

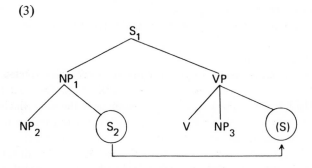

On the other hand, the rule which attaches the extraposed relative clause (S_2) to the S_1 node (or to a higher S position), as in tree (4), operates in accordance with the DC, since the position into which S_2 is attached c-commands its original position.

(4)

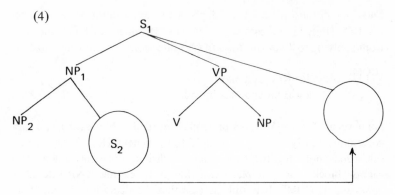

The same type of considerations apply to result-clause extraposition (see Section 2.5).

Before we consider a further example, we should note that 'core' movement rules are not restricted by the general DC alone, but also by some equivalent of the primacy condition: the moved constituent must be attached to a position c-commanding its original position, i.e. while the general DC alone would not prevent 'lowering' a constituent into a c-commanded position, 'core' movement rules allow only 'raising'. Although this does not follow from the way we described primacy so far, which was done in semantic terms irrelevant to the application of syntactic rules, the syntactic equivalent of the primacy DC requires that the moved constituent must c-command its trace, and not conversely, i.e. that the moved constituent is placed in a D-head position of a domain in which it originated.[2]

We can return now to the way *wh*-movement is restricted by the DC:

> (5a)   See diagram on next page.
>   (b)   Felix didn't realise $\underset{S_2}{COMP_2}$ [he is a failure] until whose remark.
>   (c)   *Felix didn't realise $\underset{\bar{S}_2}{[until\ whose\ remark_i}$ he is a failure] t_i.
>   (d)   *Until whose remark_i* didn't Felix realise $\underset{\bar{S}_2}{[he\ is\ a\ failure]}$ t_i.
>   (6a)   Felix didn't realise $\underset{\bar{S}}{[COMP\ he\ failed\ where]}$.
>   (b)   Felix didn't realise $\underset{\bar{\bar{S}}}{[where_i\ he\ failed\ t_i]}$.

The *wh* PP of (5a) is not prevented by subjacency from moving into $COMP_2$, which is the first available COMP if we look at a sequence like

(5a)

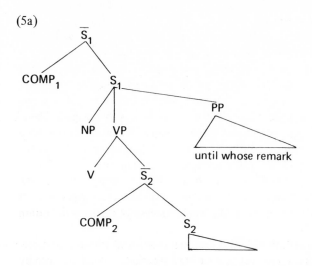

(5b) linearly. So, subjacency is not what prevents the inappropriate derivation (5c). However, since COMP$_2$ does not c-command the *wh*-constituent, the combined DC conditions we have just observed prevent this derivation, unlike, for example, the derivations in (5d) or in (6b) where the moved constituent c-commands its trace. This, then, shows that *wh*-movement conforms to the DCs independently of subjacency.

As I have mentioned already, it is not necessary for our purpose to show that syntactic rules obey the DCs directly. The crucial point is that regardless of how the restrictions on movement are captured within the syntactic theory, their results conform with the proposed DC.

This is true for the 'core' syntactic rules in any syntactic theory. Any rule which moves material into subject position within an S will satisfy the DCs since the subject NP c-commands all other material in the S. Similarly, any movement of constituents into COMP position operates within the DCs, since the COMP c-commands all other nodes in the S. And in general, any movement which attaches constituents to the S-node itself is consistent with the DCs: the same is true for all types of 'raising' rules since the node to which material is raised will c-command the position from which it was raised.

If it turns out that the domain conditions reflect some general restrictions on human language (or the human mind) it would be highly significant that no matter how the major rules of a language are organised they always turn out to operate only within these domains.

10.2 Processing Strategies

The broad application of the domain conditions suggests that they reflect restrictions on the processing ability of the mind. Obviously, the inherent properties of the mind are not accessible to the curious scholar. However, it is appropriate to hope that its options and limitations would be somewhat traceable in the actual processing of sentences by speakers. Therefore, it is appropriate to check to what extent we can find correlations between the domain conditions (DCs) and what we know about the processing of sentences. This search will be guided by the expectation that the domains that the DCs are based on will overlap with the basic units of the processing of sentences. As we shall see, this expectation is consistent with one of the competing processing-theories which have been proposed.

In reviewing the questions of what the processing units are, and how they are processed, we will restrict our attention to studies of speech perception. We shall also ignore questions of the overall organisation of the processing proceedures, e.g. whether syntactic and semantic processing apply simultaneously or in ordered stages. This question does not bear directly on the issues discussed here. However, in the presentation I will implicitly favour the first of these alternatives.

The basic assumption in speech-perception theories is that the processing of an acoustic input involves a mechanism of establishing 'closure' of units as soon as possible. The closed units are recoded, i.e. assigned more abstract mental representations and cleared from short-term memory (STM). Perceptual complexity of sentences may arise (among other cases) if the closure must be delayed, or if a closed unit must be reopened. For example, given the famous example *the boat floated on the water sank*, the tendency to establish closure as soon as possible will dictate processing *the boat floated on the water* as a clause, but then, as *sank* is reached, the closed clause must be reopened and reanalysed. The question is, then, what counts as the relevant processing units, that the parser attempts to close. On this there are two basic stands (though some intermediate variations have been proposed, too). The most prevailing assumption is that the processing unit is the clause (e.g. Fodor, Bever and Garett, 1974; Bever, 1975). This means that at the first stage of processing, speakers attempt to divide the acoustic signal into clauses. The process proceeds linearly ('from left to right'), and until the rightmost node of a clause is reached, all previous nodes are kept in STM. Only when the clause is completed is it recoded and cleared. The alternative approach defines all constituents of surface structure as perception-units, i.e. it assumes that closure and recoding apply to constituents, before the full clause is constructed. This, incidentally, has been one of the earliest analyses proposed in Fodor and Bever (1965), which the authors later rejected. It has been developed again in Kimball (1973). In Kimball's description of the process of parsing, a phrase α is closed as soon as the rightmost daughter of α (i.e. the rightmost node immediately dominated by α) is established. (This is roughly Kimball's principle five.) As soon as a phrase is closed it is 'pushed down' for further processing and cleared from short-term memory (Kimball's principle seven). This means that the mechanism of closure which sends parts of the acoustic signal for further processing applies to constituents rather than only to S nodes.

There are three types of considerations that may be used in the evaluation of processing proposals and specifically of the two hypotheses we have just considered. The first is direct experimental tests of the processing procedure (such as click-location tests). The second is an examination of the relative success of each hypothesis in accounting for perceptual difficulties or complexity (such as the 'floated boat' case I mentioned above). The third is the degree of conformity of each hypothesis with the independent findings of syntactic theory. Of these three, the direct experimental tests seem most problematic. Often the results are conflicting or unsystematic, e.g. the click-location tests are argued to support the clausal hypothesis. However, Kimball (1973) cites experiments with click-location reported in Chapin, Smith and Abrahamson (1972). Unlike other reports on click-location, this report states that clicks were attached to constituent boundaries. When a click was placed between a constituent boundary and a following clause boundary, the tendency was to perceive the click near the constituent boundary, from which the authors conclude that there is a tendency for speakers to perform closure at the end of constituents. Although this reported experiment is criticised in Fodor, Bever and Garett (1974), the results here do not seem very decisive. The second type of evaluative criteria (perceptual complexity) seems more promising, and I will return to it directly. Let us start, however, with the third criterion.

A processing hypothesis may gain some indirect support if it turns out that independently motivated restrictions on the operation of linguistic rules are consistent with this particular hypothesis. (Though, of course, the linguistic and the processing theories provide no direct proof or rejection of each other.) It is interesting to observe that the clausal-processing hypothesis correlates very nicely with the earlier beliefs that linguistic rules are restricted by the relation 'precede and command'.[3] If we state a domain-condition based on this relation it would allow linguistic rules to operate on nodes A and B only if A both precedes and commands B. In such cases, for example, node A can effect the interpretation of node B. In processing terms this means that when we process a clause all the nodes we have encountered already in this clause are still available directly, so they can affect decisions concerning the interpretation of later nodes in this clause. However, if a given node A does not command node B, this means that when we reach node B, node A is no longer available, since it is in a clause which has already been re-coded. This is illustrated below for the rule determining bound anaphora.

(7a)

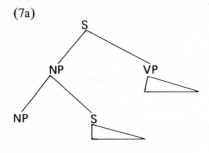

(b)   *The journalists who worked with *each of the diplomats*$_i$ hate *him*$_i$.

(8)   *Each of the diplomats*$_i$ hates his$_i$ friends.

(9)   *He$_i$ hates each of the diplomats'$_i$ friends.

The bound anaphora rule marks the pronoun as dependent for its interpretation on the antecedent. Syntactically this can be done, in this framework, only if the antecedent precedes and commands the pronoun. In processing terms this should be possible if the antecedent is available in short-term memory when we reach the pronoun. In (7) the antecedent's clause is already recoded when we reach the pronoun, so while the abstract recoded representation of the whole clause is still available, the 'antecedent' expression itself is not, and bound anaphora is indeed impossible. In (8), on the other hand, the antecedent is still unrecoded, i.e., it is available when we reach the pronoun, so it can effect its interpretation. In (9), the antecedent and the pronoun are in the same clause, but the linear nature of processing means that when we reach the pronoun the antecedent is not yet available, so it cannot determine the reference of the pronoun. If the precede-and-command-based conditions were the correct linguistic generalisation it would turn out, then, that they allow nodes to be related by linguistic rules in the same cases where the clausal hypothesis predicts that such relations should be easiest, in processing terms.

We saw, however, that this is not the correct linguistic generalisation, and our next step would be to observe that the alternative, c-command-based, domain-conditions correlate, in a similar way, with the constituent-processing hypothesis. This can be illustrated with tree (10).

(10)

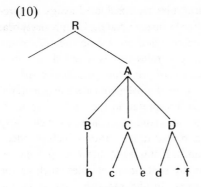

We assume that each branching constituent is closed and recoded once its rightmost node is reached. As with the previous hypothesis, once closure has applied to a given constituent, in the next stage of processing its recoded representation, but not its individual nodes, may be considered. Thus, in tree (10), when the constituent D is processed, the nodes c and e of the constituent C are no longer available, but the recoded representation of C can be considered. If, for example, C is a complex constituent, such as *letters from every candidate*, the recoded interpretation of C can control the interpretation of a pronoun in D, but not the individual node *every candidate*, which is consistent with the results we observed in our discussion of semantic-interpretation rules. Similarly, the whole constituent C can (in principle) bind a trace in A, but a node dominated by C cannot. In other words, if we reach a gap, say in the f position, material in e is not a candidate for filling this gap, since it is not available, but the whole constituent C is such a candidate. This again is consistent with the c-command restrictions on movement we discussed in the previous section.

Given this picture, it is clear that D-heads (the nodes c-commanding all other nodes in a given domain) are always the nodes which are available throughout the processing of the domain. For example, since B is not a branching constituent, its recoded representation is determined solely by b, i.e. it is identical to b. Hence b, which is a D-head of the domain A, is still available in the processing of the nodes in C and D and, consequently, b can 'influence' the interpretation of the individual nodes c–f. On the other hand, the individual nodes c–f are not available in the processing of b (i.e. they cannot 'influence' the interpretation of b), since when b is processed these nodes are either not processed yet, or are already recoded.

If the constituent hypothesis is correct, then, it would be possible to see why the independent linguistic rules we considered assign primacy to D-heads. What we described as 'primacy' material is precisely the material which needs to be available when processing the rest of the domain. In the case of interpretative rules this is material that may determine the referential interpretation of pronouns (as bound variables) or of quantified expressions. In the case of movement rules this is material that needs to fill a 'gap', or to be interpreted in the gap's position. It would follow, then, that languages will tend to organise in such a way that this type of material will be placed in a position which is indeed more available on processing grounds. If this is so, then even procedures which are not governed directly by sentence-level rules, such as the assignment of theme-rheme relations in the sentence, will show the same preference for placing the topic in D-head position.

We should note, however, that apart from the indirect support the constituent hypothesis could gain from the DCs, this hypothesis is not, as yet, independently established. Furthermore, the details of my presentation of it are not precisely identical to the proposal actually made by Kimball.[4] I cannot, obviously, attempt to establish this hypothesis here, but I would like to point out that, possibly, support for it can come from the second type of consideration I mentioned above – the treatment of perceptual complexities and ambiguities.

Let us look first at an argument based on syntactic ambiguity proposed by Kimball (1973):

(11a) Old men who have small annual pensions and gardeners with thirty years of service. (Kimball, 1973, p. 38)
   (b) See diagram on next page.
   (c) See diagram on next page.

The easier interpretation obtained for (11a) is the one corresponding to (11b). Kimball argues that this is because in processing the sentence speakers will choose the strategy that enables them to apply closure as soon as possible. If (11b) is selected, NP_2 can be closed and the nodes it dominates are removed from STM. The interpretation (11c) on the other

(11b)

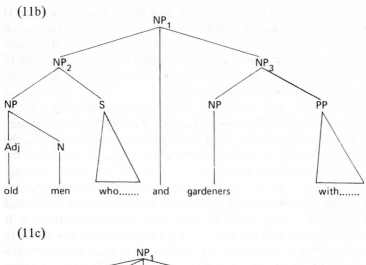

old   men   who.......   and   gardeners   with.......

(11c)

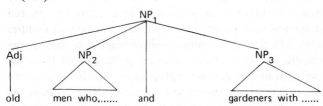

old   men who.......   and   gardeners with ......

hand requires keeping both the Adj node and (the recoded) NP$_2$ in STM until NP$_3$ is reached, at which point NP$_1$ can be closed and cleared. If closure applies only at clauses it would not make any difference which strategy is used here, since no nodes are cleared anyway from STM until the clause boundary is reached.[5]

Next, we may observe that the same arguments proposed to support the clausal hypothesis in cases of perceptual difficulties can be shown to hold for a wider range of constituents. Fodor, Bever and Garett (1974) argue that the difficulty in processing centre-embedding cases such as (12) below can be explained 'if we assume first that there is only a limited amount of short-term memory available for the perceptual processing of sentences, and second that no constituent of a sentence can be dismissed from short-term memory until it has been assigned to a sentoid' (p. 342). In other words, in these cases the closure of S$_1$ and S$_2$ cannot take place until we reach the final verb. This explanation might not be sufficient to distinguish centre-embedding from just long sentences involving, for example, conjoined constituents. So, perhaps the relevant generalisation is that it is extremely costly to hold more than two clauses unclosed in STM, i.e. to start working on a third clause while two clauses are held 'open'.

(12) [the cheese [that the cat [that the dog bit] ate] was spoiled].
      S_1 S_2 S_3
(13) Of particular interest was [an excerpt from [[an old book
                                   NP_1 NP_2 NP_3
      about Jewish prayers] in the Oxford library] in the new reader].
(14) Max [promised [to persuade Bill [to go to Chicago on Monday]
           VP_1 VP_2 VP_3
      on Tuesday] yesterday].

Whatever the precise relation between centre-embedding and closure may be, the crucial point is to observe that the same phenomenon occurs not only with clauses: the centre-embedding in (13) and (14) is just as difficult as that of (12). While in (14) it is possible to argue, within EST syntax, that this is, in fact, clausal, rather than VP-centre-embedding, in (13), clearly, no clauses are involved. The problem is that of combining the NPs and the PPs: NP_1 cannot be closed until the last PP is reached. Or, in the alternative description, two NP constituents are held open while we start processing the third. Other types of perceptual complexity involving difficulties in closing the VP are mentioned in Kimball (1973).

Although considerations of the last two types do not unequivocally establish the constituent hypothesis (since in many cases the facts allow several interpretations), they at least indicate that the plausibility of this approach is not lower than that of the clausal hypothesis.[6]

From a different direction, two recent dissertations have examined directly the psychological reality of the c-command restrictions, proposed in Reinhart (1976). Solan (1978 and forthcoming) and Goodluck (1978 and forthcoming) argue that c-command plays a role in children's grammar. Solan has shown this in the case of anaphora in child language (although his findings are not consistent with the restrictions presented in Reinhart, 1976, and here, particularly in the case of linear order). Goodluck argues that the interpretation of gaps in complement clauses by children aged 4-5 is restricted by c-command, as illustrated in her (15)-(16).

(15) The boy stands near the girl after Δ jumping over the fence.
(16) The boy is hit by the girl after Δ jumping over the fence.

While 50 per cent of her subjects interpreted the gap in (15) as controlled by *the girl* only 25 per cent came up with such interpretation for (16). Goodluck attributes the difference between children's and adults' interpretation of (15) to the children's uncertainty as to the position of the PP complement, which they may attach to the VP. However, in (16), even if the PP complement is attached to the VP, the NP *the girl* does not c-command it, so it cannot control the gap.[7]

We should note here that the correlation between the c-command domain conditions and the processing analysis is not likely to be as full and direct as I described it here. Obviously, many other factors affecting processing considerations may interfere — such as constituents' length and lexical information.[8] And, more generally, syntactic constraints can be expected at most to be consistent with processing constraints, but not identical, or directly reducible to them. In any case, if some version of the constituent-processing hypothesis is correct, this would suggest that the syntactic-domain conditions were selected by natural languages because they yield results that are easiest to process, and would strengthen the assumption that these conditions reflect some inherent properties of the mind.

Notes

1. The discussion of syntactic rules is also restricted to 'core' syntactic rules (see, e.g. Chomsky and Lasnik, 1977, and Chomsky, 1980). It is possible that the so-called 'stylistic transformations' (in which I include also rules like Q-floating) are exempt from the DCs.

2. Within a possible version of the binding analysis, this may follow from the primacy condition if we consider the relation of a constituent and its trace as a case of bound anaphora (i.e. the trace solely depends for its interpretation on its antecedent). However, *wh*-traces are not analysed as anaphors in current versions of this theory — see Chapter 6. In any case, there is no reason to expect the movement restrictions to follow directly from the primacy DC as stated, since as I argue, this condition is just the particular semantic reflection of a deeper processing constraint.

3. The correlation between the clausal hypothesis and the relation *command* was noted in a different way in Bever (1975). I ignore here Bever's remarks that subordinate clauses are held unrecoded while the main clause is processed. It seems that these remarks do not constitute an essential part of the clausal hypothesis. (As stated they do not seem to leave the original hypothesis with much content.)

4. This is primarily so since Kimball assumes that a constituent is closed as soon as its right node is established, but not necessarily closed. For example, the matrix S constituent is closed as soon as we reach the V and establish a VP. Another difference is that Kimball assumes that constituent closure is relevant only for syntactic processing, while the semantic processing applies to the whole clause.

It will also be recalled that I argued that the linear order of nodes plays no role in the application of the interpretative rule or in determining domain relations of nodes. In perception studies (including Kimball's), on the other hand, it is believed that the linear order plays a crucial role and that acoustic signals are processed from left to right. However, in view of the fact that recently 'look ahead' is granted, it is in principle possible that it will be found that c-command domains and perception units do not differ much in this regard.

5. Frazier (1978) argues that these facts could follow from her 'minimal attachment' principle which is independent of closure. So, this perhaps is not a decisive argument. However, even if we assume that we arrive at the interpretation (11b) by another principle, the fact that the reanalysis required to reach (11c) is costly may suggest that NP_2 has been already closed at this stage (i.e. independently of the closure of the whole clause).

6. Further support for the constituent analysis may come from studies of speech production rather than perception. E.g. in their acoustical analysis Danly and Cooper (1979) found that constituent boundaries within the clause are consistently marked by lengthening of the final constituent segment.

7. I have not discussed here the control of gaps of this type. However, its c-command analysis which is consistent with the DCs is proposed in Williams (1980).

8. For example, Frazier (1978) argues against most of the details of Kimball's constituent-processing analysis. Nevertheless, in her analysis constituents smaller than clauses are viewed as processing units, although which constituents 'count' is determined also by their length.

REFERENCES

Akmajian, A., and R. Jackendoff, 1970. 'Coreferentiality and Stress', *Linguistic Inquiry*, vol. 1, no. 1

Bach, Emmon, 1979. 'Control in Montague Grammar', *Linguistic Inquiry*, vol. 10, no. 4

Bach, Emmon, and Barbara Partee, 1980. 'Anaphora and Semantic Structure in K. J. Kreiman and A. E. Oteda (eds), *Papers from the Parasession on Pronouns and Anaphora* (Chicago Linguistic Society, Chicago)

Banfield, A., 1973. 'Grammar of Quotation, Free Indirect Style, and Implications for a Theory of Narrative', *Foundations of Language*, vol. 10 1–39

Bartsch, R., and T. Vennemann, 1972. *Semantic Structures* (Athenäum Verlag, Frankfurt/Main)

Bever, T.G, 1975. 'Functional Explanations Require Independently Motivated Functional Theories' in R. E. Grossman, L. J. San and T. Vance (eds), *Papers from the Parasession on Functionalism* (Chicago Linguistic Society, Chicago)

Bickerton, D., 1975. 'Some Assertions about Presuppositions about Pronominalization' in R. E. Grossman, L. J. San and T. Vance (eds), *Papers from the Parasession on Functionalism* (Chicago Linguistic Society, Chicago)

Bolinger, Dwight, 1977. 'Pronouns and Repeated Nouns' (Manuscript distributed by Indiana University Linguistics Club, Bloominton, Indiana)

— 1979. 'Pronouns in Discourse' in T. Givon (ed.), *Discourse and Syntax, Syntax and Semantics* (Academic Press, New York), vol. 12, 289–310

Bosch, P., 1980. *Agreement and Anaphora* (PhD dissertation, Ruhr University, Bochum)

Bresnan, J., 1970. 'An Argument Against Pronominalization', *Linguistic Inquiry*, vol. 1, no. 1

— 1972. *Theory of Complementation in English Syntax* (PhD dissertation, MIT, Cambridge, Mass.)

Cantrall, W.R., 1974. *Viewpoint, Reflexives and the Nature of Noun Phrases* (Mouton, The Hague)

Carden, G., 1978. 'Backwards Anaphora in Discourse Context' (Manuscript, Yale University, New Haven)

Chapin, P.G., T. S. Smith and A. A. Abrahamson, 1972. 'Two factors in Perceptual Segmentation of Speech', *Journal of Verbal Learning and Verbal Behaviour*, vol. 11, 164–73

Chomsky, N., 1965. *Aspects of the Theory of Syntax* (MIT Press, Cambridge, Mass.)

— 1971. 'Deep Structure, Surface Structure and Semantic Interpretation' in D. D. Steinberg and L. A. Jakobovits (eds), *Semantics* (Cambridge University Press, Cambridge)

— 1973. 'Conditions on Transformations' in S. Anderson and P. Kiparsky (eds), *A Festschrift for Morris Halle* (Holt, Reinhart and Winston, New York)

— 1975. *Reflections on Language* (Pantheon, New York)

— 1976. 'Conditions on Rules of Grammar', *Linguistic Analysis*, vol. 2, no. 4. Reprinted in N. Chomsky, *Essays on Form and Interpretation* (North Holland, Amsterdam, 1977)

— 1977. 'On *Wh*-Movement' in P. Culicover, T. Wasow and A. Akmajian (eds), *Formal Syntax* (Academic Press, New York)

— 1980. 'On Binding', *Linguistic Inquiry*, vol. 11, no. 1. Reprinted in F. Heny (ed.), *Binding and Filtering* (Croom Helm, London; MIT Press, Cambridge, Mass., 1981)

— 1981. *Lectures on Binding and Government* (Foris, Dordrecht)

Chomsky, N., and H. Lasnik, 1977. 'Filters and Control', *Linguistic Inquriy*. vol. 8, no. 3

Cooper, R., 1974. 'Montague Semantic Theory of Adverbs and the VSO Hypothesis' in E. Kaisse and J. Hankamer (eds), *Papers from the Fifth Annual Meeting of the North Eastern Linguistic Society* (Cambridge, Mass.)

Culicover, P.W., 1976. 'A Constraint on Coreferentiality', *Foundation of Language*, vol. 14, no. 1

Cushing, S., 1978. 'A Note on Node Self Dominance', *Linguistic Inquiry*, vol. 9, no. 2

Danly, Martha, and William E. Cooper, 1979. 'Sentence Production: Closure Versus Initiation of Constituents', *Linguistics*, vol. 17, 1017–38

Dik, S., 1978. *Functional Grammar* (North Holland, Amsterdam)

Dougherty, R., 1969. 'An Interpretative Theory of Pronominal Reference', *Foundation of Language*, vol. 5, 488–519

Dowty, D.R., 1980. 'Comments on the Paper by Bach and Partee' in K. J. Kreiman and A. E. Oteda (eds), *Papers from the Parasession on Pronouns and Anaphora* (Chicago Linguistic Society, Chicago)

Emonds, J., 1976. *A Transformational Approach to English Syntax* (Academic Press, New York)

Engdahl, E., 1980. *The Syntax and Semantics of Questions in English* (PhD dissertation, University of Massachusetts, Amherst)

Erteschik-Shir, N., 1973. *On the Nature of Island Constraints* (PhD dissertation, MIT, Cambridge, Mass.)

Erteschik-Shir, N., and S. Lappin, 1979. 'Dominance and the Functional Explanation of Island Phenomena', *Theoretical Linguistics*, vol. 6, no. 1

Evans, G., 1977. 'Pronouns, Quantifiers and Relative Clauses', *Canadian Journal of Philosophy*, vol. 7, 467–536

— 1980. 'Pronouns', *Linguistic Inquiry*, vol. 11, no. 2

Faraci, R., 1974. *Aspects of the Grammar of Infinitives and for-Phrases* (PhD dissertation, MIT, Cambridge, Mass.)

Fiengo, R., 1974. *Semantic Conditions on Surface Structure* (PhD dissertation, MIT, Cambridge, Mass.)

Fiengo, R. and Higginbotham, J., 1981. 'Opacity in NP', *Linguistic Analysis*, vol. 7, 395–421.

Firbas, J., 1975. 'On the thematic and non-thematic section of the sentence' *Style and Text* 319–34

Fodor, J.A., 1979. *The Language of Thought* (Harvard University Press, Cambridge, Mass.)

Fodor, J.A., and T. G. Bever, 1965. 'The Psychological Reality of Linguistic Segments', *Journal of Verbal Learning and Verbal Behaviour*, vol. 4, 414–20

Fodor, J.A., T. G. Bever and M. Garett, 1974. *The Psychology of Language* (Mc-Graw Hill, New York)

Frazier, L., 1978. *On Comprehending Sentences: Syntactic Parsing Strategies* (PhD dissertation, University of Connecticut. Distributed by Indiana University Linguistics Club, Bloomington, Indiana)

Freidin, R., and H. Lasnik, 1981. 'Disjoint Reference and *Wh*-Trace', *Linguistic Inquiry*, vol. 12, no. 1

Gabbai, D.M., and J. M. Moravcsik, 1974. 'Branching Quantifiers, English and Montague Grammar', *Theoretical Linguistics*, vol. 1, no. 1/2

Geach, Peter, 1962. *Reference and Generality* (Cornell University Press, Ithaca, New York)

Goodluck, Helen, 1978. *Linguistic Principles in Children's Grammar of Complement Subject Interpretation* (PhD dissertation, University of Massachusetts, Amherst. Distributed by the Graduate Linguistics Association, University of Massachusetts, Amherst)

— Forthcoming. 'Children's Grammar of Complement Subject Interpretation' in S. Tavakolian (ed.), *Language Acquisition and Linguistic Theory* (MIT Press, Cambridge, Mass.)

Gueron, J., 1979. 'Relations de coréférence dans la phrase et dans le discours', *Langue Française*, no. 44, 42–79

Gundel, J.M., 1974. *The Role of Topic and Comment in Linguistic Theory* (PhD dissertation, The University of Texas at Austin)

Hawkins, John, 1978. *Definiteness and Indefiniteness* (Croom Helm, London)

Heny, F.W., 1973. 'Sentence and Predicate Modifiers in English' in J. Kimball (ed.), *Syntax and Semantics* (Academic Press, New York), vol. 2

Higginbotham, J., 1980a. 'Anaphora and GB: Some Preliminary Remarks' in T. Jensen (ed.), *Proceedings of the Tenth Annual Meeting of the North Eastern Linguistic Society* (Ottawa, Canada)

— 1980b. 'Pronouns and Bound Variables', *Linguistic Inquiry*, vol. 11, no. 4

Hinds, J., 1973. 'Passive, Pronouns and Themes and Rhemes' (Unpublished paper, University of Tokyo)

Hornstein, Norbert, and Amy Weinberg, 1981. 'Case Theory and Preposition Stranding', *Linguistic Inquiry*, vol. 12, no.1

Ioup, G., 1975. *The Treatment of Quantifier Scope in Transformational Grammar* (PhD dissertation, CUNY, New York)

Jackendoff, R., 1972. *Semantic Interpretation in Generative Grammar* (MIT Press, Cambridge, Mass.)

— 1975. 'On Belief-Contexts', *Linguistic Inquiry*, vol. 6, no 1

Johnson, David E., and Paul M. Postal, 1981. *Arc Pair Grammar* (Princeton University Press, Princeton, New Jersey)

Kamp, Hans, 1980. 'A Theory of Truth and Semantic Representation' (Manuscript of the University of Texas at Austin, and Bedford College, London)

Karttunen, Lauri, 1969. 'Pronouns and Variables' in R. Binnick *et al*, eds), *Proceedings of the Fifth Regional Meeting of the Chicago Linguistic Society* (Chicago)

Kasher, A., 1976. 'Conversational Maxims and Rationality' in A. Kasher (ed.), *Language in Focus* (Reidel, Dordrecht)

Kasher, A., and D. M. Gabbai, 1976. 'On the Semantics and Pragmatics of Specific and Non-Specific Indefinite Expressions', *Theoretical Linguistics*, vol. 3, no. 1/2

Keenan, E., 1971. 'Names, Quantifiers and a Solution to the Sloppy Identity Problem', *Papers in Linguistics*, vol. 4, no. 2

— 1974. 'The Functional Principle: Generalizing the Notion "Subject of"' in M. LaGaly, R. Fox and A. Bruck (eds), *Papers from the Tenth Regional Meeting of the Chicago Linguistic Society* (Chicago)

— 1976. 'Remarkable Subjects in Malagasy' in C. N. Li (ed.), *Subject and Topic* (Academic Press, New York)

Keenan, E., and B. Comrie, 1978. 'Noun Phrase Accessibility and Universal Grammar', *Linguistic Inquiry*, vol. 8, no. 1

Keenan, E., and A. Faltz, 1978. *Logical Types for Natural Language* (Working Papers in Syntax and Semantics, UCLA, Los Angeles)

Kimball, J., 1973. 'Seven Principles of Surface Structure Parsing in Natural Language', *Cognition*, vol. 2, no. 1

Klima, E.S., 1964. 'Negation in English' in J. A. Fodor and J. J. Katz (eds), *The Structure of Language* (Prentice-Hall, Englewood Cliffs, New Jersey)

Koster, J., 1979. 'Anaphora: An Introduction Without Footnotes', Report no. DA 01-79 (Filosofische Instituut, Nijmegen)

Kuno, S., 1971. 'The position of Locatives in Existential Sentences', *Linguistic Inquiry*, vol. 2, no. 3

— 1972a. 'Functional Sentence Perspective: A Case Study from Japanese and English', *Linguistic Inquiry*, vol. 3, no. 3

— 1972b. 'Pronominalization, Reflexivization and Direct Discourse', *Linguistic Inquiry*, vol. 3, no. 2

— 1975a. 'Conditions on Verb-Phrase Deletion', *Foundation of Language*, vol. 13

— 1975b. 'Three Perspectives in the Functional Approach to Syntax' in R. E. Grossman, L. J. San and T. J. Vance (eds), *Papers from the Parasession on Functionalism* (Chicago Linguistic Society, Chicago)

Kuno, S., and E. Kaburaki, 1975. 'Empathy and Syntax' in S. Kuno (ed.), *Harvard Studies in Syntax and Semantics* (Harvard University, Cambridge, Mass.), vol. 1

Lakoff, G., 1968. 'Prounouns and Reference' (Indiana University Linguistics Club, Bloomington, Indiana. Reprinted in J. McCawley (ed.), *Papers from The Linguistics Underground, Syntax and Semantics* (Academic Press, New York, 1978)

— 1970. 'Adverbs and Opacity: A Reply to Stalnaker' (Mimeographed paper, University of Michigan, Ann Arbor)

— 1971. 'On Generative Semantics' in D. A. Steinberg and L. A. Jakobovits (eds), *Semantics* (The University Press, Cambridge)

— 1972. 'Linguistics and Natural Logic' in D. Davidson and G. Harman (eds.), *Semantics of Natural Language* (D. Reidel, Dordrecht/Boston)

Langacker, R., 1966. 'On Pronominalixation and the Chain of Command' in W. Reibel and S. Schane (eds), *Modern Studies in English* (Prentice Hall, Englewood Cliffs, New Jersey)

Lasnik, H., 1976. 'Remarks on Coreference', *Linguistic Analysis*, vol. 2, no. 1

McCray, A., 1980. 'The Semantics of Backward Anaphora' in T. Jensen (ed.), *Proceedings of the Tenth Annual Meeting of the North Eastern Linguistic Society* (Ottawa, Canada)

May, Robert, 1977. *The Grammar of Quantification* (PhD dissertation, MIT, Cambridge, Mass.)

Mittwoch, A., 1979. 'Backward Anaphora in Utterances Conjoined with *but*' (Paper read at the LSA Summer Meeting in Salzburg; manuscript, The Hebrew University, Jerusalem)

Montague, R., 1974. *Formal Philosophy. Selected Papers of Richard Montague*, edited and with an introduction by Richmond H. Thomason (Yale University Press, New Haven, Conn.)

Partee, B., 1973. 'Some Transformational Extensions of Montague Grammar', *Journal of Philosophical Logic*, vol. 2, 509-34

— 1978. 'Bound Variables and Other Anaphors' in D. Waltz (ed.), *Proceedings of TINLAP, 2* (University of Illinois, Urbana)

Perlmutter, D. and P. Postal, 1974. 'Relational Grammar' (Amherst Lectures, University of Massachusetts, Amherst)

Postal, P., 1970. 'On Coreferential Complement Subject Deletion', *Linguistic Inquiry*, vol. 1, no. 4

— 1971. *Cross Over Phenomena* (Holt, Reinhart and Winston, New York)

— 1972. 'A Global Constraint on Pronominalization', *Linguistic Inquiry*, vol. 3, no. 1

Postal, P. and J. R. Ross, 1970. 'A Problem of Adverb Preposing', *Linguistic Inquiry*, vol. 1, no. 1

Reinhart, T., 1975a. 'Point of View in Sentences with Parentheticals' in S. Kuno (ed.), *Harvard Studies in Syntax and Semantics*, vol. 1 (Harvard University, Cambridge, Mass.)
— 1975b. 'The Strong Coreference Restriction: Indefinites and Reciprocals' (Manuscript, MIT, Cambridge, Mass.)
— 1976. 'The Syntactic Domain of Anaphora' (PhD dissertation, MIT, Cambridge, Mass.)
— 1978. 'Syntactic Domains for Semantic Rules' in F. Guenthner and S. J. Schmidt (eds), *Formal Semantics and Pragmatics for Natural Language* (Reidel, Dordrecht)
— 1980. 'On the Position of Extraposed Clauses', *Linguistic Inquiry*, vol. 11, no. 3
— 1981a. 'Definite NP Anaphora and C-Command Domains', *Linguistic Inquiry*, vol. 12, no. 4
— 1981b. 'Pragmatics and Linguistics: An Analysis of Sentence Topics', *Philosophica*, vol. 27 (I) (Distributed also by Indiana University Linguistics Club, Bloomington, Indiana)
— 1983. 'Coreference and Bound Anaphora: A Restatement of the Anaphora Questions', *Linguistics and Philosophy*, vol. 6, no. 1
Van Riemsdijk, H., and F. Zwartz, 1974. 'Left Dislocation in Dutch and the Status of Copying Rules' (Manuscript, MIT and the University of Amsterdam; Cambridge, Mass. and Amsterdam)
Rosenbaum, P., 1967. *The Grammar of English Predicate Complement Constructions* (MIT Press, Cambridge, Mass.)
Ross, J. R., 1967. *Constraints on Variables in Syntax* (PhD dissertation, MIT, Cambridge, Mass.)
— 1972a. 'Niching' (Mimeographed handout, MIT, Cambridge, Mass.)
— 1972b. 'Sloppier and Sloppier: A Hierarchy of Linguistically Possible Open Sentences' (Mimeographed Handout, MIT, Cambridge, Mass.)
— 1973. 'Nearer to Vee' (Mimeographed handout, MIT, Cambridge, Mass.)
Sag, Ivan, 1976. *Deletion and Logical Form* (PhD dissertation, MIT, Cambridge, Mass.)
Solan, Lawrence, 1978. *Anaphora in Child Language* (PhD dissertation, University of Massachusetts, Amherst, distributed by the Graduate Linguistics Student Association, University of Massachusetts, Amherst)
— Forthcoming. 'The Acquisition of Structural Restrictions on Anaphora' in S. Tavakolian (ed.), *Language Acquisition and Linguistic Theory* (MIT Press, Cambridge, Mass.)
Thomason, R., and R. C. Stalnaker, 1973. 'A Semantic Theory of Adverbs', *Linguistic Inquiry*, vol. 4, no. 2
Wasow, T., 1972. *Anaphoric Relations in English* (PhD dissertation, MIT, Cambridge, Mass. A revised version published as *Anaphora in Generative Grammar* (Story Scientia, Gent. 1979))
Williams, E.S., 1974. 'Rule Ordering in Syntax' (PhD dissertation, MIT, Cambridge, Mass.)
— 1975. 'Small Clauses in English' in J. P. Kimball (ed.), *Syntax and Semantics* (Academic Press, New York), vol. 4
— 1977. 'Discourse and Logical Form', *Linguistic Inquiry*, vol. 8, no. 1
— 1980. 'Predication', *Linguistic Inquiry*, vol. 11, no. 1

INDEX